PRACTICING
SOCIOLOGY

PRACTICING SOCIOLOGY

TACIT KNOWLEDGE FOR THE SOCIAL SCIENTIFIC CRAFT

EDITED BY DAVID STARK

Columbia University Press   *New York*

Columbia University Press
Publishers Since 1893
New York   Chichester, West Sussex
cup.columbia.edu

Library of Congress Cataloging-in-Publication Data
Names: Stark, David, 1950– author.
Title: Practicing sociology : tacit knowledge for the social scientific
craft / edited by David Stark.
Description: New York : Columbia University Press, 2024. | Includes index.
Identifiers: LCCN 2023029256 | ISBN 9780231214001 (hardback) |
ISBN 9780231214018 (trade paperback) | ISBN 9780231560146 (ebook)
Subjects: LCSH: Sociology.
Classification: LCC HM585 .S73 2024 | DDC 301—dc23/eng/20230811
LC record available at https://lccn.loc.gov/2023029256

Printed and bound by CPI Group (UK) Ltd, Croydon, CR0 4YY

Cover design: Noah Arlow
Cover image: Shutterstock

CONTENTS

II PUBLISHING: WHAT IS YOUR PUBLICATION STRATEGY?

III REVISING: HOW DO YOU IMPROVE A MANUSCRIPT FOR PUBLICATION?

PRACTICING
SOCIOLOGY

INTRODUCTION

Vision, Decision, Revision:
Finding Topics, Audiences, and Voices

DAVID STARK

IN PREPARATION

Social scientists do research; we teach and mentor younger scholars; and we discuss theories and findings at workshops and conferences. About conducting research, we know a great deal. Professors expound at length in graduate seminars and dissertation defenses on the challenges of matching research methods to research problems; the literature on data collection, theory, and tools of analysis could fill entire libraries. Less has been written about the crafts of teaching and mentoring,[1] and still less about how to improve one's skills in presenting work to academic or public audiences.[2]

There are other activities—core to the social scientific profession—that are almost entirely in the shadows. You will not encounter them in books or articles and, regardless of how important for becoming a successful social scientist, they are seldom, if ever, addressed in the course of graduate training. I have in mind three such activities. In addition to conducting research, teaching, and presenting their work, a good social scientist must (1) come up with compelling research topics, not once but repeatedly; (2) develop a publication strategy; and (3) learn how to improve a manuscript while navigating the process of peer review.

Knowledge about such practices is not taboo, or secretive, but tacit. It is not explicit or codified, and as such is not taught in the classroom. This knowledge is acquired—sometimes painstakingly—over the course of a scholarly career.

But tacit knowledge is not precluded from being an object of conscious reflection. It might not be codified or reduced to formulas, steps, or recipes, yet it can be brought out of the shadows, illuminated, and demystified. Such reflection is exactly the task of this book.

About each of the three activities—discovering new topics, deciding where to publish, and improving manuscripts through revision—I asked ten or so prominent scholars to offer their reflections. The resulting thirty-three scholars I invited to contribute are all established figures in academia. Further still, it can be said without false modesty that they are among the most outstanding researchers and authors in their respective fields. Yet there is something that each of them shares with the PhD student looking for a dissertation topic or with the young scholar newly juggling the demands of researching, teaching, and publishing: each of them is a practicing sociologist. Like a surgeon or a sculptor, our contributors are highly skilled practitioners—in this case, of the sociological craft. Unlike dentists or attorneys, they do not have "a practice." But, like professional musicians or Olympic athletes, they practice every day.

Let me make four observations to prepare your reading. First, as you will see, none of these chapters offers recipes, formulas, or marching orders. These thirty-one chapters provide guidance for the practicing sociologist (whether the novice or the fully tenured). Yet this is not a "how-to" book. You will not be instructed, but there is much that you can learn. As you will see, moreover, the chapters are incredibly rich: they are packed with ideas, not simply about the task at hand but also with deep, sociologically theoretical insights. That is so even in the frequent cases when the author or authors seem to have adopted a casual, almost conversational tone.

Second, although the contributors were given the same question (distinctive for each activity), their answers vary widely. The great diversity of these chapters will strike you immediately. Along one axis of variation are enormous differences in style. As you will see (or perhaps I should say "hear"), one of the sources of pleasure in reading these strong writers is listening to distinctive writerly voices. Along another axis of variation is the content of their commentary. Indeed, one might think that such great variation provides no guidance at all: If the same question yields ten wildly different answers, is there really something that can be learned? In my view, the enormous differences in voice, in style, and in the intentions of the insights across the chapters are an asset, not a drawback. By confronting the reader with different—even directly contradictory—views and opinions, we affirm that on these matters of sociological practice, there is no one "best way."

Third, if there is not a clearly dominant pathway, it is also not the case that you must clear a passageway uniquely for and by yourself. You are not the first person who is navigating these multiple pathways, and you are certainly not alone. To demonstrate this, in this book you encounter scholars who are practicing sociology every day. Yes, practicing. About them we can also say that they are very practiced in their craft.[3] For the novice, these figures appear as giants. So, what do we do? Figuratively, our authors come down from their lecture hall pedestals, pull up a chair, sit down beside you, and talk, each with a distinctive voice. First one and then another, real personalities shine through, so alive. Here they are giving advice, as from one craftsperson speaking calmly to another member of the craft, not shouting it, not in a lecturing tone, being thoughtful, using humor, being caring. Frequently, they show their vulnerabilities: their manuscripts get rejected, they tear up drafts, they have doubts and worries, they curse at reviewers. But they persevere, and now, with some wonderful combination of confidence and humility, they share what they have learned. Because of this posture of talking rather than lecturing, the advice is so much more meaningful and activating. Do you see? You're not alone.

My fourth observation is how enjoyable it is to read these chapters. One of the major reasons for this is that the authors are having great fun in pulling together and putting out their thoughts. That's completely clear in the writing, and it was confirmed for me when the authors submitted their answers: almost all of them mentioned how much they had enjoyed thinking and writing about their topic. That's as it should be. There are aspects of our work life that are like a job. But being a sociologist (or a social scientist more generally) is not merely a job; it's a profession, a calling. As a vocation, it entails obligations. But obligations need not be burdens. Our work can be a joy. Perhaps the most important unstated lesson of these enjoyable chapters: throw yourself into your work and enjoy our wonderful profession.

A PRACTICING SOCIOLOGIST

Why do I refer to "practicing sociologists"? To elaborate that concept, I'll refer to the introductory remarks that I've made to the incoming PhD cohorts in the departments of sociology at Columbia (where I was twice chair) and at Cornell (where I was, for a good part of my time there, the director of graduate studies). Just as soon as everyone was settled around the table on the morning of that orientation, I'd say, "Hello, I'm David Stark and I want to welcome you to the Department of Sociology." The very next thing from me would be a pause (for dramatic effect, sure), and then I would say: "If you were in medical school, at exactly this point when you begin your training to become a physician, you would all stand up and take the Hippocratic Oath." Everyone is looking at me and at each other like, "What is this about? Why is he telling us this?" And I'd continue, "In med school, taking the Hippocratic Oath is a defining moment in which one grasps that something has changed in one's life. Sociology doesn't have a Hippocratic Oath, but I want you to understand that, from this moment on, you're not a student. You're a practicing sociologist."

Making the gesture of the basketball player shooting free throws, I'd go on to say, "I'm a practicing sociologist. I practice sociology every day." Then for the next fifteen minutes or so, I would elaborate on various ways in which the notion of practicing sociology could transform how they understood their role going forward. For example, whereas a student approaches coursework in a passive way, the practicing sociologist is more actively (critically and appreciatively) engaged. Active engagement doesn't begin and end with lobbing criticisms (the grad student equivalent of writing restaurant reviews), but with approaching every class, every seminar, every guest speaker as an encounter with a potential tool—whether a theoretical insight, a methodological innovation, or a trenchant research design—that could inform one's practice as a sociologist.

Moreover, an emphasis on "practice" means you can always improve. You must practice. Sometimes you miss, but the more you practice, the more skills you learn. It's a lifelong activity. It's for this reason that, although my undergraduates call me "Professor Stark," in interactions such as PhD seminars I am "David." Although we don't have the same status, we are all members of the same community of practicing sociologists. The same attitude applies in reverse. As I tell the participants at the beginning of the term of every PhD seminar: "I'm here to learn. The more you teach me and the more all of us can learn from each other, the better this course will be."

THE STRUCTURE OF THE BOOK

After this introduction, the major architecture of the book has three parts: (1) Encountering, (2) Publishing, and (3) Revising. For each segment, I had invited a set of sociologists to contribute to a special feature of the journal *Sociologica*.[4] So you can know the question or prompt that triggered each set of responses, I reproduce them here, as presented in my original invitation:

PART I. ENCOUNTERING: DISCOVERING A NEW RESEARCH PROJECT?

For the journal *Sociologica*, we are inviting a number of prominent sociologists to contribute to a special feature on "Heuristics of Discovery." In general terms, we're interested in how people come to work on the problems they do. We could use the word "choose," but perhaps some contributors will think that already has a decisionist bias. In an even broader sense, one could write about any aspect of work process—writing with a coauthor, matching method to research question, ways to think about data, the use of illustrations, or other topics.

PART II. PUBLISHING: WHAT IS YOUR PUBLICATION STRATEGY?

I write to ask you to reflect on your publication strategy. Some guiding questions: First, how do you know when a manuscript is ready to go? An obvious second question is about books versus articles or chapters in edited volumes. But also what about publishing in established outlets versus new journal ventures? Have you edited a volume or special issue of a journal? In general about publication strategy, what advice would you give to a young aspiring sociologist? Our telegraphic questions are merely illustrative. We cast a wide net, expecting high variance not only in your answers but also in the way you frame the question.

PART III. REVISING: HOW DO YOU IMPROVE A MANUSCRIPT FOR PUBLICATION?

We are interested in the process of improving a manuscript (article or book) for publication. We'll call the feature "Revising." Peer review is one aspect, but not necessarily. As with the previous special features, our query is open to interpretation.

Instead of summarizing the authors' contributions, in the remaining sections of this introduction, I've elected to offer some remarks of my own on the three topics, presented next as "Double Vision," "Decision," and "Revision." The temptation was strong to nominate themes prevalent across the various chapters. Perhaps even stronger was the urge to point you to lovely gems of wisdom, wit, or both. But these are too many, and they are so good. I would get lost yet one more time rereading the chapters; and in any case it would be too difficult to choose.

I know enough evolutionary theory to know that *selection* matters. Of course it does. But enough selection from me already. I've done the editorial work of selecting the topics and this cast of contributors. My guideline: read them all. Most likely, you will dip in and out. That's understandable—despite the casual tone, the chapters are dense, and, for some readers, the abrupt changes in style and tone from one author to another can be demanding. So, if you do put the book down, pick it up again, and then again.

DOUBLE VISION: ENCOUNTERING A NEW RESEARCH TOPIC

Think back to advice you received during your high school and college days. If you're like me, probably more than one person your senior said something like: "Get focused!" Perhaps more recently, a friend or an advisor, without actually employing the sports metaphor of "keeping your eye on the ball," used various expressions reminding you to keep an uncluttered, well-focused view on your path to the goal ahead.

On this matter, with his typical humor, the Yankee philosopher Yogi Berra offered: "If you don't know where you're going, you'll end up somewhere else." But Yogi's truism doesn't imply that getting and staying focused is the sole recipe for achieving goals. In fact, focus might be overrated. Of course, periods of intense focus are required lest you wander, aimlessly adrift. But unremitting focus on the given course could be just as detrimental. As we are biological organisms, it is our *peripheral* vision that is particularly sensitive to detecting movement. Without peripheral vision, our long-ago ancestors would have been devoured by large predators on the savannah; and it is precisely by *not* focusing that one can move quickly through a fast-moving crowd in the 42nd Street Times Square subway station.

For this reason, one of the epigraphs of my book *The Sense of Dissonance* was a passage from Dante's *Purgatorio*: "Fix not thy mind on one place only" (Stark, 2009). The object of study in that book was at the organizational level. In that context, Dante's injunction could be read as a warning to organizational decision makers of the dangers of locking in to prior successes. To thrive, even to survive, in rapidly changing environments requires something like an organizational peripheral vision.[5] The findings from my three ethnographic case studies suggested the positive effects of an organizational double vision: to the question "What's valuable?" answer by keeping multiple evaluative frameworks in play.

Applying this insight to our first practical challenge—encountering a new research problem—in place of the maxim "Stay focused," I'll substitute, "Pay attention." To make the case for this approach, let's start with a passage from "An Excess of Fact," an essay by Lee Friedlander, one of America's greatest photographers. Recalling an experience in adolescence in which he was "bitten by the mysteries of photography" and "learned its practical possibilities," Friedlander writes:

> The camera was a kind of net and what it caught had something to do with what was true, or truth in an excess of fact. The net is indiscriminate unless you point it and then are lucky. I might get what I hoped for and then some—lots of then some—more than I might have remembered was there. I only wanted Uncle Vern standing by his new

car (a Hudson) on a clear day. I got him and the car. I also got a bit of Aunt Mary's laundry and Beau Jack, the dog, peeing on the fence, and a row of potted tuberous begonias on the porch and seventy-eight trees and a million pebbles in the driveway and more. It's a generous medium, photography (Friedlander, 1996:103).

To some, Lee Friedlander would be an odd choice if one is questioning the absolute value of focus: in the typical Friedlander photograph, *everything is in focus*. There's a lot going on in a Friedlander photograph, but not because it's frenetic or blurred. Instead, using reflection, shadow, and bold composition, Friedlander guides our attention. Look. You see here? Now look again; something else, and something different yet again. Pay attention. Windows are a recurring device. It is through car windshields that Friedlander (2010) sees America. Car windshields provide a framing, and then we notice the side-view mirror, a framing within a frame, and within it, an entirely different perspective on the setting. Shop windows can be mirrors reflecting what is behind the camera. But the same reflecting window can also be partially seen through—where there is a shadow, sometimes a shadow cast by the photographer. For Friedlander, the shadow reveals. By using it as something to be *seen through*, it is almost as if the shadow is illuminating a part of the scene that would otherwise be hidden.

So, I suggest reading the passage from Friedlander's essay again, this time replacing "the camera" and "photography" with "sociological research." Sociological research is a generous medium, casting a net that catches more than we see on first observation. If you are lucky and paying attention, your next research project will be one that was there in the shadows of one or another of your prior projects. It might be a minor finding that seemed odd at the time, or a line of investigation that you considered but put to the side, or an opening into a neighboring (or even distant) field to which you now turn your attention.

While you're attentive to materials and insights that are there in the shadows of your prior projects, don't forget the mirrors showing what's right behind you, just over your shoulder, so to speak. The cars from which Friedlander guided us to see America were not moving at the time he photographed from them. Like with the equally stationary shop windows, the cars' side-view and rear-view mirrors reflected not something from the past but something that was simply *behind* the photographer. Yet, in the remarkable visual vocabulary through which Friedlander's style had such a great and lasting impact on American photography, those reflected images were there, quite literally, right *in front of* the photographer.

Upon reflection, I recognized this process when I was close to completing a book on the political and economic transformations (some were saying "revolutions") in Eastern Europe after the fall of the Berlin Wall and the collapse of the Soviet Union. I was not yet on the lookout for a new topic. If I had not been paying attention, I might have locked in to my prior successes and continued, path dependently, to study Eastern Europe, or property transformation, or democratization. I didn't entirely stop doing any of those things, but I did encounter a new research problem—the so-called digital revolution that was happening right in front of my eyes, whether in Silicon Valley or Silicon Alley. My research in Eastern Europe had given me some preparation for studying the digital transformation in the United States. For one thing, I was somewhat immunized against the hype that surrounded the digital revolution. Moreover, I had some conceptual tools—notions about the "heterarchy" of value or the "network properties of property," for example—that gave me preparation to get started in the new field.[6] But it could not be just a matter of observing a new setting through exactly the same lenses: that starting point gave me some advantages but could also cloud my vision if I was not aware of its limitations.

Concepts and methods, like all the screens upon which we project our representations, conceal at the same time that they reveal

(Girard and Stark, 2007). Strictly speaking, one cannot pay attention to one's blind spot, but one should be attentive to the ways in which it allows *and* limits one's vision.[7]

Turning to peripheral vision, I find it helpful to read work that is not at the core of the field I'm researching. Of course, one must be familiar with the current debates. But that crowded, consecrated core is overshadowing other excellent work at the periphery of the field. That's where it can also pay to pay attention. Read work (and go to talks) by researchers who are reading (and thus being influenced by) different stuff than you. That way, you can be influenced by papers that you yourself have never directly encountered.

In my own case, the best way to promote peripheral or double vision is to work on more than one project at a time. As many of the chapters in the book indicate, that next project can appear by serendipity. In my experience, it doesn't matter how the second (in parallel, at the same time) project comes about. What matters is that it has to be different enough from the other. A recent paper of mine is exemplary in this respect. While working with one set of coauthors on an experimental study of how racial diversity affects performance (Levine, Reypens, and Stark, 2021), I was simultaneously working with a different coauthor on a network analytic paper on patterns of attention (Prato and Stark, 2022). Without the latter, I doubt that I would have come up with the core concept that was signaled in the title of the experimental paper: "Racial Attention Deficit."

That paper also shows a process that I'll call *being prepared to be surprised by your obsessions.* At first glance, this seems to be at odds with the line of argument I've been making, characterized as being alert to the dangers of becoming captivated and then captured by one's previous successes. Let's look closer. In the situation at hand, the topic was race, an area in which I was not an established researcher. The sense of novelty was amplified, moreover, by the fact that I was still new to experimental techniques. The novelty of methods, but even more the novelty of my engagement in a new field, was part of the attraction, multiplied by knowledge that the problem was important and a realistic anticipation that the research was likely to be consequential. And so, it was with a strong feeling of surprise that suddenly one day I discovered that I was now, in this research on race, once again grappling with a fundamental problem that had animated my theoretical interests and my empirical research already from the middle of the 1980s—the problem of worth. It was back then, in 1986, that I had written about how the tool makers in the Hungarian factory I was studying had used the opportunity of forming an intrapreneurial partnership in an attempt to gain recognition of their worth. Yes, the experimental research (like the network analytic research with Matteo Prato) was about who was paying attention to whom. But in a deeper sense, I recognized that it was about recognition.

The situation is familiar enough—one encounters something as a surprise and then, in the very next moment, it immediately seems completely obvious. Indeed, it was a surprise. I had not deliberately set out to create a research design to study the problem of worth in the context of race. When Sheen Levine and I started to work on the project, we had finished a study showing that ethnic diversity contributes to error detection by disrupting conformity. The new project, with a postdoc named Charlotte Reypens, would be something about race and observational learning. During the initial period of research design, and even during the early pilot studies, nothing in our conversations was about concepts of worth and recognition.

It was not the first time that I had been surprised to find that the problem of worth (or some similarly fundamental theoretical preoccupation) had been there in the shadows. Was I returning to an old problem? Yes, as in a musical composition, the theme was coming around again, returning. But, taking this new turn, it was not a simple repetition. Paying attention means being open to the world and to its new problems and challenges. Paying attention also means being prepared to accept your obsessions when they catch you by surprise.

DECISION: FINDING YOUR AUDIENCE

In his chapter here, Shamus Khan observes that in order to have publications, you must first have written something publishable; so his take on publication strategy is about his *writing* strategy. I'll take up a similar line of thinking: to have a publication strategy you must first know your audience. For writing at the beginning stages of one's academic career, I interpret this expression literally; rather than a general *idea* about your audience, it helps to write for people you actually know, or at least have particularly in mind.

Let's start with the dissertation. Of course, you will be writing for your advisor. That's already part of the problem. Writing for just one other person definitely won't do it, no matter how smart, thoughtful, and kind that person is. Widening the circle to the three or four other members of your dissertation committee is a step out, but not far enough. Your friends, your close pals in your graduate program, are good because that gets you started thinking about writing for your peers. I write my best when I'm writing for my peers. That's as it should be because science is very much peer-to-peer. So it follows that, as the audience for your dissertation and your first publishable papers, you should be *targeting other PhD students*.

Before elaborating on several reasons behind this targeting, a word about my own experience. I was not, nor should you be, thinking of an abstraction known as "other graduate students in sociology." No, I really do mean particular people. In the case of my first academic publication (Stark, 1980) and then my dissertation, at the center of my audience were Michael Burawoy, Magali Sarfatti-Larson, and Erik Olin Wright. "Yeah, right," you say, "two of the three became presidents of the American Sociological Association!" That's true, but not the point. At the time I was writing, they were just a few years my academic senior. As I recall, when I met each of them, they were writing their PhD dissertations.

Erik, Michael, and Magali were not students with whom I hung out in my department. We would later become friends, but at the time we were friendly acquaintances. I was reading their work, I had heard them speak on different occasions, and we had all participated at a wonderful conference on labor process theory where I was one of the presenters. Meeting, communicating, interacting—this is the key. Your target audience consists of other researchers in your field. You need to get out and meet them. Go to workshops and conferences (and not necessarily the biggest ones), introduce yourself, and offer to read and comment on their work. It's as part of a community of researchers that you will write for an audience that is interested in your work. Your faculty advisors want you to finish; but from the peers in your broader community, you get something more. From that community of peers you'll get criticism and encouragement, but even more important, a sense of urgency, even a kind of pressure: "Get that piece out, it's an important part of what we're doing, we need it, c'mon do it."

As your ideas develop, you will write for broader, anonymous audiences. The question is how to develop your ideas so you have something worth offering. In my case, it helped to have particular scholars in mind. Aim high. Think about the people who are having or will have an impact on the field, the ones whose ideas grab you. If you can meet them, do so. If not, still reach out. Write personally to scholars you admire.

Posting on social media might help you reach an audience, but it's not a substitute for making a connection to particular others. The way to raise the standards of your work is to have in mind and write for people with very high standards. As a young researcher, I wrote for Claus Offe, one of Europe's most outstanding sociologists. I had heard him speak several times while I was a graduate student fellow at Harvard's Center for European Studies. It was only later that I made his acquaintance. Even before then, I sent Claus my papers, frequently in manuscript. I wasn't terribly preoccupied with the number of people I was reaching. What mattered more was the quality of the people who knew and appreciated my research. It was my great fortune that Pierre Bourdieu and Janos Kornai also helped me in this way.

Over time, the audiences that I had in mind for any particular piece became less embodied. I say "audiences" because there was a long period in which many of the major pieces I was publishing were intended for two or more research communities, something about which I had not been explicitly aware until this writing. These include a book addressed to economic sociologists *and* political sociologists (Stark and Bruszt, 1998); a social sequence analysis of network positions targeting historical sociologists *and* network analysts (Stark and Vedres, 2006); several studies written for economic sociology *and* science and technology studies (Beunza and Stark, 2004, 2012); and a piece advocating cultural network analysis addressed to network analysts *and* cultural sociologists (De Vaan, Stark, and Vedres, 2015).

There have been other, more peculiar audiences. Writing about the economic and political transformations in Eastern Europe in the 1990s (Stark, 1996; Stark and Bruszt, 1998), I had in mind contemporary readers, of course. Yet, even more important, the real audience I was writing for was one that, I hoped, would read my work some twenty-five or more years in the future. Why? At the time, the prevailing view was that the countries of the former Soviet bloc were in transition, with the outcome known in advance: they would become liberal democratic societies with free elections and free markets. The only question was which country was wearing the yellow jersey leading the race to the promised land. For those who looked at the world through the distorting lens of the transitologists' crystal ball, the present wasn't interesting. For me, it was this messy present that was so fascinating. I proposed to analyze it as best I could without the optics of an imagined future, in hopes that some reader in the future would be interested in learning what was happening in the five or so years on either side of 1989.

Perhaps my most peculiar, certainly the most singular, audience was for an op-ed piece that my coauthor and I published in the *New York Times* in December 2015 (Levine and Stark, 2015). About a year earlier, Sheen Levine and I had published an article that used experimental methods to test the effect of ethnic diversity on market outcomes (Levine et al., 2014). We had found that markets of ethnically diverse traders outperformed those that were ethnically homogeneous. The message of the paper: racial/ethnic diversity deflates price bubbles and leads to less mispricing because it disrupts conformity. The paper received considerable attention in the press, especially in the financial pages of some major newspapers. The opportunity to write an op-ed piece appeared when we learned about a major affirmative action legal case that was being heard by the U.S. Supreme Court. Abigail Fisher, a white student, had sued the University of Texas on the grounds that she was denied admission to the law school because of racial discrimination. Her attorneys, we learned, were making the argument that there was no scientific evidence supporting the claim that racial diversity contributed to a better learning environment. Our experimental study was not in an educational context, but markets are a kind of learning environment, and the error detection that we documented in the diverse setups was a form of learning. So, drawing on the lessons of that study, we submitted 1,000 words to the *New York Times*.

The editorial board of the *Times* expressed interest in the piece, provided that it could be published on the morning of the day of the oral hearings for that Supreme Court case. That gave us about thirty-six hours to revise the paper, responding to the very demanding conditions of the *Times* fact-checkers and working closely with a member of the editorial board. In that back-and-forth, we were able to read between the lines to infer that the editorial board of the *New York Times* had a very clear and precise audience in mind: Justice Anthony Kennedy, the swing vote on the Court. Coming to this realization, we were better able to interpret subtle cues, for example, directing us to several important prior cases, including an important opinion written by Justice Sandra Day O'Connor. We are under no illusions that our piece made a difference. But it was interesting to learn that the intended audience for that opinion piece was the justice who would go on to write the majority opinion in the case of *Fisher v. University of Texas*. The Court decision upheld the lower court decision (i.e., ruled against Fisher). Whether they are known to you personally or persons whom you will never encounter, knowing your audience is the first step in a publication strategy.

REVISION: GIVING VOICE TO YOUR IDEAS

Revision can begin from the first lines put to the page. Putting one's thoughts in writing with the foreknowledge that they will be revised can be a blessing or a burden (or both). On the one hand, it can be liberating to start writing without worries. Not carelessly, but *carefree*. On the other hand, knowing that revision is always possible, but then starting it too soon can be debilitating. Word processing provides both sides of these possibilities. It is for this reason that my son, a very gifted writer, sometimes elects to use a manual typewriter when writing a first draft. The backspace functionality of the electronic keyboard, making it easy to delete a word or catch a spelling error, he found, creates a subconscious inclination toward correction. The manual keyboard encourages a freer style. Who cares about typos when one isn't even concerned that everything comes in complete sentences? Just bang it out, hit the carriage return, and move on to get another phrase on the page.

   With some material to work with, the more deliberate phase of writing/revising turns phrases into sentences. For me, those must always be grouped as paragraphs. For an academic paper, the paragraph is the basic unit of writing. Paragraphs have sentences, of course. And first and last sentences of paragraphs are privileged.

But it's with paragraphs that one makes an argument. It's for this reason that I would never write with double-spacing. I prefer to use single-spacing, with a hard carriage return at the end of a paragraph so that each thought unit stands out clearly.

But preferences and modes of writing differ. The point is to find what works for you. I sometimes wish I could write worse first drafts. In principle, I see the virtue of Samuel Beckett's edict: "Fail. Fail again. Fail better." In practice, at least when it comes to the mechanics of writing, I'm more in the continuously-revising-while-writing mode. Most important, if I'm now reconciled to the problem that my first drafts are in some ways too good, I know that they're not perfect—and might never be. "If the world were perfect," said Yogi Berra, "it wouldn't be."

At some point while writing, I will start to think about the title. The importance of a good title cannot be overstated—not just because it helps the reader, but because the process of thinking about it *helps the writing*. In not insignificant ways, the process of revising can be seen through the lens of working to find the right title.

The timing of the appearance of the good title can vary considerably. In my own experience, most good titles have come about only after the project was well on its way. If the typical project gets completed at, let's say, version 6.0, then the final title is there by version 3.0 or so. That would have been the case for some of my titles: "Recombinant Property in East European Capitalism" (1996), or "Tools of the Trade: The Socio-Technology of Arbitrage in a Wall Street Trading Room" (with Daniel Beunza, 2004), or the already mentioned "Racial Attention Deficit" (2022). Sometimes the work of getting the fitting title was painfully protracted right up to the joyful moment when it clicked, for example, *The Sense of Dissonance: Accounts of Worth in Economic Life* (2009). At one extreme, "Structural Folds: Generative Disruption in Overlapping Groups" (with Balazs Vedres, 2010) didn't show up until the paper was in the revise-and-resubmit phase at *AJS* in something like version 8.0, if not more. Less often, and at the other extreme, the final title happened during the very first session of writing, such as "Put to the Test: For a New Sociology of Testing" (with Noortje Marres, 2020). And in one entirely singular case, the title "Permanently Beta" came first and then Gina Neff and I (2004) decided to write the paper.

When the right title happens is much less significant than *how* it comes about. Or, more accurately, from the standpoint of making the argument, actually finding the right title is less important than *what results from the process of searching* for it. This should be understood within the broader context of writing and revising. While the process of writing involves understanding how a given phrase or sentence or paragraph or section fits in relation to what came before and what will come after, revision involves two quite different aspects.

The first (less related to title) is discovering what needs to be expanded and what needs to be trimmed (or deleted altogether). I think about this as fulfilling the criterion of *needs to know*. In intelligence services, "need to know" refers to who (which agents or agencies) needs to know and at what level of clearance and specificity. Analogously, while revising, ask: Does the reader need to know this? If the reader doesn't need to know it in order to be able to grasp and be convinced by the argument, cut it. In parallel, also ask whether there is something else that the reader needs to know. If so, it must be included, and perhaps expansively.

The second aspect of revision is compression. To find the appropriate title, one must grasp the key concepts of the project. At first, it might take you many pages to figure it out. That's an idea in long form, but the underlying concept should be compressed and expressed (i.e., better if it is compressed expressively). Here's the one-sentence summary of my 1996 *AJS* paper: capitalism in Eastern Europe is not being built *on* the ruins of communism, but *with* the ruins of communism. There are various ways to express that concept, pointing to how property change is not a transition but a transformative recombination. It's one thing to have a concept; another to be able to express it succinctly; and yet another to give it a name. A concept might take a sentence, or at least a phrase, to state. Naming it can be done well in three words or less. Robert Merton was particularly gifted at this, giving us, for example, "unintended consequences," "role strain," and "self-fulfilling prophecy."

I was fortunate to come up with "recombinant property." But as important as the naming was the process of repeatedly looking for ways to compress and express the key ideas. Generating titles is a simple heuristic for doing so. It can come with making diagrams and trying different metaphors. While revising, I'll often make lists of title candidates. Those that don't work as the overall title will sometimes make excellent subheadings. Fail. Fail again. Fail better.

The writing is finished; I've revised the project in response to comments from friends and colleagues in the field; it was sent off to a journal or publisher; and now I've received the "we-regret-that-we-cannot-accept-revise-and-resubmit-please-respond-to-the-reviewers" letter from the editor. Judging from a good number of the contributors to this volume, my initial reaction to the reviewers' comments is not idiosyncratic: "Where does this journal find such idiots?" would be the apt characterization. But, of course, they're not (all) idiots. And so, waiting at least some days to let my temper cool, my coauthors and I frequently adopt the following tactic: we read the reviewers' comments out loud. I'll read several, then each coauthor does, going slowly, taking turns, reading deliberately. Heard in one's own voice or that of a trusted other, the comments can now have a different effect. From item to item: "That's a valid point; we should incorporate it." "Here the reviewer doesn't grasp our argument, but that's our problem, we need to restate it more clearly." "OK, but we don't agree, we'll have to deal with that." And so on.

So voiced, the reviewers' comments help us gain distance from the text. We can now see its flaws—and not just those indicated by the reviewers. We can now map out a strategy for revision. We've made notes on how to respond to reviewers, but those comments recede in importance as we get involved in conducting new analysis, reworking the introduction, and sometimes making radical changes in the architecture of the paper. Now, we're excited about revising.

After being more or less satisfied that we have a version we really like, we turn again to the reviewers' comments for the purpose of preparing our explicit response. We go down the list of reviewers' criticisms and suggestions, checking off:

- Yes, that's been dealt with, and this one, too, and that one as well.
- Hmmm. Here, we disagree with reviewer A, but on this same or similar point, we agree with reviewer B. So, no problem—we say we agree with reviewer B.
- Oh, that's such a good phrase. There's a sentence in that middle section where we can make some adjustments to incorporate it. Thank reviewer A.
- Whoops, we forgot about that, but we can take care of in a footnote.
- On this point, we disagree with reviewer B. We need to say so and to be very explicit about why we have that disagreement.

Once, a few years ago, a close friend told me, "David, I've finally learned how to write for the reviewers." I was saddened, and I said so. My friend is a great writer with a wonderful voice. We don't write for reviewers, I told him; we write for audiences. If you really do revise your paper for three reviewers, you have almost guaranteed that the paper will find its intended audience—three readers, and only three.

Over the past few decades, the reviewing process has evolved so it is now widely accepted that the reviewer's role is almost exclusively to detect errors. Some reviewers will resist this confinement, but lest journal pages be filled with articles that are absolutely flawless yet entirely uninteresting, editors and editorial boards must be adamant that error detection is only one of the tasks of the editorial process. Editors are overwhelmed, so the responsibility to resist the preoccupation with error detection is up to authors and audiences. Do not let the editorial process repress your voice. To be good, sociology needs more voices. We need new voices, excellent voices. If the so-called major journals do not offer readers articles with strong authorial voices, then readers should find other journals that do. As a writer, use the revision process to identify your audience and better voice your ideas. Clearly expressed, your voice will find its audience.

I hope that you will be able to take several reading sessions listening to the wonderful set of sociological voices in the chapters that follow. They write from considerable experience as researchers and as authors. I speak for all of them: We hope that the knowledge you gain from this book will be matched by genuine enjoyment while reading it. It has been a pleasure sharing with you our reflections on the tribulations and joys of practicing the sociological craft.

NOTES

1. As an exception, see Becker (n.d.).
2. About presenting in public, also exceptionally, see Stein and Daniels (2017). About writing, there are some excellent guides, including Becker (2008) and Eco (2015).
3. Exceptionally, one of the authors, Eric I. Schwartz, is not a sociologist. But as the editorial director of a major university press that is a leading publisher of books in sociology, Schwartz is a prominent figure in sociology, understood as a *field* (see Fligstein and McAdam, 2012) in which some participants are not themselves sociologists.
4. I am coeditor-in-chief at *Sociologica*, where these essays were originally published in three special symposia: "Heuristics of Discovery" (vol. 12, no. 1, 2018); "What Is Your Publication Strategy?" (vol. 13, no. 1, 2019); and "Revising" (vol. 16, no. 1, 2022).
5. On the importance of organizational peripheral vision, see Prato and Stark's (2022) network analytic study of observational learning.
6. On heterarchy, see Stark (1999, 2001). On recombinant property, see Stark (1996).
7. In terms of the anatomy of human perception, one's blind spot (where the optic nerve meets the retina) is what allows one to see. But at that spot itself, one is blind. For insights building on that observation, see especially von Foerster (1984) and Esposito (2013).

REFERENCES

Becker, Howard S. *Performing Social Science.* San Francisco: Wise Guy Press, n.d. http://www.howardsbecker.com/images/books/pss-lo-res.pdf.

Becker, Howard S. *Writing for Social Scientists: How to Start and Finish Your Thesis, Book, or Article,* 3rd ed. Chicago: University of Chicago Press, 2008.

Beunza, Daniel, and David Stark. "From Dissonance to Resonance: Cognitive Interdependence in Quantitative Finance." *Economy and Society* 41, no. 3 (2012): 383–417. https://doi.org/10.1080/03085147.2011.638155.

Beunza, Daniel, and David Stark. "Tools of the Trade: The Socio-Technology of Arbitrage in a Wall Street Trading Room." *Industrial and Corporate Change* 13, no. 2 (2004): 369–400. https://doi.org/10.1093/icc/dth015.

De Vaan, Mathijs, David Stark, and Balazs Vedres. "Game Changer: The Topology of Creativity." *American Journal of Sociology* 120, no. 4 (2015): 1144–1194. https://doi.org/10.1086/681213.

Eco, Umberto. *How to Write a Thesis,* translated by C. M. Farina and G. Farina. Cambridge, MA: MIT Press, 2015. Originally published in Italian in 1977.

Esposito, Elena. "Economic Circularities and Second-Order Observation: The Reality of Ratings." *Sociologica* 7, no. 2 (2013): 1–10. https://doi.org/10.2383/74851.

Fligstein, Neil, and Doug McAdam. *A Theory of Fields.* Oxford and New York: Oxford University Press, 2012.

Friedlander, Lee. *America by Car.* San Francisco: Fraenkel Gallery, 2010.

Friedlander, Lee. "An Excess of Fact." In *The Desert Seen,* 103–106. New York: Distributed Art Publishers, 1996.

Girard, Monique, and David Stark. "Socio-Technologies of Assembly: Sense-Making and Demonstration in Rebuilding Lower Manhattan." In *Governance and Information: The Rewiring of Governing and Deliberation in the 21st Century,* edited by D. Lazer and V. Mayer-Schoenberger, 145–176. Oxford and New York: Oxford University Press, 2007.

Levine, Sheen S., Evan P. Apfelbaum, Mark Bernard, Valerie L. Bartelt, Edward J. Zajac, and David Stark. "Ethnic Diversity Deflates Price Bubbles." *Proceedings of the National Academy of Sciences* 111, no. 52 (2014): 18524–18529. https://doi.org/10.1073/pnas.1407301111.

Levine, Sheen S., Charlotte Reypens, and David Stark. "Racial Attention Deficit." *Science Advances* 7, no. 38 (2015): 1–9. https://doi.org/10.1126/sciadv.abg9508.

Levine, Sheen S., and David Stark. "Diversity Makes You Brighter." *New York Times,* December 9, 2015. https://www.nytimes.com/2015/12/09/opinion/diversity-makes-you-brighter.html.

Marres, Noortje, and David Stark. "Put to the Test: For a New Sociology of Testing." *British Journal of Sociology* 71, no. 3 (2020): 423–443. https://doi.org /10.1111/1468-4446.12746.

Neff, Gina, and David Stark. "Permanently Beta: Responsive Organization in the Internet Era." In *Society Online: The Internet in Context*, edited by P. N. Howard and S. Jones, 173–188. Thousand Oaks, CA: SAGE, 2004.

Prato, Matteo, and David Stark. "Observational Learning in Networks of Competition: How Structures of Attention among Rivals Can Bring Interpretive Advantage." *Organization Studies* 44, no. 2 (2022): 253–276. https://doi.org/10.1177 /01708406221118672.

Stark, David. "Ambiguous Assets for Uncertain Environments: Heterarchy in Postsocialist Firms." In *The Twenty-First-Century Firm: Changing Economic Organization in International Perspective*, edited by Paul DiMaggio, 69–104. Princeton, NJ: Princeton University Press, 2001.

Stark, David. "Class Struggle and the Transformation of the Labor Process: A Relational Approach." *Theory and Society* 9, no. 1 (1980): 89–130. https://www .jstor.org/stable/656824.

Stark, David. "Heterarchy: Distributing Intelligence and Organizing Diversity." In *The Biology of Business: Decoding the Natural Laws of Enterprise*, edited by J. Clippinger, 153–179. San Francisco: Jossey-Bass, 1999.

Stark, David. "Recombinant Property in East European Capitalism." *American Journal of Sociology* 101, no. 4 (1996): 993–1027. https://www.jstor.org/stable/2782236.

Stark, David. *The Sense of Dissonance: Accounts of Worth in Economic Life*, Princeton, NJ: Princeton University Press, 2009.

Stark, David, and Laszlo Bruszt. *Postsocialist Pathways: Transforming Politics and Property in East Central Europe*. Cambridge: Cambridge University Press, 1998.

Stark, David, and Balázs Vedres. "Social Times of Network Spaces: Network Sequences and Foreign Investment in Hungary." *American Journal of Sociology* 111, no. 5 (2006): 1367–1411. https://doi.org/10.1086/499507.

Stein, Arlene, and Jessie Daniels. *Going Public: A Guide for Social Scientists*. Chicago: University of Chicago Press, 2017.

Vedres, Balazs, and David Stark. "Structural Folds: Generative Disruption in Overlapping Groups." *American Journal of Sociology* 115, no. 4 (2010): 1150–1190. https://doi.org/10.1086/649497.

von Foerster, Heinz. *Observing Systems*. Seaside, CA: Intersystems Publications, 1984.

I

ENCOUNTERING

Discovering a New Research Project

1

THE ART OF RECOGNIZING
WHAT YOU OUGHT TO HAVE
WANTED TO LOOK FOR

ANDREW ABBOTT

In an email message responding to my request for a contribution to this special feature, Andrew Abbott mentioned several reasons for declining the invitation. One of these was so appropriate to the topic that I am excerpting it here and publishing it with Professor Abbott's permission.

—The editor

I've just been in the middle of preparing a big lecture for the university here and so on this invitation I'll need to decline. It's odd, in a way, because one of the ways I *do* get new problems is illustrated by the talk I just gave. The Divinity School asked me to give the Nuveen Lecture, their big lecture for the year. It's kind of a dare: they ask a member of the faculty outside the Divinity School to talk to *them* about religion. But I was asked only in June, when my writing schedule for the Fall Quarter was already all set, because I had decided to teach a seminar on the drafts of my theory book, even though the chapters weren't all done or—in some cases—even started. By committing to teach uncompleted and even unwritten chapters, I was tying myself to the mast, hoping to force myself to finish the entire book manuscript in the Fall Quarter. But the Divinity

School invitation could be used to force me to apply the whole argument to a particular social institution, and to come up with all the reasons why one should follow my theoretical path. So I did it anyway, forcing myself to write for three hours every weekday morning for the first four weeks of the quarter.

And of course it proved extremely helpful. The mere exercise of applying the theory enabled me to wrench it free from its roots in my reactions against aspects of quantitative methodology. Having to cut a quarter of the talk at the last minute taught me what was essential and non-essential. Having to address a lay audience taught me that all the details had to be left out (and should go into footnotes in the book), something I was already learning from teaching the class. (One of the failings of my work has always been that I write at too many levels at once. It makes the texts unreadable, sometimes. But this kind of exercise forced me to a single level.)

So one place to get obligations is from outside, to see that you really ought to have wanted to give the talk you have been asked to give. As I said in *Digital Paper* (2014),[1] the art of research on found data from the library or on the internet is not to find things that you want, but to recognize when it is that you have run into something that you ought to have wanted to look for. The answer to every problem is always staring you in the face. But so also are a lot of wrong answers. The art of research is knowing how to tell the difference.

NOTE

1. This book underscores this point a number of times and in various contexts—both specific ones, like reading and document search, and more general ones, like conceptualization and problem structure. See pages xii, 1, 24, 30, 91, 104, 140, and 245.

REFERENCES

Abbott, Andrew. *Digital Paper: A Manual for Research and Writing with Library and Internet Materials.* Chicago: University of Chicago Press, 2014.

2

KEEPING ONE'S DISTANCE

Truth and Ambiguity in Social Research

DELIA BALDASSARRI

To the memory of Enzo Rutigliano

I t is not yet clear to me why certain topics become part of my research agenda, although I suspect a mix of political and personal interest, serendipity, and social influence is at play. I do have, however, a good sense of *what drives me while doing research*, meaning what I look for in the data, how I "treat" my subjects, and how I interpret their observed and unobserved behavior. Here I discuss two seemingly contradictory principles: a naïve commitment to the search for the truth, and a strong belief in the generative role of ambiguity and multivocality in the unfolding of social life.

First, I am driven by some sort of naïve commitment to the search for the truth. Not that I believe in its epistemological existence, but I find it useful to act as if there is something "definitive" to discover that, once revealed, other people would be able to see too. This naïve commitment affects the way I do research, in a way that is best captured in one of Italo Calvino's short stories: *The Count of Monte Cristo* (Calvino, 1967). In it, both Edmond Dantès and Abbé Faria linger in the dungeons of the prison of Monte Cristo/Château d'If. They both speculate upon the possibility of escaping; Dantès describes their strategies as follows:

> Faria proceeds in this way: he becomes aware of a difficulty, he studies a solution, he tries out the solution, encounters a new difficulty,

plans a new solution, and so on and on. For him, once all possible errors and unforeseen elements are eliminated, his escape can only be successful: it all lies in planning and carrying out the perfect escape. I set out from the opposite premise: there exists a perfect fortress, from which one cannot escape; escape is possible only if in the planning or building of the fortress some error or oversight was made. While Faria continues taking the fortress apart, sounding out its weak points, I continue putting it together, conjecturing more and more insuperable barriers. The images of the fortress that Faria and I create are becoming more and more different: Faria, beginning with a simple figure, is complicating it extremely to include in it each of the single unforeseen elements he encounters in his path; I setting out from the jumble of these data, see in each isolated obstacle the clue to a system of obstacles, I develop each segment into a regular figure, I fit these figures together as the sides of a solid, polyhedron or hyper-polyhedron, I inscribe these polyhedrons in spheres or hyper-spheres, and so the more I enclose the form of the fortress the more I simplify it, defining it in a numerical relation or in an algebraic formula (Calvino, 1967:143–144).

Consider the two strategies. Faria and Dantès look for, respectively, the realizable, perfect escape or a perfect, inescapable fortress and they adjust their everyday search practices accordingly. They implement two different approaches to the same goal: breaking out. Two approaches, that, nonetheless, lead to different outcomes. While Faria directly searches for a breakout, he generates a more complicated fortress. By pursuing "the multiplicity of possible things" (Calvino, 1967:147), he discovers an infinity of possible errors, and thus escaping becomes impossible. In contrast, Dantès searches for the perfect fortress, in which break out is impossible. While Faria dismantles the fortress piece by piece, Dantès constructs more and more impeding barriers. In so doing, he captures the geometric essence of the fortress, and thus simplifies it. Such simplification, far from being a pure analytical exercise, is instead the product of a continuous try out/ examination of the real fortress.

> But to conceive a fortress in this way I need the Abbé Faria constantly combating landslides of rubble, steel, bolts, sewers, sentry boxes, leaps into nothingness, recesses in the sustaining walls, because the only way to reinforce the imagined fortress is to put the real one continuously to the test (Calvino, 1967:144).

Paradoxically, Faria's spasmodic attempt at removing all possible errors and unforeseen elements does not lead to an escape, but to a more complicated fortress, while, in contrast, Dantès's conjecture of the inescapable fortress allows him to find the possible discrepancies between the real fortress and the imaginary one and thus plan his actions accordingly:

> And so we go on dealing with the fortress, Faria sounding out the weak points of the wall and coming up against new obstacles, I reflecting on his unsuccessful attempts in order to conjecture new outlines of walls to add to the plan of my fortress-conjecture. If I succeed in mentally constructing a fortress from which it is impossible to escape, this conceived fortress either will be the same as the real one—and in this case it is certain we shall never escape from here, but at least we will achieve the serenity of one who knows he is here because he could be nowhere else—or it will be a fortress from which escape is even more impossible than from here—and this, then, is a sign that here an opportunity of escape exists: we have only to identify the point where the imagined fortress does not coincide with the real one and then find it (Calvino, 1967:151–152).

What does breakout stand for? In theory, it may symbolize different things, either social achievements (such as freedom, emancipation, or salvation) or cognitive fulfilments (such as knowledge or self-consciousness). In general, we can think of it as the search/call for truth. Indeed, in the Christian tradition there is an intimate relationship between freedom and knowledge:

You will know the truth, and the truth will set you free (John, 8, 32).

And this relation has maintained its prominence during the Enlightenment, even though a rhetoric of salvation was substituted by a rhetoric of emancipation and knowledge (partly) replaced faith.

What Dantès's and Faria's story suggests is that beliefs about the possibility of a breakout strongly affect research practices and eventually their outcomes. In other words, the type of empirical evidence one looks for and digs up depends on his/her orientation to knowledge: diverse images of reality will emerge depending on whether one proceeds by making the fortress increasingly more complex, or by simplifying it, capturing its mathematical form.

There is a general tendency in sociology, more than in any other social science, of capturing social reality in its complexity and multiple layers of meaning. And this seems a sensible way to proceed, given that the social phenomena we are interested in are usually quite complicated. However, maybe because I am a bit lazy, my instinct is often to tell the simplest story possible. Not because I do not believe that reality is complex—I indeed witness many Farias around me taking the fortress apart—but because I think our only chance at walking away from the fortress is to capture its analytical essence and thus reduce its complexity. My reliance on analytical categories, (simple) formal models, behavioral games, and field experiments can be understood in this framework. Sketching the bare bones of a formal model (Manzo and Baldassarri, 2014; Baldassarri and Bearman, 2007), studying human interdependence within the minimalist constraints of a behavioral game (Baldassarri, 2015), as well as embedding unobtrusive field experiments in everyday life (Baldassarri and Abascal, 2017) are all ways in which I try to capture geometric complexity through simplification. What many would see as arid, ahistorical, empty of context and meaning, is for me the final test in which the real fortress gets compared to the hypothetical one—the one from which it is impossible to escape—and only if there is a difference, then a break-out is possible.

This predilection for analytical simplicity however combines with a second, almost orthogonal tendency to consider the generative role of ambiguity and multiplexity in shaping social relationships.

To give you an example of what I mean by the positive role of ambiguity, let's consider the (mostly American) concept of going on a "date." To me, this was a cultural shock, because in the culture I come from there is no equivalent attempt at predefining the content of a relationship of this kind, the first solo encounter between two individuals. Or, at least, there is no explicit attempt at drawing a line between romantic and non-romantic relationships. This is an event defined by its potential, in which fluidity is maximal, and defining ex ante the boundaries of the relationship does inexorably mean to constrain it, and therefore limit its possibilities. To label it a "date" kills the romance! A romantic relationship unfolds from the ambiguity that underlines courtship, the multiple and sometimes contrasting signals, e.g., dressing up but remaining casual, choosing a romantic restaurant but avoiding the candlelight cliché, showing interest but not falling in love, etc.

Of course, a romantic relationship is a very personal, peculiar event, but the same positive role of ambiguity can be seen in many other patterns of relations, involving individuals as well as institutions. In general terms, we should think of ambiguity as a property of the situation, rather than of the actors themselves. Ambiguity can generate from many factors, including the fact that actors have imperfect information, multiple and even contrasting desires, an inadequate or limited understanding of the situation, of their own means and of other people's intentions, sometimes even scarce control over their own will, thus limited control over their course of action.

I'm here less concerned with the ambiguity that derives from imperfect information, misperceptions, cognitive biases, and other individual limitations. These have already been the object of extended investigation in the social sciences. What I want to highlight is the *relational* dimension of ambiguity, the fact that the meaning of social action is contingent on how it is perceived by other individuals, and how it cumulates into a sequence of actions. Moreover, social actions might be multivocal, sometimes even deliberately oriented at providing noisy signals.

I have the sense that in the social sciences we tend to think of ambiguity as a limitation, either as a distortion from the model of perfect information (and rational action) or a situation in which individuals and organizations are under stress, in which actors experience multiple and counteracting tendencies, a potential source of misunderstanding, wrong calculation, or a possible cause of unattended consequences.

In contrast, I tend to think about the ambiguity that permeates social actions and interactions as a necessary precondition for the unfolding of social relations, a buffer space that allows shifts in roles, fluid understanding, partial disclosure, and might contribute to preventing direct confrontation, and conflict.

Ambiguity conceived in these terms is complementary to the concept of social role; it captures what is left out, what we miss when we constrain individuals to categories, expected behaviors, and obligations that are defined by their socio-demographic profile and status. Ambiguity should not be conceived as an alternative to social roles, but instead as the fertile terrain that provides the preconditions for roles to be defined, negotiated and, more importantly, for contrasting roles (and identities) to be carried out simultaneously. The roots of this complementarity can be easily found in Merton's role-set theory (Merton, 1957).

So, what does this attention to ambiguity add to our research? The most important thing is that it prevents the researcher from the *risk of role reification,* in which actors are stuck, crystallized into a set of categories, labeled as working class, Evangelicals, mothers, Latinos, Southerners, Democrats, and then expected to follow courses of action that are coherent with the labels we give them.

Here's three pieces of scholarship that well exemplify how ambiguity and multivocality can have a generative role in the explanation of social action. Eric Leifer, in "Interaction Preludes to Role Settings: Exploratory Local Action" (1988), argues that in settings in which roles are not "given," in which roles are not yet established, actors have to strategically interact to acquire desirable roles. During the interaction that precedes the establishment of roles and social hierarchy, individuals should avoid claiming a coveted role until there is evidence that it will be conferred. Otherwise, they will reveal their intention and desires, thus giving an advantage to other people competing for that role. In general, explicit status claims are dangerous, because people are exposed to the possibility that the status won't be conferred: "The same actions that confer status can also take it away, depending on the responses they elicit." As an alternative, Leifer discusses a distinct action ideal, called "local action," that is intended to suppress role differentiation. It is a non-role-specific action, "that, ex ante, leaves open a range of roles, and ex-post, does not prove inconsistent with any role that might be claimed later" (Leifer, 1988:868). The relative status of individuals remains fluid until ambiguity failures occur and roles emerge from local interactions. In these terms, interaction preludes role setting. Roger Gould built his theory of status hierarchies on similar principles.

In addition to being a strategic tool that individuals deploy in the competition to achieve desirable roles, however, ambiguity is also a mean for individuals to juggle their different, and sometimes alternative identities. In his *Insurgent Identities* (1995), a study of the Parisians protests of the nineteenth century, Gould asks how the collective identity of workers emerges as such and becomes a mobilizing identity. Instead of categorizing individuals as workers, he considered the multiple identities that were available to the actors, from their gild affiliation to the neighborhood where they lived, and shows how patterns of social interactions—the web of interpersonal relationship in which people are embedded—are fundamental in eliciting certain identities and neglecting others, thus producing an alignment of interest and identity. Class *in se* becomes class *per se*: the initial ambiguity of multiple potential identities is resolved through social interaction.

Finally, Padgett and Ansell in their "Robust Action and the Rise of the Medici" (1993) describe the birth of the Renaissance state in Florence deploying Leifer's concept of local action. According to them, the Medici's political power emerged from their capacity to span across the network disjunctures within the élite. The Medici's party was a "mixture of contradictory interests and crosscutting networks" (Padgett and Ansell, 1993:1262). At the basis of Cosimo de Medici's action there is the notion of multivocal identity, where *multivocality* is intended as "the fact that single actions can be interpreted coherently from multiple perspectives simultaneously" (Padgett and Ansell, 1993:1263). It is through this multivocal action that interest remains opaque, hidden. In more general terms, they conclude: "Ambiguity and heterogeneity, not planning and self-interest are the raw materials of which powerful states and persons are constituted" (Padgett and Ansell, 1993:1259).

As it should be clear from this last example, this perspective suggests a theory of action that is alternative not only to classical rational choice, but also to many means-goal explanations. The main difference between Leifer's theory of local action and these other theories of action, however, doesn't have to do with the rationality of the actors or their level of agency. The real difference concerns the focus of observation, namely rational action theory is centered on the individuals and their motivations, while local action starts from relationships. Consistently, scholars working on this vein have found in social network analysis a very powerful analytical instrument. In fact, acknowledging the primacy of relationships is a way to maintain the composite and contradictory nature of individuals, and therefore keep alive the source of their ambiguity.

Some readers might wonder whether this focus on ambiguity and multivocality is simply another way of saying that individuals are complex creatures, and thus cannot be categorized and quantified. It is not. What I have in mind is instead the basic dualism that, according to George Simmel, "pervades the fundamental form of all sociation. The dualism consists in the fact that a relation, which is a fluctuating, constantly developing life-process, nevertheless receives a relatively stable external form" (Simmel, 1971:351).

Simmel builds on the analytic distinction, and dialectic, between forms and life-process: according to him, the stream of life, its potentiality and energy, in order to realize itself, inevitably has to be constrained by forms: "our inner life, which we perceive as a stream . . . becomes crystallized, even for ourselves, in formulas and fixed directions often merely by the fact that we verbalize this life. Even if this leads only rarely to specific inadequacies . . . there still remains the fundamental, formal contrast between the essential flux and movement of the subjective psychic life and the limitations of its forms. These forms, after all, do not express or shape an ideal, a contrast with life's reality, but this life itself" (Simmel, 1971:352).

Thus, forms are the realization of the life-process, their crystallization. Life-process is always more than forms, but can only express itself by becoming forms. Focusing on the network of social relations in which individual and institutions are embedded is a powerful way to capture these forms. We need, however, to remember the enduring discrepancy between life contents and their objectification in relational forms, and keep alive the tension between individual possibilities and their realization. Only in this way we would avoid the *risk of form and network reification*. Some hard-core structuralists have run into this problem in the past. Now, the same problem is visible in most research based on large-scale networks, in which big data comes at the expense of information about the nodes and the nature of their relationships.

To avoid social structural reification, we should recognize individual possibilities and agency, as well as the historical and social constraints actors face, and the ways in which they overcome them. Consider the episode from the *Odyssey* of Ulysses and the Sirens. The Sirens have the power of charming by their song everyone who heard them, leading mariners to destruction. Ulysses needs to pass by the Sirens' island, but simultaneously wants to listen to their voice. His solution is to stop the ears of his seamen with wax, so that they should not hear the strain, and to have himself bound to the mast. Furthermore, he instructs his people, whatever he might say or do, by no means to release him till they have passed the Sirens' island.

In a popular interpretation of this episode, Elster (1979) treats Ulysses as a rational decision maker and the episode is an example of pre-commitment: a decision is taken at time o to bind the decisions one can make at time 1. In contrast, Horkheimer and Adorno (1988) put Ulysses's behavior in relation to the historical context and broader social order in which he is acting. First, Ulysses has multiple and contrasting goals: he wants to get home, but also wants to satisfy his own curiosity, thus listen to the Sirens. Moreover, he has a specific position in the social structure; he has power over his subordinates and exercises it, in order to prevent potential weaknesses of his own will, and therefore maintain his social status. The entire journey, and this episode in particular, can be read as an allegory of modernity, and the growing control that the bourgeois individual has over myth. In sum, while through Elster's lens we are presented a mythology of individual efficacy, Adorno and Horkheimer's dialectic reveals the historical, relational, and contextual preconditions that enable Ulysses to cross boundaries, to overcome his own limitations in a new and creative way. This is not by chance: a dialectical method is, first and foremost, the rejection of all reifications, and stands in contrast to positivist and scientific models of science that turn to myth "by failing to reflect on their own practices" (1988). This leads me to a final question: If we agree that ambiguity and multivocality have a positive role in determining the unfolding of social life, should they have a role in our research activity?

I believe that keeping alive the sources of contradiction in our research practices can be potentially useful. It is in this spirit that I decided to title this little exercise in self-reflection "Keeping One's Distance," after a beautiful two-page fragment in *Minima Moralia* in which Adorno (2007) shows how "distance and self-criticism is not a safety-zone but a field of tension. It is manifested not in relating the claim of ideas to truth, but in delicacy and fragility of thinking" (127). In other words, in the "concrete awareness of the conditionality of human knowledge" (Adorno, 2007:128). If there is something that I should reveal about my way of doing research, it is this intellectual tension.

REFERENCES

Adorno, Theodor. *Minima Moralia. Reflections on a Damaged Life*, translated by E. F. N. Jephcott. New York: Verso, 2007. Originally published in German in 1951.

Baldassarri, Delia. "Cooperative Networks: Altruism, Group Solidarity, Reciprocity, and Sanctioning in Ugandan Farmer Organizations." *American Journal of Sociology* 121, no. 2 (2015): 355–395. https://doi.org/10.1086/682418.

Baldassarri, Delia, and Maria Abascal. "Field Experiments across the Social Sciences." *Annual Review of Sociology* 43 (2017): 41–73. https://doi.org/10.1146/annurev-soc-073014-112445.

Baldassarri, Delia, and Peter Bearman. "Dynamics of Political Polarization." *American Sociological Review* 72 (2007): 784–811. https://doi.org/10.1177/000312240707200507.

Calvino, Italo. *t zero*, translated by W. Weaver. San Diego, CA: Harcourt Brace, 2007. Originally published in Italian in 1967.

Elster, Jon. *Ulysses and the Sirens: Studies in Rationality and Irrationality*. Cambridge: Cambridge University Press, 1979.

Gould, Roger V. *Insurgent Identities. Class, Community, and Protest in Paris from 1848 to the Commune*. Chicago: Chicago University Press, 1995.

Horkheimer, Max, and Theodor Adorno. *Dialectic of Enlightenment*, translated by J. Cumming. New York: Continuum, 1988. Originally published in German in 1947.

Leifer, Eric M. "Interaction Preludes to Role Setting: Exploratory Local Action." *American Sociological Review* 53 (1988): 865–878. https://doi.org/10.2307/2095896.

Manzo, Gianluca, and Delia Baldassarri. "Heuristics, Interactions, and Status Hierarchies: An Agent-based Model of Deference Exchange." *Sociological Methods and Research* 44, no. 2 (2015): 1–59. https://psycnet.apa.org/doi/10.1177 /0049124114544225.

Merton, Robert K. *Social Theory and Social Structure.* Glencoe, IL: Free Press, 1957.

Padgett, John F., and Christopher K. Ansell. "Robust Action and the Rise of the Medici, 1400–1434." *American Journal of Sociology* 98, no. 6 (1993): 1259–1319.

Simmel, G. *On Individuality and Social Forms.* Chicago: University of Chicago Press, 1971.

3

NOTES FOR "HEURISTICS OF DISCOVERY"

PETER BEARMAN

ACKNOWLEDGMENTS

Comments from Mark Hoffman, Alessandra Nicifero, and Adam Reich are gratefully acknowledged, as is support from the Interdisciplinary Center for Innovative Theory and Empirics (INCITE) at Columbia University.

Thinking about the problems the editor posed to us—how do we pick topics, what heuristics do we follow, what work processes do we use, and so on—made me realize that the hardest thing for me about any project is knowing when it is finished. That is one of the reasons why I've sometimes waited years between finishing papers and submitting them to journals, essentially unchanged after years spent in a box, or file cabinet. *Relations into Rhetorics* was written in 1985 and mailed to the press in 1992; *Chains of Affection* was written in 1998, but not published until 2004; *Becoming a Nazi* was written in 1992 and published almost a decade later, in 2000. Early on in my career I thought this was a disorder caused by a very negative review of my first attempt to publish *Generalized Exchange* in 1984 (finally published in 1997), which consisted, in its entirety, of the following lines: "This must be a word processor error because the tables come from one paper and the text comes from another."[1] But this still happens to me now, and today there are papers I will come to think as really good which remain deeply in the closet. I've overcome whatever stress I had about reviewers and I now understand that the delays, early on in my career, and now, are just because my papers are waiting for me to understand what their contribution could be. And that sometimes takes a long time to see.

Knowing when something is finished reflects what contribution we want to make in the first place. The contributions that I try to make share the ambition of creating beautiful things that have not been seen before. In this regard I think of my work as aesthetic in orientation. I think of the conventions that structure scientific work as comparable to the frames that bound canvasses in painting—constraints that one works with because they make many of the hard decisions easier; they take them off the table. Because these constraints vary with the style of work, they also bound the character of the objects one can create, and so the choice of topic and style or problem and method are inextricably woven together. Not all papers are going to succeed entirely on the beautiful object dimension, and part of trying to figure out when a paper is finished is coming to grips with the fact that for whatever reason, usually a bad starting point, it can't achieve what I had imagined, but that still, there is some part of it; a figure, a turn of phrase, an idea, that is beautiful enough.

We always wonder, or I always wonder, why people work on the problems and projects that they work on. Maybe that same curiosity was the motivation for this issue, on the part of the editor. It seems worth saying here that our methods are sometimes designed to provide answers to causal questions (though the typical explanation in our field is a just-so story) and sometimes the work I do also explicitly addresses causality. I have the perception that getting some causal estimation right motivates much work in our discipline—but for me, that is a secondary goal. I only mention this because, for those whose ultimate goal is different than mine, it is unlikely that my thoughts on the broad topic of heuristics for creating new objects and heuristics for knowing when to mail one's work to journals and presses will be at all useful.

So, in terms of structure, for this chapter, I'll talk about two heuristics that I use, connect them to work of mine by way of example, and then finish with the three things I learned from Harrison White.

HEURISTIC I: USE RELATIONAL DATA OR INDUCE A RELATIONAL CONTEXT

I still browse the shelves of others' offices and libraries looking through books and archives and record repositories for relational data that appear systematic enough to exploit in one way or another. That is how I found the data structure—221 221×221 square matrices identifying with a letter code how people living on Groote Eylandt on the eve of detribalization referred to one another using one of roughly twenty-one distinct kinship terms—that was at the heart of a paper I wrote on *Generalized Exchange* (Bearman, 1997). I knew that project was essentially finished when I was able to discover and reveal the hidden structure of their kinship system induced from a block model of kin terms. This structure was a perfect cycle; built from hundreds of violations of stated norms, a cycle based on categories that natives could not articulate but which actually produced, on the ground, a theoretical ideal, long imagined but never seen, a cycle for generalized exchange. I think I discovered the micro-mechanism undergirding the generation of cyclic exchange, the pursuit of balance in a context of stark intergenerational asymmetry in partner "choice." But what sealed the deal was thinking about an amazing photograph of a trial by ordeal that took place on the beach, one day. A man stole a woman who he felt should be his wife but who was given to another man, whom he killed in the resulting fracas. By explicit native norms he was in the wrong for the theft, and therefore the murder. By the hidden structure revealed from the block model, he was the rightful spouse; the murdered man was an illegitimate interloper. All of the men on the island gathered. They stood fewer than 100 feet from the thief. The photo captures the moment immediately before they each threw a spear at him. They all missed. I remember thinking: "*Now that is beautiful.*" And sometime later, I mailed the paper off.[2]

I only once made the mistake of building a data set that was not at its core relational. That was for a project on desertion from the Confederacy (Bearman, 1993), and the paper was only saved by realizing that I could induce relationality (of sorts) by imagining that people who were listed next to one another in the census ought to live next to each other, since the census taker in 1860 had to walk from household to household to enumerate residents. By inducing relations through spatial proximity on the home front I could embed soldiers simultaneously in two communities: one arising from the units in which they served, the other arising from the micro-contexts—below the level of counties or towns—in which they could return. And from that, I could infer something about the ways in which the structure of their social relations shaped their identity, and hence their actions, at least with respect to desertion. What sealed the deal for me in this paper was that I could find a partition of household numbers which matched (in one case perfectly, in another closely) desertion timing for late but not early deserters. For me, the beautiful discovery was that localism—an identity that arises from relations with others—not interests (abstract or concrete) brought men into and out of the confederate army, at least from North Carolina. Sometimes, one can build beautiful relational data structures but elements critical for the project are totally elusive. From my work with *Add Health*, I had become familiar and enamored with multilevel models. I thought then and still think now that they help us capture an aspect of the essentially Russian-doll reality of the contexts in which we are embedded and that they help us understand the ways in which context shapes our sense of self, and hence our action in the world. When I came to Columbia I wanted to shift back to historical work, and I thought a long time about what a model historical project—that is, a project which could serve as a model for a wide array of different research problems—would look like. And I understood that it would require a multilevel framework, with rich and very granular temporal data, on a large, interlinked population of actors, whose linkages were also multilevel.

Driving those methodological considerations down to something realizable was more complex. After a lot of thought, I had the idea that I could undertake a study of mutinies if I could induce a data structure that captured every boat on the seas and every person on each boat at multiple moments in each day that the boat was on the water. Boats could be linked by sharing ports; and by sharing men; men could be linked by their sharing boats. Mutinies as a repertoire of action took off at a certain point—one could clearly see that there was an epidemic of them and so I needed then to capture boats over a long *durée*, before mutinies took off and after they largely disappeared. I first looked in the Atlantic, but the boat data was too imprecise. Then, Emily Erikson discovered the East India Company Archive—a book which listed every boat that ever departed from England for the East under the aegis of the Company (and since they had a monopoly, that was pretty much every boat) and the individuals, above ordinary seamen, who were on it. The data were so precise and so uniform that we had the idea that we could measure long-term changes in climate based on trip durations only to discover that climatologists had actually already done it! By inducing boat overlap from sharing a stay at an Eastern port and by inducing ties between people by modeling their career mobility, as they moved from boat to boat over the course of multiple voyages (a similar strategy to what I had done in *Relations into Rhetorics* [1993], for preachers), we realized we could build the network structure that facilitated learning about how to mutiny.

The thing about mutinies, though, is that like all social action they are motivated for some reason, and that, anecdotally at least, the reason was about the conditions on board—whether there was food, water, the maggot situation, cholera, the character of the punishment meted out by the Captain, getting stuck in the doldrums, and so on. Voyage logbooks, built from entries recorded every four hours, provided insight into ship conditions at a level of temporal granularity that was unprecedented. My plan was to get a sample of logs for boats that experienced a mutiny and those that did not, capture their network position, and understand quite precisely how knowledge about how to mutiny shaped the likelihood of actually doing it, if the conditions warranted. Emily went to England to extract the logs. After the first few arrived it became pretty clear that the plan was very deeply flawed. I had forgotten to consider the obvious fact that when boats experienced a mutiny the first thing to disappear was the logbook. So that project failed.

But because there was a relational data structure we were able to model the emergence of global capitalism (Erikson and Bearman, 2006). And here there was a special joy in being able to discover that the British were able to expand beyond the Dutch because their captains were cheats and crooks. What could be more beautiful than a single figure which suggested that capitalism as a global system arose from malfeasance?

HEURISTIC II: DISCOVER AND REPRESENT MULTIPLE STANDPOINTS

My screen saver reminds me throughout the day when I open my computer that "it is better to travel through a single land with a thousand pairs of eyes than a thousand lands with a single pair of eyes." I found this sentence years ago in R. D. Laing, the *Politics of Experience* (Laing, 1967). Laing attributes the quote to Proust, and a friend of mine—a Proust expert—found something kind of like it in *In Search of Lost Time*,[3] but the Laing version is too distant to say anything other than "attributed to Proust." Provenance aside, this aphorism shapes my thinking about how we are to understand the social world. I wish I could say that I have, but I've never been able to make it through Proust. But from what I understand, *In Search of Lost Time* is about continuity. And that makes sense because understanding how continuity happens is irresolvable without being able to capture what contexts look like from multiple points of view, at every moment in time. And, not really as an aside, but relevant to the question of how one chooses topics, my interest now is to understand continuity, which I think has always been one of the hardest problems facing the discipline.

In ethnographic contexts, it is possible to capture the orientations of actors by standing on the edge of actors' perceptions as they are seeing. Because one is in the setting, the good ethnographer can see how the multiple orientations compose the whole setting. In historical work this is much more difficult. Even situating ourselves within the framework of single actors is difficult. How can we see what actors saw without imputing our standpoint to them? How can we preserve the multiplicity of standpoints that characterizes a single setting? I've been working on this problem for a very long time. Interestingly, one of the reasons that classificatory kinship systems are so attractive to work with is because they radically simplify, through an incredible expansion of the language of kinship, the multiple standpoint problem. In classificatory systems every person in one section of the tribe can agree on the relations of every other pair of pair of persons in the tribe. As White (1963) argues, "Of course I can always agree on how two people are related to each other by putting myself in one of their places as ego, but it is only in a classificatory system that I as ego can group others in exactly the same clusters of equivalence as they do" (81–82). Which is how it came about to be that all the men on Groote Eylandt, at the same moment, missed in their trial by ordeal.

In *Blocking the Future* (1999), Moody, Faris, and I interwove multiple life stories extracted from residents of a single Chinese village to induce a history of interlinked events that covered a half century of massive social change. We exploit the fact that actors' life stories arise from different standpoints—they have to since the life story is the narrators' theory of how s/he got to where they are (wherever they are). We know that the standpoint of the life story is not the standpoint that the actor had at the moment of their action, but we know with equal certainty that it is not ours. Stacking those life stories on top of one another like we used to stack transparencies in grade school reports makes it possible to induce a single context from the multiple stories that cross it. Like the giant crab-like spanning tree in *Chains of Affection* (2002), the beautiful object at the end of *Blocking the Future* (1999) is built from local action, but could never be seen by a single perspective. It is a history of a small village that *has to be*—randomly re-wiring whole chunks of the past don't change the structure—but which no one can see by themselves. And that is what we mean, I think, when we think about continuity. Each actor, doing their thing, on the short chains they are embedded in, contributing to each present in such a manner that most anything that happens preserves the opportunity structures they and others face, just as they were, for the next event, and the next.

In one of the best papers I have ever had the fortune of collaborating on—a paper written around 2008 on the conflict in Northern Ireland, with Hrag Balian, and partially published only in 2018 (Balian and Bearman, 2018)—this central idea is pushed to the limit. Here the data are all of the thousands of author-victim killing pairs, perfectly time-stamped, unfolding as a sequence of killings carried out by different groups. At any specific moment each group, relative to all others, can try to achieve a coveted end—revenge for a prior killing, dominance over other groups—but as with talk in meetings they cannot all act (speak) at once, and the next killing whether theirs or that of another group, changes the structure for everyone, producing new opportunities. The paper conceives of a way of capturing which opportunities each group can see relative to all other groups at every moment in time. They look back through a window to their past with other groups. Network ties are no longer dots connected by edges; they are vectors of events extending over different calendric periods. And so, the image of history is not a graph linking one event to another from an Archimedean standpoint outside of the graph, but instead a series of multiple sequences seen from every perspective simultaneously. Inducing a picture of the dozens of interwoven event sequences in the Northern Ireland conflict from each groups' perspective was, for me, just staggeringly beautiful. It is inserted here, as figure 3.1. The lines are group-specific histories. They start when groups have a motive to kill and stop when they no longer have one. Is it any wonder that civil conflicts last for generations if any specific moment in time is embedded in one or more events sequences defined by the presence of a reason to kill?

Is this history as an accordion real? Simmel may or may not have said somewhere that facts are overrated and that if one can think

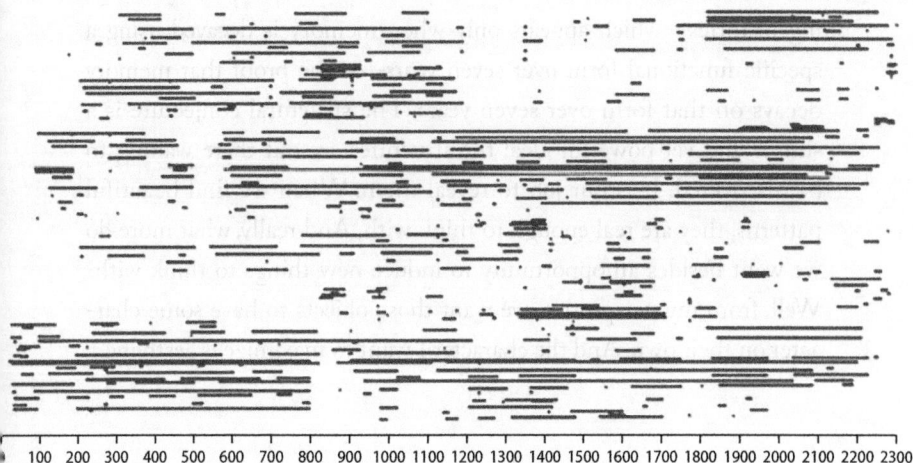

FIGURE 3.1 History as an accordion.

Note: The *x*-axis is a count of killing events, from 1 (the first killing) to 2,300 (of more than 3,000). Each moment is embedded in multiple unfolding event sequences; each actor is embedded on multiple lines; the past for each actor has multiple durations, and there is no uniform time.

something, it is as good as if it were an actual fact.[4] This is a version of what I take to be the structural conjecture, which I learned from Harrison White. The reason this makes sense—and this is another thing I learned from Harrison White—is that people are like plants in a hothouse. They just naturally get all intertwined. But what distinguishes people from plants (and following Levi-Strauss, from animals as well) is that they define some ties as ties that they cannot have. And the pattern that is revealed by the absence of ties points our way towards understanding the cultural rules that structure social life. This is why the vast majority of work on social networks says so little about social structure. Social structure arises from the absence of ties, not the presence. The so-called network science revolution which just looks at the presence of ties can't really get to structure beyond epiphenomenal features, like power laws. But that is a digression.

The importance of the structural conjecture is hard to underestimate for finishing projects. One example of this comes from the work of Kate Stovel, whose discovery of a structure in county lynching histories—which appears only when memory is decayed using a specific functional form over seven years—is the proof that memory decays on that form over seven years. The structural conjecture is a simple and yet powerful idea: the structures are out there waiting to be discovered. It is our job to reveal them. When we find beautiful patterns, they are real enough to think with. And really, what more do we want besides an opportunity to induce new things to think with? Well, from my perspective, we want those objects to have some character on their own. And the character I want to maximize is aesthetic.

CONCLUSION

We all pursue our work for different reasons. I'm interested in discovering structures that can exist but are not known (which is the same as creating new objects). There are lots of ways to discover structures.

The two heuristics I've discussed just happen to be the ones that I use and find useful for discovery. Even better, they also provide great stopping rules. Speaking of which . . .

CODA: THE THREE THINGS I LEARNED FROM HARRISON WHITE

For this to be a heuristic it has to be something like: "Remember the three things I learned from Harrison White." These are (1) Trust your students, they are smarter than you; (2) Being completely wrong is better than being just a little wrong; (3) Look at things in reverse; (4) Leave technical problems for technical people.

NOTES

1. For younger-generation readers who do not know what a word processor was, they were short-lived machines that bridged the gap between typewriters and computers. They were new in 1984 and the reviewer was right—I used one. These kinds of reviews make one sensitive to theory/data gaps.

2. Gerry Marwell, the editor of *ASR* who first rejected the sociology version of the paper—the earlier rejection was from an anthropology journal—wrote a little note on the paper which he sent back, which said: "You should talk to a senior colleague about how to write a paper." He crossed out "senior" and wrote "junior." He crossed out "junior colleague" and wrote "anyone." It took a long time to publish that paper because sociology reviewers didn't believe the idea that people could and did follow norms that they could not articulate and which operated on categories which they had no words for. In short, they didn't believe sociology was possible.

3. "The only true voyage, the only bath in the Fountain of Youth, would be not to visit strange lands but to possess other eyes, to see the universe through the eyes of another, of a hundred others, to see the hundred universes that each of them sees, that each of them is . . ." (Proust, 1993:343).

4. I don't know where he said that, if he said that; and the special thing about that idea is that it doesn't actually matter if he said it, since I can think with the idea that he said it, which is sufficient.

REFERENCES

Balian, Hrag, and Peter S. Bearman. *Pathways to Violence: Dynamics for the Continuation of Large-Scale Conflict.* Manuscript, 2008.

Balian, Hrag, and Peter S. Bearman. "Pathways to Violence: Dynamics for the Continuation of Large-Scale Conflict." *Sociological Theory* 36, no. 2 (2018): 210–220. https://doi.org/10.1177/0735275118777000.

Bearman, Peter S. "Desertion as Localism: Army Unit Solidarity and Group Norms in the U.S. Civil War." *Social Forces* 70, no. 2 (1991): 321–342. https://doi.org /10.2307/2580242.

Bearman, Peter S. "Generalized Exchange." *American Journal of Sociology* 102, no. 5 (1997): 1383–1415. https://doi.org/10.1086/231087.

Bearman, Peter S. *Relations into Rhetorics: Local Elite Social Structure in Norfolk England, 1540–1840.* New Brunswick, NJ: Rutgers University Press, 1993.

Bearman, Peter S., Robert Faris, and James Moody. "Blocking the Future: New Solutions for Old Problems in Historical Social Science." *Social Science History* 23, no. 4 (1999): 501–533. https://www.jstor.org/stable/1171636.

Bearman, Peter S., James Moody, and Katherine Stovel. *Chains of Affection: The Structure of Adolescent Romantic and Sexual Networks.* New York: Columbia University Academic Commons, 2002.

Bearman, Peter S., and Katherine Stovel. "Becoming a Nazi: A Model for Narrative Networks." *Poetics* 27, no. 2–3 (2000): 69–90. https://doi.org/10.1016/S0304 -422X(99)00022-4.

Erikson, Emily, and Peter S. Bearman. "Malfeasance and the Foundations for Global Trade: The Structure of English Trade in the East Indies, 1601–1833." *American Journal of Sociology* 112, no. 1 (2006): 195–230. https://doi.org/10.1086/502694.

Laing, Ronald D. *The Politics of Experience.* New York: Pantheon, 1967.

Proust, Marcel. *In Search of Lost Time, Volume 5: The Captive & The Fugitive,* translated by C. K. S. Moncrieff and T. Kilmartin. London: Chatto & Windus, 1993. Originally published in French in 1923 and 1925.

Stovel, Katherine. "Local Sequential Patterns: The Structure of Lynching in the Deep South, 1882–1930." *Social Forces* 79, no. 3 (2001): 843–880. https://www.jstor.org /stable/2675611.

White, Harrison C. *Anatomy of Kinship.* New York: Prentice-Hall, 1963.

4

HEURISTICS AND THEORIZING
AS WORK ON THE SELF

MICHELA BETTA AND RICHARD SWEDBERG

The topic of heuristics is attracting increased attention in U.S. sociology, as evidenced by a growing number of works on this topic (e.g., Becker, 1998; Abbott, 2004; Martin, 2014; Swedberg, 2014). The term "heuristics" itself is situated somewhere between the following two poles in social science discourse: rules of thumb on the one hand and discovery on the other. Its meaning as discovery was the original, dating to Antiquity. The notion of heuristics as rules of thumb, which people use in situations of uncertainty, was introduced some decades ago by Amos Tversky and Daniel Kahneman (Kahneman and Tversky, 1974; for a related approach, see Simon, 1989).

While our own preference is for heuristics understood as discovery, what we will argue in this note is that there also exists a third meaning, which is not part of the semantic history of heuristics but which is important for understanding the current role of heuristics in social science. According to this meaning, heuristics do not only consist of "tricks" and "moves" and "good advice" that sociologists follow, in the hope of making a discovery. Heuristics in sociology is also part of something larger, namely a new and developing area of knowledge. And this new area of knowledge throws in its turn a new light on heuristics: not only on what it is but on what it can become.

Today's attitude towards heuristics among sociologists, we suggest, is part of a larger and more important development in social science which is still taking shape. During the last ten or so years a new field of knowledge has slowly begun to open up; and the knowledge of tricks, moves and advice is part of this field. This new field of knowledge is *theorizing*. Theorizing is about sociologists becoming aware of what they are actually doing when they work with theory, and also being aware of how they can use this knowledge to shape their work.

Social scientists have concerned themselves with what they are doing and with the forces that shape their behavior for a long time. This concern has crystallized into different forms of knowledge, one of which is the sociology of knowledge or, more precisely, the sociology of sociology. Reflexivity and the sociology of ideas are more recent, related approaches. All of these express first and foremost an awareness that the works of sociologists is not the result of objective consciousness, but instead deeply influenced by their authors' upbringing and related social forces. You grow up in a specific family, in a specific class; you work in a specific profession, and so on. All of these factors will influence how a sociologist handles research, including theory.

This type of knowledge, however, is general in nature and blunt; it lacks the specificity needed when dealing with complex phenomena such as thinking and language. Knowing that someone is a member of a certain family, a certain class, and so on does not tell very much about what will happens in the head of that person (even if has its obvious uses). The errors will also typically be of the oversocialized type.

This type of knowledge fails in another way as well: it cannot be translated into a positive program for how to do research, including how to do theory. In this respect reflexivity and related perspectives are mute and of less value.

But we know that there also exist books and articles that tell social scientists how to do research with some precision. There are plenty of these on topics such as sociological methods and theory construction; and they view as their primary task to spell out how you should go about things when you do social science, including theory. In doing so, they are at the same time both helpful and insufficient.

They are helpful in that they provide answers to question such as the following: How is a model built, a survey conducted, a theory constructed? Their drawbacks, especially when it comes to heuristics in the sense of discovery, are equally obvious. They mainly focus on the context of justification and have little if anything to say about the context of discovery.

To this should be added that they do not describe how research is done in a realistic way, with all of its ups and downs, dead ends and inspirational parts, and so on. They present "the story-book version of scientific inquiry," to cite Merton (1968) in *Social Theory and Social Action* (16). Merton also approvingly cites a physicist who once said that scientists are "professionally trained to conceal from themselves their deepest thought" and to "exaggerate unconsciously the rational aspect" of work done in the past (Merton, 1968:6–7).

It is precisely here that theorizing comes into the picture. Theorizing represents an attempt to portray how things are *actually* done, and how theory is *actually used* in research. The searchlight is directed straight at what the social scientist does for two reasons. First, by proceeding in this way, social scientists will become aware of what they are currently doing; and second, they will also learn what they *should* be doing.

At this point it is possible to note some interesting parallels between theorizing and moral action; and the reader may suddenly realize that the topic of theorizing is not so different from what constitutes the central topic in Foucault's *History of Sexuality* (Betta, 2016a, 2016b). This is *the creation of the self as an object of knowledge.*

In the case that Foucault (1985) is concerned with, there is what he calls *"ethical work"* (*"travail éthique"*; 27); and in the case that is discussed in this note, there is a concern with what Merton calls *"theory work"* (Levine, 2006:239).

According to Foucault (1985), ethical work originally took the form of "care of the self" and this happened in ancient Rome. In the important introduction to volume two of *The History of Sexuality*, where this new Roman form of ethics is discussed, the reader is told the following about the creation of the ethical self as an object of knowledge:

> In short, for an action to be "moral," it must not be reducible to an act or a series of acts conforming to a rule, law, or value. Of course, all moral action involves a relationship with the reality in which it is carried out, and a relationship with the self. The latter is not simply "self-awareness" but self-formation as an "ethical subject," a process in which the individual delimits that part of himself which will form the object of his moral practice, defines his position relative to the precept he will follow, and decides on a certain mode of being that will serve as his moral goal. And this requires him *to act upon himself, to monitor, test, improve, and transform himself* (28, emphasis added).

Foucault then goes on to show how knowledge is created when the actor views himself/herself as an object to work on. He also describes how this type of knowledge becomes a new field or discourse with its own structures and rules.

What links the projects of ethics and theorizing to one another is that they both lead to the creation of a new discourse of knowledge, which not only describes what someone is doing but also what *should* be done to reach a goal. The actors, to repeat, create this new field through their thinking and the acts entailed. Personal and impersonal rules are created and anchored, first in practices and then in institutions.

To return to heuristics. The bits and pieces of knowledge about heuristics that so far have been collected and held up as useful to the individual sociologist are part of the formation of a much broader and more general area of knowledge. And it is also through this new area of knowledge that the emerging notion of heuristics in social science is best understood. Again, the discourse is constituted through the theoretical practices of the social scientist. Heuristics joins in this way a set of issues and activities that all are part of theory work, such as how to use analogies, metaphors, induction, deduction, explanation, generalization, and so on. Heuristics interacts with these other techniques or tools of thinking; and it also comes into being with their help, in the concrete acts of research.

The area of theorizing, which is created in this way, seems to be increasingly recognized in today's social science (e.g., Swedberg, 2017). It is developing alongside traditional theory and the history of social science, both of which have atrophied over the last few decades, overshadowed by the quick and brutalist progress of methods in the social sciences. Heuristics, in other words, is one of the many mental techniques that help to shape the theorizing self, and also allows this self to express itself in thought and practice in the form of research. This is a promising development that will hopefully continue.

But turning into a new field of knowledge, about to be established in social science, theorizing will also have to go through the process of being scrutinized, classified, and probably neutralized by the powers that control the discourse in social science. These powers are currently poorly understood even if they are strongly felt.

If this neutralization of theorizing happens or not depends also on how deep the transformation of the self of the social scientist will be. Tricks and moves and good advice touch only the surface, but when heuristics turns into serious work on the theorizing self, it reaches considerably deeper. How deep, and what will be found at these depths, we do not know. Research in cognitive science may have to be brought in at this point, and probably also advances from some other sciences.

But in discussing the possible neutralization of theorizing, the reader should also be reminded of the intellectual tradition that Foucault comes from as well as theorizing itself. Another reason for returning to Foucault at this point is the need to say something more about the parallels between ethical work and theorizing.

Foucault was not only influenced by some of the best minds in the great tradition of French social thought, such as Gaston Bachelard and Georges Canguilhem. He was also, from the very beginning of his career, deeply immersed in the work of Immanuel Kant, as exemplified by his early translation and introduction to Kant's *Anthropology from a Pragmatic Point of View* (Foucault, 2008). It was, however, another work by Kant that fascinated Foucault the most, and which he kept coming back to time and again in his writings and lectures. This is the short article by Kant that can be seen as the first and also the founding document in the history of theorizing: "What Is Enlightenment?" (1991).

Here we find, for the first time in modern philosophy, a thoroughly democratic concern with thinking—how to go from obedience and conventional thought to learning how to look at the way in which you think, in order to be able to think for yourself (*Selbstdenken*; Arendt, 1992:32). Kant outlines many of the obstacles to be overcome in a concrete manner. You must not, most importantly of all, hand over your right to think to somebody else.

The Kantian project of the thinking self, which can be described as persons who act on themselves by teaching themselves how to think, has been carried on and further developed by many philosophers, including Charles Sanders Peirce (1992a, 1992b) and Hannah Arendt (1978, 1992). This is the broader tradition to which theorizing, as well as heuristics, belong, whether they take place inside or outside the university. Its motto was given by Kant (1991) and is still valid today: "Have the courage to use your *own* understanding!" (54, emphasis added).

REFERENCES

Abbott, Andrew. *Methods of Discovery: Heuristics for the Social Sciences*. New York: W. W. Norton, 2004.

Arendt, Hannah. *Lectures on Kant's Political Philosophy*. Chicago: University of Chicago Press, 1992.

Arendt, Hannah. *The Life of the Mind. Thinking* (Vol. 1). New York: Harcourt Brace Jovanovich, 1978.

Becker, Howard S. *Tricks of the Trade: How to Think about Your Research While You're Doing It*. Chicago: University of Chicago Press, 1998.

Betta, Michela. *Ethicmentality. Ethics in Capitalist Economy, Business, and Society*. Dordrecht, Netherlands: Springer, 2016a.

Betta, Michela. "Foucault's Overlooked Organisations: Revisiting His Critical Works." *Culture, Theory and Critique* 57, no. 3 (2016b): 251–273. https://doi.org/10.1080/14735784.2015.1078252.

Foucault, Michel. *Introduction to Kant's Anthropology*, translated by R. Nigro. Los Angeles: Semiotext(e), 2008.

Foucault, Michel. *The Use of Pleasure: The History of Sexuality, Volume 2*, translated by R. Hurley. New York: Random House, 1985. Originally published in French in 1984.

Kahneman, Daniel, and Amos Tversky. "Judgment under Uncertainty: Heuristics and Biases: Biases in Judgments Reveal Some Heuristics of Thinking under Uncertainty." *Science* 185, no. 4157 (1974): 1124–1131. https://doi.org/10.1126/science.185.4157.1124.

Kant, Immanuel. "An Answer to the Question, What Is Enlightenment?" In *Kant: Political Writings*, edited by H. S. Reiss, translated by H. B. Nisbet, 54–60. Cambridge: Cambridge University Press, 1991. Originally published in German in 1784.

Levine, Donald N. "Merton's Ambivalence towards Autonomous Theory: And Ours." *Canadian Journal of Sociology* 31, no. 2 (2006): 236–243. https://doi.org/10.2307/20058698.

Martin, John L. *Thinking Through Theory*. New York: W. W. Norton, 2014.

Merton, Robert K. *Social Theory and Social Structure*, enlarged 3rd ed. New York: Free Press, 1968.

Peirce, Charles S. "How to Make Our Ideas Clear." In *The Essential Peirce*, edited by N. Hauser and C. Kloesel, 124–141. Bloomington: Indiana University Press, 1992a.

Peirce, Charles S. *Reasoning and the Logic of Things*. Cambridge, MA: Harvard University Press, 1992b.

Simon, H. "The Scientist as Problem Solver." In *Complex Information Processing: The Impact of Herbert A. Simon*, edited by D. Klahr and K. Kotovsky, 375–398. Hillsdale, NJ: Lawrence Erlbaum, 1989.

Swedberg, R. *The Art of Social Theory*. Princeton, NJ: Princeton University Press, 2014.

Swedberg, R. "Theorizing in Sociological Research: A New Perspective, a New Departure?" *Annual Review of Sociology* 43 (2017): 189–206. https://doi.org/10.1146/annurev-soc-060116-053604.

5

CURIOSITY DIDN'T KILL THE CAT

BARBARA CZARNIAWSKA

When I was first asked how I came to work on the problems I have chosen, I thought that the answer was obvious and simple: curiosity. The longer I thought about it, though, the more complex the answer became. I finally counted at least four reasons for my choice of research topics.

Curiosity is still number one. My doctoral dissertation was a combination of my knowledge of psychology and economics; the result was a speculative model of motivation to work, of which I was rather proud. Yet I was still curious about whether it would work in practice. I presented it to managers I was meeting at courses we were offering at the University of Warsaw and asked them for anonymous, written comments. They all agreed: the model was truly impressive, but it would never work in this country (Poland) at that time (the 1970s). Somewhere else, perhaps: USA?

When I went to MIT on an ACLS fellowship, I decided to check this possibility. First, I discovered that "motivation to work" was simply a euphemism for "control"; second, I discovered that those U.S. corporations I studied applied control mechanisms that were much closer to those thought to be typical for centrally steered economies than were the rather muddled controls employed in Polish state-owned enterprises.

No wonder the results were not appreciated in either Poland or the USA. Actually, when I submitted one of my first English-language articles to a journal, its editor told me that it seemed that I wrote this to satisfy my own curiosity. He meant it (with best of intentions) as a constructive critique, but I didn't understand how it could be otherwise—and I still don't.

Nevertheless, I was soon to discover that there could be other reasons to choose a research topic: I would call it *contingency*. When I immigrated to Sweden, the job I was offered required that I study public-sector organizations. I considered it an enormous if necessary sacrifice. Studying public-sector organizations in Poland meant summarizing a plethora of boring laws and bureaucratic rules that applied to them. Little did I know that there could be different kind of studies with far-from-boring results. So when the next contingency offered me an opportunity to join the Power and Democracy project, I did it without hesitation. I had to admit, though, that within the project I studied what I wanted and how I wanted to study it.

Yet another reason to start (and continue for a long time!) a research interest was the *infectious enthusiasm of my colleagues and later coauthors*. Thus, Bernward Joerges convinced me that city management is a fascinating subject and Orvar Löfgren later persuaded me that the management of overflow is equally worthy of attention. Ten years on each, and I am not sure I am done.

The final reason, which relates only to my gender studies, I would call *disbelief*. I cannot believe that eighty years after Maria Curie Skłodowska or forty years after Maria Ossowska (a Polish sociologist who initiated studies of science), the situation of women in science is, if not worse, certainly not much better than it was in their time. I cannot believe that after the long chain of women rulers, beginning with Cleopatra and continuing with Empress Catherine the Great, Queen Victoria, Queen Elizabeth, and Angela Merkel, women are still not supposed to rule countries. My disbelief could be related to the fact, that when (and where) I was growing up, the idea of women becoming housewives was extremely exotic; some antique prejudice. Alas, it came back with force even in Poland, which is another reason for my disbelief. What is worse, this study topic seems to be inexhaustible.

6

FOUR MECHANISMS FOR FINDING (AND BEING FOUND BY) RESEARCH PROBLEMS

PAUL J. DIMAGGIO

ACKNOWLEDGMENTS

I am grateful to the Institute for Advanced Study, School of Social Science and to New York University for support of the sabbatical during which I wrote this paper.

Sociology faces outward: it addresses problems in the external world and uses the tools of science to subdue them. We have no William James, who developed a viable psychology (in part) by reflecting on his own inner experience, nor a Piaget, who made many observations on which his seminal development theory was based from the comfort of his children's nursery. Thus, an opportunity to reflect on my own intellectual development—to play Piaget to my own Jacqueline, Laurent, and Lucienne—is a treat and a challenge.

I shall do the best I can, but I would warn any student who hopes to draw guidance from this account to proceed with caution, for two reasons. First, my experience is at best only relevant to one type of scholar. Isaiah Berlin (1953) famously elaborated upon Archilochus's distinction between the fox (who knows many things) and the hedgehog (who knows one big, important thing). I am far at the vulpine end of the fox-to-hedgehog continuum, at times to the point of intellectual ADHD. I'm not sure I'd recommend this approach. When it works, others take up a question or idea and push it forward on their own, saving one the trouble. When it doesn't, promising lines of research wither on the vine; and, in any case, one spends much more on intellectual start-up costs than one's more erinaceous peers.

The second reason applies to any essay of this kind. Neuroscientists who study people with brain injuries have found that they can produce elaborate and plausible accounts of their behavior even when they are unaware of its causes (Gazzaniga, 1989). The reader is warned that the human talent for producing dubiously coherent accounts reaches its pinnacle in autobiographical reconstruction. To constrain my capacity for unintentional confabulation, I have assembled a data set consisting of my published papers, books, and book chapters, to which I shall refer throughout.

FOUR MECHANISMS

Four mechanisms have led me to research problems: experiential; semi-stochastic; stochastic; and crescive. Experiential problems come about when you seek explanations for puzzles that life presents. Stochastic problems come out of the blue, often but not always at the initiative of others. Semi-stochastic problems emerge directly from the last thing you were thinking about, with no direct history before that. Crescive problems are itches that demand scratching: theoretical or methodological dilemmas that one has encountered in multiple research projects and can no longer avoid. After describing the mechanisms at greater length and discussing how they have figured into my own work, I will test a few hypotheses about the relationship between mechanism and reception on a data set comprising ninety-six of my own books, book chapters, and journal articles.

Experiential

This mechanism was most influential at the beginning of my career; or at least it seems that way, probably because most of my experience since graduate school has been as a professional sociologist (this is not as sad as it sounds), which makes it difficult to distinguish this mechanism from the others. I classify 5.3 percent of my publications as experientially based. One of several possible accounts of why I became a sociologist begins in Nashville, Tennessee, where good fortune landed me after college, having used my Sociology BA to get a job as a research assistant to Richard Peterson, then in the midst of his seminal work on the production of culture. For a semi-pro rock critic and aspiring songwriter like me, getting to work with a gifted and experienced scholar who was as into music as I, not to mention meeting song publishers, recording artists, and charter members of the Grand Ole Opry, pretty much sealed my fate and led to my first three publications and an extended interest in the production of culture.

An equally plausible account of my sociological origins begins in a fifth-grade classroom in Swarthmore, Pennsylvania, where I undertook observation during my first year in my college's teacher certification program. At the time, my school was part of a district that served children from two very different communities: Swarthmore, a prosperous suburb populated by high-income professionals that boasted the highest incidence of BMWs in the state; and Morton, a blue-collar town, equally monoracially white, where most employed parents worked making helicopters in the Boeing-Vertol plant or in small businesses that served the former. As it happened, this made my classroom a privileged site for looking at class differences in education: it consisted of two groups of children with different local identities, strongly differentiated by social class, more or less randomized by gender, and racially and linguistically homogenous.

The first thing I learned was that some kids were smarter than others: they were more attentive, they answered questions more eagerly and more accurately, they had better vocabularies, and they just *seemed* smarter. The second thing I learned was that the kids who seemed smart were almost all from Swarthmore and the kids who seemed less able were almost all from Morton. The third thing I learned, after observing for a while and getting to know the kids, was that the first and second things I learned were wrong. The little Swarthmore boy with the constantly upraised hand was more anxious than gifted, and the silent and sullen Morton girl turned out to be the most cognitively sophisticated and articulate in the class, though a difficult family situation kept her from concentrating on academics. How was it, I wondered, that social class predicted my initial impressions of intelligence so perfectly, while predicting the underlying construct (as revealed by longer-term observation) so poorly? Could it be that something about the home-school fit made middle-class kids more able and motivated to *perform* being smart, even in the absence of underlying differences in intellectual acuity?

In my first year of graduate school, I described my experience to one of my professors, Mike Useem, who mentioned that a young French sociologist, Pierre Bourdieu, had been doing interesting work, as yet untranslated, that I would find instructive. I read everything I could find by Bourdieu, as well as Bernstein on language, Bowles and Gintis on school structure, and Collins on credentialism and educational expansion, and ended up writing a dissertation on social class, aesthetic taste, and school success that generated some of my earliest papers (e.g., DiMaggio, 1982). I have continued to work on related topics, though with declining frequency, ever since.

Semi-Stochastic

Much of the time (45.6 percent of papers), my intellectual progress has been semi-stochastic, in that each project is influenced by a previous one, while lacking direct connection to any that proceeded it. At times, a project or paper leads in this way to several others, which may therefore give an impression of planfulness; but more often, this pattern produces a multi-tendriled tree, in which any given project may generate several new directions. As a result of my interest in class, culture, and education, and drawing on earlier work with Richard Peterson on how the center of gravity for the country music audience had shifted from Southerners to the white working class (Peterson and DiMaggio, 1975), I collaborated with Michael Useem on a meta-analysis of the U.S. audience for the arts, supported by the National Endowment for the Arts. The Endowment asked that we go beyond synthesizing findings of audience research by arts organizations to studying why the research was undertaken and how the results were used (Useem and DiMaggio, 1978).

Answers to the first question (managers perceived that opportunities for government funding would increase and that such opportunities would require them to diversify, or at least to pretend to care about, the composition of their audiences) led me to research on organization-environment relations. Answers to the second (the results were used symbolically, used to stimulate conversation, or not used at all, and their perceived utility was unrelated to the research quality) led me to Carnegie School research on limited rationality and organized anarchies. Together, working on these papers cultivated a career-long engagement with organization theory, a field in which I had previously had little interest.

The branches that grew out of this project were several and diverse. Taking an organizational perspective on audiences encouraged me to think about alignment between class and aesthetic taste as itself a product of organizational systems, which led to historical work on the origins of high culture (DiMaggio, 1982) and on developments in public cultural policy that seemed responsible for the managerial jitters Useem and I had noted (DiMaggio, 1991). It also led me to study the managers themselves to understand how institutional change occurred through demographic succession and changing recruitment channels (DiMaggio, 1987). Because several fields I studied were rife with contention over these new directions, it made sense to use network analysis to examine the structure of the managers' professional affiliations; this in turn led to an engagement with network analysis (which I had studied in graduate school but had not yet used) and, more broadly, with clustering and subgroup-detection algorithms, that has continued through the present (DiMaggio, 1986).

Stochastic

Some projects or papers (32.2 percent) come to one out of the blue, with limited relation to anything that has preceded them. At times, the source is an organizational role. My involvement with Yale's Program on Non-Profit Organizations led to a series of papers on the nonprofit sector (e.g., DiMaggio and Anheier, 1990); and my engagement with Princeton's Center for Cultural Policy Studies to several papers on basic data resources for studying cultural participation and nonprofit arts organizations (Kaple et al., 1998)—not necessarily at the top of my personal agenda, but important tasks that our Center was best positioned to carry out. My participation in the General Social Survey led to work on a module of questions on economic behavior, which generated a paper on a new topic (albeit one of long-standing interest), the role of personal networks in consumer and housing markets (DiMaggio and Louch, 1996).

Many papers (55.3 percent) that I classify as stochastic are among the 39.6 percent of publications that resulted from invitations rather than emerging out of my own research programs.[1] Some of these stem from opportunities that are too interesting to decline. In general, one should decline them anyway, but at times the temptation is too great and the results are fruitful. A Social Science Research Council working group on New York's centrality in the urban network led to my only publication in urban sociology and the only one on power (DiMaggio, 1993). A fortuitous conversation with Filiz Garip, then writing her dissertation at Princeton, led to our joint realization that apparently different problems we were each tussling with might have a common solution, resulting in several papers about network externalities and economic inequality (DiMaggio and Garip, 2011). More recently, participating in a symposium about an outstanding paper on rational action and institutions provided an excuse to review the role of saloon keepers in politics during the Gilded Age and undertake a mini-project on Southern senators' connections to slavery and subsequent political careers in the 1840s: departures from any reasonable research trajectory but thoroughly enjoyable nonetheless (DiMaggio, 2017).

Crescive

So far, I have avoided the language of choice in describing the way projects and I find one another. The crescive mechanism, which accounts for 6.3 percent of the publications, represents the exception. There are problems that nag at one for a long time, compelling one's attention until one finally does something about them. Such problems may present themselves as theoretical or methodological. But I prefer to call them "theorodological" because behind every really knotty theoretical problem is a methodological challenge (because the solution often requires a new way of looking at data) and beneath any good methodological problem are theoretical choices.[2]

Toward the beginning of my career, most of these problems presented themselves as theoretical. In recent years, they have been largely methodological. My most cited paper, "The Iron Cage Revisited" with Woody Powell, was something like this: I had been studying small, community-based arts organizations that sought to combat class biases in access to the arts; Woody had been studying small publishers who tried to find alternatives to commercialism; and we were both interested in collectivist organizations in other fields that sought alternatives to bureaucracy. Our collaboration was an effort to understand why mission-driven organizations had so much trouble remaining distinctive, often ending up resembling the very bureaucratic organizations to which they had hoped to be alternatives (DiMaggio and Powell, 1983). Second example: in describing the experiential mechanism, I noted the influence, first, of my engagement with popular music and, second, of my experience in the Swarthmore schools. In graduate school I pursued these interests separately, which led me to feel as if I was writing under two personas: an organization theorist who studied artistic innovation, and a Bourdieusian student of cultural reproduction. An invitation from Howard Becker to prepare a paper for an ASA thematic session enabled me to fuse these two intellectual halves, by thinking seriously about the way in which systems of cultural classification interact with social organization and the ways in which formal organizations affect cultural hierarchies (DiMaggio, 1987). Finally, from early in graduate school I noticed that theories of social reproduction were based upon constructs like the "correspondence principle" (Bowles and Gintis, 1976) or *habitus* (Bourdieu, 1977), that made strong assumptions about social cognition without reference to research in social or cognitive psychology.[3] At the time, psychologists, in recovery from behaviorism, provided little guidance; but the problem of finding a cognitive grounding for the sociology of culture continued to fester until psychologists finally provided suitable materials (DiMaggio, 1997).

More recently, a search for methods appropriate to theoretical intuitions has motivated much of my research. Given the magnificent diversity of the social world, and people's facility for assembling beliefs and sentiments into surprising packages, I have long felt that studies of beliefs and attitudes too often assume that one model fits all. If we believe, as I do, that people organize the same ideas in very different ways and that, further (and more controversially), such differences in domain construals can rarely be reduced to groups defined by one or even two social identities, one needs an inductive method to detect population heterogeneity in attitude and opinion data. In this case, my major contribution was assembling a strong research team and scheduling repeated meetings until Amir Goldberg (2011) came up with a brilliant solution, Relational Class Analysis (RCA), which we and others have used to good effect to examine heterogeneity in several domains (DiMaggio and Goldberg, 2018; DiMaggio, Sotoudeh, Goldberg, and Shepherd, 2018). Similarly, inspired by Bakhtin's work on multivocality, I long searched for ways to identify multiple voices, frames, or themes in texts. The work on RCA led to meeting a computer science colleague, David Blei, who had created a text-analysis program, LDA topic models, which did just that. The conversation led to a joint paper on the utility of topic models for cultural analysis (DiMaggio, Nag, and Blei, 2013) and ongoing work in that vein.

Do Some Mechanisms Lead to More Influential Papers than Others?

To address this question, I conducted an OLS regression analysis in which the dependent variable was logged citations (given dispersion in the raw count) and where independent variables included dichotomous mechanism indicators (stochastic omitted) and a vector of controls.[4] Raw citation totals are a poorer measure of influence than weighted centrality measures, but the latter were unavailable. And "influence" via citations may be a less important indicator for someone reflecting on or planning a scholarly career than, for instance, personal satisfaction with a research product or even enjoyment in its production. But without having much sense of the stability of subjective measures or the extent to which they may have been contaminated *post hoc* by knowledge of citations counts, I stick with the more conventional indicator.

The model predicted a respectable amount of variance in logged citations (33.04 percent) even without distinguishing journal quality (which would have added explanatory power) or exploring interaction effects. Because older papers had more years in which people could cite them, I assumed that age would be associated with number of citations, and it was significantly so. Books and chapters received slightly more citations than papers (p < .10). Papers on economic sociology, organizations, stratification and the Internet were cited more than papers on culture, networks, social attitudes and nonprofit organizations. A rational agent–centered model would expect a scholar's best work to be internally motivated, and to emerge from long-term engagements with tightly related research questions. From this perspective, we would expect invited papers to have less impact than papers for which the motivation is internal, and papers with a history, even a semi-stochastic one, and, *a fortiori*, those of crescive origin, to have more impact than those whose origins are purely stochastic. A pragmatist might also expect experientially-based papers to be especially fecund, and someone vainer or with more faith in individual agency than me might predict that sole-authored papers would surpass multi-authored ones.

Pragmatists may not be happy with these results, nor will agency enthusiasts with a heroic view of the lone scholar. Neither experientially based nor sole-authored papers have been cited more than others. (And, for multi-authored papers, it didn't matter whether or not I was first author.) Pragmatists and believers in agency will take heart, however, in the success of papers that emerged crescively through repetitive encounters with obdurate problems. The poor performance of invited papers, especially compared to crescively generated ones, provides strong support for the importance of doing what one feels is important. At the same time, there is little support here for a rational model of path-dependent problem selection, as papers that flowed logically from prior research received no more citations than stochastically generated publications. Discipline is important, but the

TABLE 6.1 PREDICTORS OF LOGGED CITATIONS TO DIMAGGIO'S PUBLICATIONS (SELECTED VARIABLES ONLY)

	Unstandardized *coefficient*	p
Experiential mechanism	.130	.734
Semi-stochastic mechanism	-.153	.372
Crescive mechanism	.898	.011
Sole-authored	-.022	.775
Invited	-.551	.008
N	96	
Adj. R²	.330	

Note: Dependent variable from Google Scholar. Omitted mechanism is "stochastic." Excludes reviews, working papers, reports, and ephemerata. Model controls for years since publication and substantive topic.

stochastic mechanism introduces quasi-random elements into one's intellectual life in ways that can be productive, entertaining, or both.

So, what lessons can we take from this? Probably none, as citations are a rough estimate of influence and a poorer indicator still of satisfaction; and, moreover, the model just explains variance among one sociologist's publications; and it is not at all clear that the results would be robust to a different distribution of mechanisms. Gathering similar data from a few hundred other sociologists (especially with some hedonic measures) might identify modal patterns, each with its own distinct correlates of relative publication success. Until then, it is probably best to understand one's intellectual predilections, do work that addresses problems one finds challenging and important, and hope that enough other people agree to support one's research habit for six or seven decades.

NOTES

1. The distinction is not always clear-cut, in that at times I have responded to invitations with papers that I had already written or wanted to write. I classify as "invited" only those papers that I would have been unlikely to have written

were it not for the invitation. Surprisingly (to me at least), the percentage has been stable over the course of my career.

2. Princeton University's Center for the Study of Social Organization sponsored a monthly "Theorodology Workshop" for several years and presented "Theorodology Awards" to Andrew Abbott, Mike Hannan, Arthur Stinchcombe, and Harrison White for lifetime contributions at the intersection of methods and theory.

3. Basil Bernstein (1973), who grounded his claims in his research on sociolinguistics, was the notable exception.

4. I compiled citations from my Google Scholar personal page, using the regular Google Scholar listings to add data on several papers that are omitted from my personal listing, summing references to the same paper under slightly different names, and cross-checking across the two sources to try to minimize error. That said, it is clear that Google Scholar introduces considerable noise to the measure. Independent variables were years from publication, authorship (1-sole authored, else 0), dummy variables for books and chapters (journal articles omitted), whether the publication stemmed from an invitation rather than my personal agenda, and binary variables indicating whether the paper dealt with topics in culture, organizations, networks, economy, internet, attitudes, or nonprofits (with many papers falling into more than one category). Full results available on request. Analyses were conducted using Excel 2016's regression utility (from the Data Analysis Add-In).

REFERENCES

Berlin, Isaiah. *The Hedgehog and the Fox*. London: Weidenfield & Nicolson, 1953.

Bernstein, Basil. *Class, Codes and Control, Vol. 2: Applied Studies toward a Sociology of Language*. London: Routledge & Kegan Paul, 1973.

Bourdieu, Pierre. *Outline of a Theory of Practice*, translated by R. Nice. New York: Cambridge University Press, 1977. Originally published in French in 1972.

Bowles, Samuel, and Herbert Gintis. *Schooling in Capitalist America*. New York: Basic Books, 1976.

DiMaggio, Paul. "Cultural Capital and School Success: The Impact of Status-Culture Participation on the Grades of U.S. High-School Students." *American Sociological Review* 47, no. 2 (1982): 189–201.

DiMaggio, Paul. "Culture and Cognition." *Annual Review of Sociology* 23 (1997): 263–287. https://doi.org/10.1146/annurev.soc.23.1.263.

DiMaggio, Paul. "Layers of Endogeneity: How Porous Boundaries between State and Society Complicate Institutional Change." *Rationality and Society* 29, no. 1 (2017): 80–90. https://doi.org/10.1177/1043463116685662.

DiMaggio, Paul. *Managers of the Arts.* Washington, DC: Seven Locks, 1987.

DiMaggio, Paul. "On Metropolitan Dominance: New York in the Urban Network." In *New York: Capital of the American Century*, edited by M. Schefter, 193–218. New York: Russell Sage Foundation, 1993.

DiMaggio, Paul. "Social Structure, Institutions, and Cultural Goods: The Case of the U.S." In *Social Theory for a Changing Society*, edited by P. Bourdieu and J. Coleman, 133–166. Boulder: Westview, 1991.

DiMaggio, Paul. "Sociological Perspectives on the Face-to-Face Enactment of Class Distinctions." In *Facing Social Class: How Societal Rank Influences Interaction*, edited by S. Fiske and H. R. Markus, 15–38. New York: Russell Sage Foundation, 2012.

DiMaggio, Paul. "Structural Analysis of Organizational Fields: A Blockmodel Approach." *Research in Organizational Behavior* 8 (1986): 335–370. https://doi.org/10.2307/2094962.

DiMaggio, Paul, and Helmut K. Anheier. "The Sociology of Nonprofit Organizations and Sectors." *Annual Review of Sociology* 16, no. 1 (1990): 137–159. https://www.jstor.org/stable/2083266.

DiMaggio, Paul, and Filiz Garip. "How Network Externalities Can Exacerbate Intergroup Inequality." *American Journal of Sociology* 116, no. 6 (2011): 1887–1933. https://doi.org/10.1086/659653.

DiMaggio, Paul, and Amir Goldberg. "Searching for Homo Economicus: Variation in Americans' Construals of and Attitudes toward Markets." *European Journal of Sociology/Archives Européennes de Sociologie* 59, no. 2 (2018): 1–39. https://doi.org/10.1017/S0003975617000558.

DiMaggio, Paul, and Hugh Louch. "Socially Embedded Consumer Transactions: For What Kinds of Purchases to People Use Networks Most?" *American Sociological Review* 63, no. 5 (1998): 619–637. https://doi.org/10.2307/2657331.

DiMaggio, Paul, Manish Nag, and David Blei. "Exploring Affinities Between Topic Modeling and the Sociological Perspective on Culture: Applications to Newspaper Coverage of U.S. Government Arts Funding." *Poetics* 41 (2013): 570–606. https://doi.org/10.1016/j.poetic.2013.08.004.

DiMaggio, Paul, and Walter W. Powell. "The Iron Cage Revisited: Institutional Isomorphism and Collective Rationality in Organizational Fields." *American Sociological Review* 48, no. 2 (1983): 147–160. https://doi.org/10.2307/2095101.

DiMaggio, Paul, Ramina Sotoudeh, Amir Goldberg, and Hana Shepherd. "Culture out of Attitudes: Relationality, Population Heterogeneity, and Attitudes toward Science and Religion in the United States." *Poetics* 68 (2018): 31–51. https://doi.org /10.1016/j.poetic.2017.11.001.

Gazzaniga, Michael S. "Organization of the Human Brain." *Science* 245, no. 4921 (1989): 947–962. https://doi.org/10.1126/science.2672334.

Goldberg, Amir. "Mapping Shared Understandings Using Relational Class Analysis: The Case of the Cultural Omnivore Reexamined." *American Journal of Sociology* 116, no. 5 (2011): 1397–1436. https://doi.org/10.1086/657976.

Kaple, Deborah, Ziggy Rivkin-Fish, Hugh Louch, Lori Morris, and Paul DiMaggio. "Comparing Sample Frames for Research on Arts Organizations: Results of a Study in Three Metropolitan Areas." *Journal of Arts Management, Law and Society* 28, no. 1 (1998): 41–66. https://doi.org/10.1080/10632929809597278.

Peterson, Richard A., and Paul DiMaggio. "From Region to Class, the Changing Locus of Country Music: A Test of the Massification Hypothesis." *Social Forces* 53, no. 3 (1975): 497–506. https://doi.org/10.2307/2576592.

Useem, Michael, and Paul DiMaggio. "An Example of Evaluation Research as a Cottage Industry: The Technical Quality and Impact of Arts Audience Studies." *Sociological Methods and Research* 7, no. 1 (1978): 55–84. https://doi.org /10.1177/004912417800700103.

7

THE EDUCATION OF A SOCIOLOGIST

MARION FOURCADE

An essay like this is an uncomfortable exercise. Sociologists, of all people, should be suspicious of the explanatory value of introspection. Perhaps the first, necessary, step therefore is to reflexively question why, of all the eminent sociologists out there, I ended up on this short list, and why I accepted the invitation. It is somewhat fitting that I started writing this piece on a plane, returning from a conference on moral economies. I gave a presentation on Marcel Mauss's *The Gift*. The wheels of the academic world, like all social worlds, are oiled by solidarity, solicitation, and reciprocal exchange. My name did not come up randomly. My selection was built on preexisting relations and mutual appreciation, deep enough for the invitation to have been extended, though shallow enough for me to feel that many others might have served in the role just as well. There is no right or wrong about this, just normal social life.

This particular invitation is a small honor, not only because the other writers in this issue are so distinguished, but also because the ostensible purpose of the exercise is to make my scholarly life and trajectory relevant to others. Both of these reasons are psychologically pleasing, in their way. But they remain uneasy to navigate. Sociological honesty requires one try, at a minimum, to avoid two common mistakes: the error of seeing one's life as a sequence of purposeful choices; and the error of seeing it as a succession of random events.

It demands a sincere acknowledgement of the chance encounters and broader structural forces that made certain career and intellectual paths possible—in my case, everything from my family's devoted commitment to culture and education (my mother, as my paternal grandmother, taught in primary school) to my marriage, quite young, to a French engineer who would become an economist,[1] to the people I met in graduate school and ended up collaborating with.

I went into sociology almost by default. My passions in college (and my real strengths) were literature and philosophy, and I always assumed that this is what I would study if I succeeded the entrance exam to the *École Normale Supérieure*. But I worried about being confined to a teaching path if I did, and I made the somewhat more instrumental choice of a dual degree in economics and sociology. I thought it would give me more options. I loved both disciplines. I was seduced by the beautiful mechanics of economic models, the ability to explain large-scale phenomena (I was particularly drawn to macroeconomics) with a few equations. I realize now that what I really loved, up to a point, was the math. But even then, I knew that sociology gave me much more plausible insights into the world around me, though they appeared in a less well-ordered way. Economics was precise, but sociology felt accurate. Meanwhile, the man who would become my husband was studying physics. By the time he turned to economics, I had almost given up on the field. I had come to the realization that—unlike him—I was not well suited to the skills that would be required of me after undergraduate work. Instead, I started an interdisciplinary master's program in "social science." It was there that I first put my knowledge and fascination for economics to work by writing a thesis on one of my intellectual heroes, Albert O. Hirschman. I admired (and perhaps felt a hopeful kinship with) Hirschman's iconoclasm, his lack of respect for disciplinary boundaries, and his personal and political commitments. In 1992, I benefited vicariously from the established pipeline that routinely drafts French engineers into American universities. Had my husband not been advised to pursue his studies across the Atlantic, I would never have considered applying to a graduate program in the United States. Harvard rejected my initial application but my school in France had a visiting program there, and so I went anyway. We arrived in Cambridge on a hot and humid summer day. As a visitor I took classes with the first-year graduate cohort and ended up reapplying to the PhD program the following year, with a project on fiscal sociology and the supply-side movement in American economics.

That year I was also pregnant with my first child. Some faculty members were oblivious to my growing belly, while others—none more ardently than Orlando Patterson, who later became my adviser—were generous and supportive. Harvard's offer of a full fellowship came the day after my daughter was born at a hospital in Boston. The following September, I formally started my PhD with a six-month-old baby. Much of my stipend was immediately recycled back to Harvard, via the university's childcare center.

Needless to say, as a young mother my years at Harvard were a bit of a blur, but through the training I received I did develop a tremendous fondness for the comparative and historical sociology practiced by Orlando Patterson, Theda Skocpol, Yasemin Soysal, and Libby Schweber. It is no doubt through their influence that I started to conceive of my dissertation as a three-country comparative study of the economics profession, using a mix of historical material and interviews with present-day actors. I wanted the project to address, as it were within the same movement, the institutions of the field and the intellectual content of economic knowledge. So, I also read of lot of original texts by economists. The project was ambitious, and it would take me many years to complete my first book, *Economists and Societies*.[2] It is the kind of thesis that I would never have been able to write in France. But in the heyday of American macro-historical sociology, anything seemed possible.

And yet for some, that wasn't enough! When we moved to Stanford in 1996, John Meyer, who later became a sort of shadow adviser, encouraged me to think of my country cases as exemplars of the much more general phenomenon of the worldwide rise of economics. I still remember how he said to me: "but everyone goes like this," his arm making an ascendant move. I started methodically collecting data from around the world. I tracked the institutionalization of economics departments, economics associations, finance ministries, and central banks in every country, anything I could get my hands on. My article on "The Construction of a Global Profession" came out of that suggestion. My time at Stanford also produced a fecund collaboration with a graduate student there, Evan Schofer (now at UC Irvine), with whom I shared an interest in the articulation between global forces and national ones.

The study of economics has remained the strongest anchor of my work, however. It is through our common interest in the field that Sarah Babb (who had written an outstanding book on Mexican economists) and I started our collaboration on the "Rebirth of the Liberal Creed," drawing on our combined knowledge to compare the neoliberal policy shift in two mid-income and two high-income countries. It informs my recent publications on power relations in the social sciences ("The Superiority of Economists") and on the rise of business schools, as well as a newly launched project (with Etienne Ollion) on gendered writing across the disciplines. My fascination with the field has not abated, perhaps because now I also see its workings up close. I can see Economics from my house. While the combination of closeness and distance is not always easy to navigate on the personal front, it comes with endless (and precious) opportunities to observe the tacit knowledge operating in the field, and to casually identify interesting topics. For instance, my project on the valuation of nature came out of an off-hand remark someone made at a social event I attended. If the French had hired the proper economists after the *Amoco Cadiz* oil spill, he said, they would have done just as well as the state of Alaska against Exxon. My curiosity was piqued, and off I went, interviewing people and exploring archives to study how courts in France and the United States had dealt with compensations for ecological damage in these cases. The research that came out of that project ("Cents and Sensibility") followed a very inductive approach, in an effort to understand my cases holistically and do justice to the sheer cultural density of the processes at work in science, the courts, and politics. I had started with economics, but it ended up being about a lot more than that.

Economics had provided me with a somewhat unexpected point of entry into "economic sociology," a field that had been formally reorganized in the late 1990s. This was an exciting time. By 1998 we had moved to Princeton, which was perhaps the center of the intellectual revival of the field, with a distinctive approach centered on the intersection between culture and economy and dominated by Viviana Zelizer, Frank Dobbin, Paul DiMaggio, and Michèle Lamont. But the most decisive encounter, perhaps, was with fellow graduate students. At Princeton I met Kieran Healy, who became a friend and coauthor. Perhaps the fact that we were both foreigners brought us closer together. Our common interest in morality, judgment, and classification in the economy did the rest. To be sure, we came from two different universes, but in a strange way the confrontation between his reflexive (in the French sense!) Anglo-empiricism and my spontaneous retreats into French theory made our collaboration more stimulating. Twenty years later, we are writing our first book together, after a series of theoretically oriented articles about the inescapably moral nature of economic actions and institutions ("Moral Views of Market Society"), the importance of classification processes in markets ("Classification Situations"), and the emergence of new forms of capital in the digital economy as technologies of scoring increasingly underpin the differentiated processing of individuals in market and nonmarket settings ("Seeing Like a Market"). While our approach to social stratification in the digital society builds upon two empirical projects, each of which is led by one of us—a quantitative project on how to think about the role of credit scores in inequality, and an interview-based project on the harvesting and circulation of digital data—in many ways our styles have converged so much over the years that every new piece feels a bit more like the product of one mind rather than two.

I began my academic life as a comparative-historical sociologist. I continue to do historical work (on wine classifications in France and the United States) and my self-presentation on my website still says that "I am a comparative sociologist by training and taste." But in many ways I have left comparative-historical sociology behind. Perhaps the comfort and peace of mind afforded by tenure at an American university has made me less dependent on sticking to my specialization. What I do know is that I never would have thought that one day my mind would be so obsessively fixated on the frontier of technological progress. From algorithms to killer robots, from fake news to virtual reality, from gene editing to trans-humanism, the industry that is bustling outside my door in Silicon Valley is compelling me not simply to ask sociological questions, but also to question sociology's ability to comprehend, with the tools at hand, the world that is being made today. It is that sense of wonder and dread, I think, that is propelling my accidental, but quite determined, foray into developing a social theory of the present.

NOTES

1. He and I owe a lot to these social origins and to the French higher education system.
2. *Economists and Societies* was published in 2009, nine years after I finished my PhD.

8

WHEN A DISSERTATION
CHOOSES YOU

ERIC KLINENBERG

When I first told the professor whose work made me want to study sociology at Berkeley that I planned to write a dissertation about a massively lethal heat wave that had just happened in Chicago, he immediately advised me that it was a terrible idea.

He had a point.

Elite sociology departments, as I'd later learn, have little interest in the environment and even less in disasters. Intellectually ambitious work in our field is about everyday social processes, not extreme events. We analyze social facts, not ecological or meteorological conditions. And, student beware, when we study current events and crises we can easily get distracted by political rather than scientific concerns. The heat wave, my professor explained, should be an object of criticism, and those responsible for the unnecessary suffering it induced should be denounced. But a dissertation in sociology needs an object of *analysis*. He kindly, perhaps wisely, encouraged me to leave his office and find one. The trouble, one I likely share with other contributors to this volume, is that the problem of the heat wave had already chosen me. Part of this stemmed from biography. I grew up in Chicago and had long been fascinated by its neighborhoods, its political culture, its durable racial segregation, its ruthless violence, and, most intriguingly, its collective pride in being a "city that works." I was also interested in political ecology and had worked for an environmental group while I was an undergraduate. When I began graduate school in the fall of 1995, I was trying to understand how emerging concerns about global warming being issued by climate scientists might be relevant for sociology. Although I had just moved to California, I felt compelled to return to my native city and investigate what happened. I was lucky, because the heat wave turned out to be far more interesting than my professor (and I) had imagined, and there were all kinds of genuine scientific puzzles to explore. For instance, the mortality rate during the event far exceeded what the best health and climate models predicted, leaving epidemiologists to speculate about why it was so deadly. Sociology offered tools for replacing their guesses with concrete evidence. That was just the beginning. Predictably, the city's poor neighborhoods were disproportionately affected by the heat wave. But there was surprising variation among them, with several areas showing surprising resilience. Again, sociological research methods could help explain why.

The more closely I examined the heat wave, the more vexing sociological questions I identified: Why did so many people die alone? Why were men, who were so much less likely than women to age alone, so much more likely to die during the disaster? Why did city leaders decide not to issue a heat emergency and ignore the plan they had prepared for this very situation? Why did the government provide public services to people who didn't really need them, while neglecting the people and places that were most at risk? Why did the editors of the city's largest journalistic organization assign a large team of reporters to uncover the reasons that so many people died, and then bury the story after deciding it wasn't worthy of sustained attention? Why did the catastrophe, one of the worst in modern American history, prove so easy to deny, ignore, and forget?

Each of these questions became a peg for my dissertation chapters, and intellectually, I was hooked. My professor got it, too, albeit only after I did a lot of writing to flesh out the problems I would tackle.

I decided that he wouldn't be the right person to chair the committee, but his skepticism helped motivate me, and his critical voice, which of course I'd internalized, forced me to dig deeper and think more sociologically. It still does. In my final months of graduate school, I became close with an eminent professor in a different field whose work blended social science, political history, and psychoanalysis. When he advised me, he rarely asked questions about research methods or inferences or theory building. Others would cover that. Instead, he probed for the underlying reasons that I was so interested in questions about isolation, ecological collapse, racial inequality, the soft violence of an unnatural disaster, and the collective "will not to know" about rampant social suffering in the city I still called home.

One day, at his favorite lunch spot, the outdoor restaurant at the campus art museum, I asked him how he chose topics for the essays he'd been writing. "At this point," he said, "I prefer to have someone else choose projects for me. It's actually one guy, an editor (at a prestigious review of books). He gets me. He sees things I'd be interested in, things that I probably wouldn't see myself. He's been giving me assignments for a few years now, and he's had some great ideas. I trust him. And each time he puts me onto something I wind up learning a lot more than I would if I chose something on my own."

Fifteen years later, a book editor I'd worked with called me and asked if I could come to his office and meet a comedian.

Chosen, again.

9

HEURISTICS FOR DISCOVERY

JOHN LEVI MARTIN

I imagine that I am not alone in insisting that I do not choose my topics, but rather, the topics choose *me*. They do this in just the way that, say, a potato chip decides that you will eat it—by lying there, in plain view, looking all crispy and salty. But I still think I have some useful things to say, some prescriptive, some descriptive—some about good heuristics for sociology, and some about the heuristics I have used—which, unfortunately, were not always the same thing.

WHAT IS DISCOVERY?

To do this, I will rely on an extended metaphor. I will try not to repeat arguments made in *Thinking Through Statistics*, *Thinking Through Theory*, and especially chapter 2 of *Thinking Through Methods*. But first, I want to take seriously the charge to consider heuristics for *discovery*. There are, so far as I am aware, very few major discoveries in sociology—perhaps less than ten. A discovery isn't just an idea, or an argument. And simply being able to find data that don't contradict your claim doesn't mean you've discovered something. A discovery is something that involves some degree of surprise (even if the discoverer suspected it was there, other people didn't), and, after it happens, is the subject of relatively wide consensus. Of course, every now and then something that was "discovered" is later determined to be a mirage. But we call things discoveries when we think they aren't.

The social sciences as we know them really started with a discovery, one dating back to the political arithmeticians of the seventeenth century. This discovery was that certain aggregate ratios (such as the birth rate and the suicide rate) were extremely stable. This does not surprise now, but it did then, and has remained a very robust finding. Another example of such a discovery was Zipf's law of the distribution of city populations. For many years, this was scoffingly dismissed by sociologists as sheer coincidence, or, if robust, still irrelevant to theory. But it has remained an important fact and helped guide some of the most theoretically advanced work in social science, namely economic geographic/regional systems theory.

In sociology we have many claimed discoveries that unwind relatively quickly because they are cobbled together out of implausible theoretical assumptions. That is, it's only a "discovery" if you ignore all the unproven, supporting axioms. Of course, many scientific discoveries require a certain background acceptance of theory. For example, in geology, the pivotal discoveries that the magnetic orientation of the poles reverses over time, and that there is crust being produced at certain ridges under the sea, required people to accept some theories about the relation of current rock formations to historical processes. But those axioms had good justification, they've proven pretty robust and still are widely accepted.

So first, let's hold ourselves to somewhat high standards when it comes to what constitutes discovery, and we won't count as discoveries claims like "social capital is important." Why not? Well, for one thing, "social capital" isn't a natural kind, but a hodgepodge that no one's really thought through. It doesn't really hold together under investigation, such that we could make general statements about it that aren't either empty or wrong. But more important, other sciences don't want to give out prizes for things like "algae is important" (though it is). Second, if, we don't make discoveries, what *do* we do?

I think most sociology is an attempt to shift the balance of the evidence one way among a set of contending explanations for a generally accepted phenomenon. That may not be discovery, but it still can be science.

Before discussing heuristics for sociology, then, we need to decide whether it is worth trying to maximize the chance of a real discovery, at the cost of being unable to do decent sociology. For the heuristics that are most likely to maximize the chance of making even minor discoveries may not be very good at anything else, and if the chance of making discoveries is very small, this might be a bad bet.

BACKTRACKING

Let me give one example of an all-purpose heuristic that I have used upon occasion, and that does work for one kind of discovery. Sometimes we are sure that something *has* to exist, but we just don't know quite what or where it is. For example, think about setting out to discover the source of the Nile. This is very different from discovering America. The way you discover America is to be so bone-headed dumb that you literally run aground on something you didn't think was there. That's an unplanned discovery, and unplanned discoveries can have a lot of fun and drama to them. In contrast, if you want to discover the source of the Nile, you can set out looking for it, because you're going to be pretty sure that it's *somewhere*—or at least, there are going to be *some* sources of the Nile. It's just ("just"!) a matter of tracing it out (and up—it's got to start somewhere higher than where you are now).

However, the reason that sociologists aren't thrilled about trying to use this heuristic ("just trace it backwards") is the same reason that Sherlock Holmes would rarely bother borrowing the bloodhound to trace back the steps of someone whose mucky shoe he found. And the reason was, you trace back that smell, no matter where you start, and you end up in the same huge pile of s—t. We can call it capitalism, modernity, hegemony, society, or whatever. Certainly, what an infinite number of mediocre papers on "reproduction" have shown us is that if you rush out randomly into the bushes and try to trace back, you end up with all the other lost students, out there on Hegemony Hill.

When we try to follow the heuristic in a more focused, and disciplined, fashion, and trace the *specific* source of a clearly delimited class of phenomena, we tend to be frustrated—we're trying to find the peak of a very craggy mountain, where we can't see far ahead, and constantly face forks where we have to go one way or the other. Not surprising that many methodologists increasingly tell us that the answer is, don't even *try* to go uphill—don't look for causes—go *downhill* and look for *effects*.

But, if we are interested in discovering, we need to take the heuristic of back-tracing more seriously. In fact, killing off our enthusiasm for questions of the form "where did it come from?"—a cauterization of our fundamental sociological curiosity—will devastate our field, since our strength must be, at least in part, in answering the sorts of questions that regular people have about the world, and those questions are rarely "how much will y change if we twist the x dial?" and more like "where the heck did y come from, anyway?" Even a snoring drunk can roll down a hill—that shouldn't win any prizes.

But tracing back rarely involves just charging off into the first bushes you see with a machete. One has to start from the well-established parts of the Nile and work upwards, and then make choices when there are forks. There are three problems we run into. The first is when you come to an impassable zone—an unscalable height, an unfordable river, and so on. Most important here is when there are reproductive phenomena or strong selectivity issues. The second is when you simply lose the trail. Sociologists can be better than they are at saying, "and here we must stop for the scent disappears." Finally, very often, if you do follow the trail with determination, you find that it leads you right out of the jurisdiction that you've been given permission to explore—that is, you need to start working with experts from other fields, such as psychologists, anthropologists, or (perhaps most importantly) historians.

The times when I have actually set out to trace back and discover something were ones in which I was brought up quickly to the limits of my training and ability. Some of those have been intellectual history: my first paper tried to figure out where the idea of a "sexual revolution" came from, and I probably got this wrong. At the time, I didn't know about the work of Otto Gross, and that almost certainly was pivotal (I dated it only to the end of the First World War). Much of the article is still right, but I should have turned to a German historian. My most solid claim to a discovery has to do with the relation between two different ways of interpreting Coombs's noncompensatory factorization. I had started to understand, with the help of James Montgomery, that there were two different versions of this, and figured that, there's got to be *some* place where these two things fork off each other, and if I'm patient, I can find it. In this case, I had to learn some math and demonstrate that it comes from the question of whether the lattice of all possible states is lower semi-modular (I published this last year and I have already forgotten what this all means). The problem is, this is probably something that mathematicians knew a long time ago.

Maybe that's a particular example, but I think it's not at all uncommon for serious backtracking to lead you into other fields. As far as I can see, Durkheim was just flat out wrong about this idea that a social fact always has to be traced back to another social fact. Good news for sociology if that were true, but there's no reason to think that the world works that way. So, I don't think the "discover the source" heuristic is one to recommend (certainly, I've had no success with my most fundamental sociological impulse, the desire to "find the source of politics").

PRINCIPAL CITIES

I'd really like to stick with this metaphor—not necessarily that we are trying to discover the source of the Nile, but that we are trying to learn about a country. And by this, we mean to learn about its general geomorphology—What is the land like? How is it structured and arranged? The metaphor can help to clarify the implications of a number of heuristics.[1] If you wish to "see France," does that mean to go to Paris? In some ways yes, and in others no, in that while Paris is the apex of France, most of France is not Paris—and Paris is distinctive in a very particular way. It's special, and it's cool, I suppose, but it is, above all else, a concentration of *people*. You don't go there to see the landscape as much as to see what people have done with it. An example of the Paris-equivalent in the realm of subfields of sociological endeavor is the problem of intergenerational mobility. It is a busy city of scholars communicating with each other, and, for that reason, recognizably bad work is usually weeded out rather quickly. If you want to do good work, do you move to the city? There are advantages in starting where people have done a lot. The stumps are out, the swamps are drained. But, like the country kid moving to the city, it can be a lonely place for you to get started—the people already there seem to know what is going on, and you don't. You sit in your little apartment alone at nights, watching *Mr. Ed*, while they are (or so you believe) at champagne bashes. Perhaps they aren't, but it is true that those who come from clusters that have been working on these issues *are* ahead of you.

But there's a deeper problem, or so I now believe, with the "principal cities" approach. While the work done is usually better than the work done elsewhere, it tends, like a city, to be highly artificial. Remember, in this metaphor, the thing we are trying to discover is less what the citizens do, than physical geology of the terrain. But it's those sorts of people-doings that make cities what they are. Cities are certainly somewhere, but they tend to be in unusual places (usually by at least one river, sometimes a confluence of different waters). And sometimes they fundamentally change the terrain, or make it impossible to really see. So they're relatively hard places to make geological discoveries.

I'm not saying there aren't great archeological digs going on in cities. But just as in real life, when you do that sort of excavation, you're still usually finding *earlier* cities, on top of which yours was built. Further, cities are relatively hard places to make discoveries, since there are so many watchful eyes about. When there are discoveries in cities, it's often the result of being able to get new data.

To return to the case of stratification, a great deal of time was spent trying to estimate parameters from layered 7×7 tables. That was progressive in a way, but it was "indoor" research. It was arguing over relatively small issues of a model constructed for purposes of convenience, and one that didn't always hold up to the "look out the windows" critiques. But it gave everyone something to do, and it was beautiful in an aesthetic way, so we stuck with it.

Cumulative social science is an important goal. But so is the reality check. I consider one of the few discoveries of sociology to be David Grusky's work on micro classes. He had a talk in which he simply showed something like a 300×300 occupational inheritance matrix done as a 3D frequency plot. It fundamentally changed my understanding of the American class structure in a way that none of those arguments about whether ϕ could or could not be compared across samples did. That's what I mean by fundamental geomorphology.

So in cities, I think there are only two types of discoveries. One is the discovery of better data that allows you to avoid assumptions that everyone has had to make before. The other is the realization that you've been digging in the wrong place entirely, and, sadly, that does happen—you can be the killjoy who discovers that the city is built on a fault line or in the shadow of Vesuvius and has to be abandoned. That sort of negative discovery is a real contribution, but it's not as satisfying as the positive discovery. And maybe it's not even as satisfying as good old fashioned, Lewis and Clark, exploration and mapping. That's often the first step to a serious geomorphology, and I don't think we've done enough of it.

One key to a great Lewis and Clark heuristic is that you try to get somewhere that might be rather arbitrary (for example, it might come from political or identity concerns), but is still far away. To get there, you need to traverse lots of different types of difficult territory. You can avoid some of it, but not all. You learn about the nature of the Rocky Mountains when your goal is on the other side of them. Weber, perhaps, did some seriously good comparative sociology, because he was trying to walk by himself from coast to coast. He didn't get there, but by gum, by the time he died, he had mapped a fair amount of what could be mapped at the time.

From here on, I'd like to make a case for heuristics of mapping. I'll talk about what has worked for me, what hasn't worked, and what I'm hoping to try soon.

FOLLOW THE SHINY

Of course, I must begin by admitting that if I do in fact decide what to do next, my consciousness has not been let in on the secret of that decision process. So rather than invent a plausible argument about how these decisions are made, I'll give a more accurate, if vague, report on the feeling I have, which is that rather than choosing my tasks, I merely accept them. That sort of relation to an external (possibly only virtually external) leading force—what Weber called an "object"—is easy to justify when (as in Weber's vision) it pulls you by the hair in a straight line. But it is no less a pull when it hops and skips all over the place. I trust that it knows what it is doing, because it hasn't let me down yet.

The way it appears to me is a bit like a halo of shininess that bobs beckoningly in certain areas, and I dutifully follow. While "mission from God" probably somewhat overstates the coherence, "Attention Deficit Disorder" probably understates it. Of course, most things I do branch off from previous projects. Finishing one isn't really finishing, and it points you in the direction to the next. But one branch may slowly ebb in force, and so something else starts to take its place.

At that point, I believe that I follow a simple three-part algorithm. First, look around for the shiniest thing you can see. Second, attempt to go towards it. Third, if it does not *obviously* increase in shininess, drop it and look around for something else that is shiny. This is not an altogether bad way of proceeding. While it does give disproportionate attention to things that are near, those are often ones we are in a better position to attack, as we have already some of the conceptual and methodological infrastructure in place. The emphasis on "obvious increase" in shininess as a key part of this heuristic means that one avoids chasing will-o'-the-wisps—but it also means you aren't guaranteed to be moving across the terrain at any time. Still, to the extent that one spends a fair amount of time moving from one place to another in more or less the same area, one is presumably in a reasonably good place for research. On the other hand, the shiny does move, and leads to variation in the terrain one explores.

Following the shiny (FTS) then is a nonrandom if somewhat obscure way of traversing the countryside before us. And the random-walk aspects of the strategy can be improved upon if one has some general knowledge of the likely organization of the land based on past experiences. I'd like to contrast the pros and cons of this to other heuristics.

To some extent, FTS sits in the middle between two other heuristics. On one pole, we have the "hunker down" heuristic— wherever you are, that's where you stay. This is not at all a bad heuristic, especially if you happen to be in an area that has real scientific importance for a larger view of the whole. There is a reason why a geologist might go to the middle of the desert in Oman to do research. That's because it's one of the only places on the globe where ocean crust (which is qualitatively different from land crust) is above the water.[2] It's a strategic site for the study of the planet, and you could spend a career there.

When I was in college, my advisor always advised me that in every sociology paper, your second paragraph is about how your topic of study is a "strategic site" for examining the theoretical questions you are interested in. Because it wasn't true in my case—I was interested in the site for other reasons—I soured on the very notion, associating it (correctly, empirically) with dishonest salesmanship. But we shouldn't forget that it *is* great to choose a site because it has unique advantages in untangling a theoretical question. And for some projects, you really need to be there for a long time to make progress—if you want to study geology in the Antarctic, you can't just waltz in and waltz out. You need to go somewhere where others have already established a well-stocked base camp.

So I very much appreciate this heuristic, and I'm actually trying to move in that direction. I don't have as much to say about the opposite pole, which I'll call "airport science." Here, like the traveling salesman who thinks he's been to all these different cities but has only seen the airport and the Ramada Inn, we have people who think they've done many different projects because they've dealt with different *easy data applications*. I don't think we should be jealous of work that scholars from other disciplines do even when they poach on what was once our investigatory site, but in this case, I think there is a problem for sociology in the fact that we are increasingly expected to compete with pressures from what is euphemistically called "social science." It's great to have outsiders bring fresh methods and fresh eyes, but a lot of this is airport science, often done by modelers who just don't know anything about what they are modeling. (Of course, some outsider modelers know a *lot* about the substance; I continually point to Dirk Helbing as an exemplar worthy of emulation.) But we should go to airports to study airport phenomena (like queuing)—not to do fundamental geomorphology. You study Twitter data if you are interested in how people use narrow band broadcast communicative technologies—not to see where ideas come from.

You might think I am simply saying, my wandering is okay, and others', not. But I know that there is a difference between FTS and airport science, and it is objectively measured in the effort/publication ratio. You know you're not going from airport to airport, but wandering through swamps and hedges, where you need to put in 1,000 hours to get a third tier publication! The key to the airport strategy is that you write papers, but you don't really solve problems. You can perhaps make a real contribution with this strategy when there is a data set for which slapping an existing method on it will yield a significant substantive finding that others have missed. But that's pretty rare. Airports, like cities, are pretty crowded places. Even if someone did drop a twenty dollar bill on the floor, odds are you won't find it.

ADVANTAGES AND DISADVANTAGES OF FTS

The "follow the shiny" heuristic, however, has its own problems. Moving from one place to another meant that I spent a fair amount of time doing entry-level work in a host of different tangential fields. That has been immensely rewarding as a way of life, and I can't say I regret that. And there's an intellectual upside to this as well. The savage man, says Adam Smith, does many tasks in an uncertain environment, and accordingly is forced to exercise his ingenuity over and over again. Perhaps what he makes is not quite as well made as that composed in a society with a mature division of labor, but he has a great deal more fun.

I'm not claiming that FTS leads to a well-rounded personality (if there is such a thing, I certainly don't have one); the heart of Smith's point is a bit different. True, you aren't completely one-sided, but what is essential about the average person in a nonindustrial society, according to Smith, is that he or she is constantly being forced to respond to problems, as opposed to the factory worker incessantly repeating a simple action. I have always preferred to do a project that required a new solution, than one that involved application of well-known solutions—and I think this was an error I am trying to correct. But I want to take with me this key principle. If you choose your projects by your tools—which is an extremely sensible heuristic—you can get very far. But it's a bit like having one sort of vehicle (such as a big motorboat), and being able to go anywhere that it is suitable for. You can definitely outrace the canoes where things are good for you. The problem is, if the river gets shallower, you get stuck, and if you have to actually port across land, you're totally out of luck. You have nothing to do but retrace your steps and go home. An amazing thing to learn is that you aren't actually a slave to your own technology. I always tell the story of my friend Andy Helck, teaching me auto-mechanics as we worked together on his slant 6 Dodge engine. "We can't get that out unless we have a tool that has a box wrench on one side, is 25" long, with a 30 degree bend." Where can we get one? "We can't." I assumed that this meant we had to abandon the project. But he continued, "We're going to have to make one." Sometimes to solve a problem, we have to visualize a second problem.

Now I'm dubious about our capacity to come up with heuristics for discovery, or even for generating problems, by simply using our noggins. We can come up with quests, but impossible quests aren't problems. Nor is it really a problem if everything around you is lousy. Problems are things with solutions. And I think that the way we come up with problems is not from deduction or reflection, but from the *Gestalt* experience of "insight." Here one sees all at one time a solution, often an indirect one, and therefore a problem appears as a true problem, a *solvable* problem. Part of what the Gestalt psychologists identified as intelligence involves the capacity to substitute one problem for another. To return to the geographical metaphor, if I can't get there from here, from where *could* I come closest? Can I get *there*?

Sometimes we can handle this in a straightforward fashion (thus Polya teaches us to solve proofs by attempting to find the problem that we *can* solve that is closest to this problem). But in other cases, getting to the place from which you can solve the problem involves taking a "detour" (*Umweg*) whereby we seem to go *away* from our goal to get closer. To do this, it appears that it requires that sort of flash of insight—an appreciation for what the overall constellation of the field affords us—that is resistant to being turned into an algorithm (as C. S. Peirce emphasized).

And so I think that the advantage of doing FTS for at least a while is that by forcing a spirit of invention, doing a little sociological "outward bound" (can you survive in the wild with nothing but an 80486-based computer and FORTRAN?), one sees a wider class of problems. I'm increasingly horrified that, perhaps motivated by the admirable concern for rigor, more and more sociologists seem to think that it is acceptable not only to choose their problems by what their tools are good for—that makes a lot of sense—but even to prefer the wrong tool if it is fancier or of greater precision. People will go to great trouble estimating what they swear up and down is the "right" model, even though it requires that they ask the "wrong" question—for example, they'll blatantly ignore the most obvious confounders, or use a model that makes strong and false *substantive* assumptions, because this allows them to use a technique that has been declared "best" by someone who doesn't care about getting the right answer to the question at hand. And often, other methods are going to do far better at approximating the right answer, even if they are cruder. I'm delighted for you if you have a Lamborghini Centenario, but if you need to get up a dirt road and it can't make it, what the hell's wrong with taking your dad's old F250?[3]

So what makes something shiny to me isn't that the substance is "cool" or that the methods are "state of the art" or that if you write about it, you can sell a lot of books. It's seeing that there's a way to solve a problem—and for this reason, very often, my ideas come from a particular data structure—in a few cases, actually stumbling across data in books (like a new piece forthcoming, or so I am told, in the *Journal of Social Structure*, analyzing the social networks produced by a sufferer of multiple personality disorder).

But that meant that I got better at knowing how to solve problems in general than about any particular thing. I don't feel that bad about this, because so many of the "things" that sociologists seem to know about aren't really about the social world anyway, in the same way that, in our metaphor, the city isn't really the same thing as the country—often we sociologists don't know the world, we just know *knowledge* (at best—putative knowledge at worst). But still, there are some sociologists who really know a lot about something, the way Claude Fischer really knows about Americans' social relations.

To return to the metaphor, the FTS heuristic can lead one to become a good woodsman—to have a general sense of how to get by outdoors without losing one's orientation, to have a sense of the regularities in the organization of land and landscape. But one lacks the detailed knowledge of the particular soil conditions and flora that someone who grew up there and did subsistence agriculture would have. And, not having spent enough time in the cities to really have "the knowledge" (as cab drivers in London call a total memorization of all streets), one isn't really likely to enjoy or contribute to the projects in the good cities. And for the bad ones—the Sodoms and Gomorrahs of social investigation—well, they deserve what's coming to them, and the sooner, the better, I say. So one can be a good teacher, with a stock of valuable lessons disproportionate to one's years, without yet making any particular discovery.

CORRECTING THE HEURISTIC

And that would be fine, except that there is a question, I suppose we could call it a theoretical question, that's been nagging me since I started in on sociology in college. It's a question in what was once understood as the sociology of knowledge but I think is better understood as political psychology—how people understand the social structure they are in and develop insightful beliefs that allow them to navigate these structures in ways that are ecologically rational, in that they have a correlativity to that structure. (Of course, locally rational beliefs can be 100 percent wrong and in fact suicidally insane. They're no less impressive for all that.) To me, this is the great wonder of social life, and I don't believe we really understand the first thing about it. And I don't think we currently can. Our methods, and our theories, build in assumptions that prevent us from understanding the true meaning of political knowledge (and in this way all social knowledge is political knowledge).

So a lot of what I've spent my time on are attempts to figure out what are the theoretical and methodological blocks to us even formulating the right questions here. And while I am no closer to an answer, I do think that, in part because of the new attention to cognition in sociology, and the perestroika of political science, we are in a better position to collectively make substantive progress on what might well be a very good, if difficult, problem. So now it might be time to hunker down.

NOTES

1. If you are impatient with metaphor, my dear little scientists, bear in mind that sociology itself has been, to a first approximation, a centuries-long attempt to think through the implications of the metaphor *society ~ organism*, and a great deal of insight has come via a critical examination of the strengths and limitation of that metaphor!

2. I am grateful to Joe Martin, who did research in Oman, for telling me about this.

3. As an aside, I am always struck by the way that I get accused of telling people they shouldn't study, for example, influence, if I say that even with longitudinal data, identification assumptions are too implausible to be worth doing. They are shocked when I suggest that they might need to use an entirely different method, such as participant observation, if they really want to learn about influence. The truth is, probably they don't. That's like having to take that hot, dirty bus out of the air-conditioned airport.

10

NIKLAS LUHMANN'S CARD INDEX

The Fabrication of Serendipity

JOHANNES F. K. SCHMIDT

*The following article is a revised and shortened version of: Schmidt,
J. F. K. (2016). "Niklas Luhmann's Card Index: Thinking Tool,
Communication Partner, Publication Machine." In A. Cevolini
(ed.),* Forgetting Machines: Knowledge Management Evolution
in Early Modern Europe *(pp. 289–311). Leiden, Netherlands/
Boston: Brill.*

THE SOCIOLOGY OF NIKLAS LUHMANN

Niklas Luhmann (1927–1998), Professor of Sociology at Bielefeld
University from 1968 to 1993, was one of the last advocates of a
so-called "grand theory": Over the course of his forty years of
academic work, he developed a universal theoretical framework—
i.e., sociological systems theory—capable of covering nearly the
entire spectrum of social phenomena. In doing so, he placed great
emphasis on conceptual and terminological consistency and was
receptive to theoretical developments not only in sociology but in
other academic disciplines such as philosophy, law, theology, biology,
and cybernetics in particular. Since the 1960s, Luhmann published
a bewildering wealth of articles and books year after year, and at
the time of his death, his list of publications comprised more than

500 titles on diverse topics, mostly part of his central research interest: a theory of society.[1]

Luhmann studied law from 1946 to 1949 and then first worked as a senior civil servant in public administration. In the mid-1950s, before he had any institutional affiliation with academia, he was already conscious of the fact that the notes he took from his readings at the time[2] would not be collected for a limited publication project but for a far more extensive endeavor, eventually for a lifelong project. The shortcomings of the common methods of organizing notes by collecting them in folders motivated him early on to start a card-based filing system.[3] In organizing his research in this way, Luhmann adopted a system of organizing knowledge that had emerged in the wake of early modern scholarship, along with the rapidly growing number of available publications since the sixteenth century and the practice of excerpting that followed: card indexing.[4] He went on to develop the potential for systematic knowledge production inherent in this filing technique to perfection by devising a very specific system of organization and referencing which seems to be an analogical pre-adaptive advance of the modern form of digital database. Luhmann's card index allows the production of new and often unexpected knowledge by relating concepts and thoughts that do not have much in common at first sight: one could say that it makes—to use Robert Merton's term[5]—*serendipity* possible in a systemically and theoretically informed way.

NIKLAS LUHMANN'S CARD INDEX

Luhmann's card index consists of approximately 90,000 handwritten cards in A-6 format organized in two collections. The first collection, approximately created between 1951 and 1962, a time when Luhmann was on his way from a legal expert with interests especially in constitutional law and administrative sciences to a systems theoretical sociologist, is based primarily on his readings in political science, administrative studies, organization theory, philosophy, and sociology. It consists of approximately 23,000 cards, which are divided into 108 sections by subjects and numbered consecutively, two bibliographies comprising about 2,000 titles, and a keyword index with roughly 1,250 entries. The second collection (1963–1997), now clearly reflecting a sociological approach,[6] is divided into eleven top-level sections with a total of about 100 subsections. It consists of approximately 67,000 cards, including a sizeable but obviously incomplete bibliographical apparatus with roughly 15,000 references and a keyword index with 3,200 entries.

The bulk of the collections (approximately 75,000 cards) consist of notes documenting the results of Luhmann's readings, but also his own thoughts and theoretical arguments and concepts. The notes resulting from his readings are not simply excerpts; what mattered to him was "what could be utilized in which way for the cards that had already been written. Hence, when reading, I always have the question in mind of how the books can be integrated into the filing system."[7] As a consequence he normally did not put the notes made during reading directly into the collection, nor did he file them in exactly the same way that he had taken them while reading; in fact, in the evening he transferred the often only rudimentary records he made during the day into new notes according to his special filing technique. Furthermore, his main concern was not to develop an idea to maximum sophistication before including the note into the collection; rather, he operated on the assumption that a decision on the usefulness of a note could only be made in relating it to the other notes—and therefore would (in many cases) be a matter to be decided *in the future*: by rereading the note in the context of new notes compiled afterwards or in the context of an inquiry, i.e., in using the card index as a database for new thoughts and publications. Furthermore, this being the case, it was not clear right from the beginning where the note to be added would be inserted into the collection—this was a decision that was made in the course of preparing the respective note for filing; and normally there was *more than one possible solution* to the question where to place the note in the collection due to the specific structure of the collection.

These issues draw the attention to the *four special characteristics of the file collection* which are the prerequisites for its main function of producing new knowledge: a specific system of organization and method of card integration with specific rules of numbering, an internal system of linking, and a comprehensive keyword index. All this together makes Luhmann's card index a complex cognitive system with a creativity of its own, a "second memory" as he called it. This ability was not totally independent from its creator, of course, but it was leading systematically to ideas that do not lie at hand—even surprising the person who was the author of cards. Without doubt there was a personal unity between the author and the reader of the notes, but on the other hand there was a difference between these two insofar as the factual complexity and the evolutionary history of the collection intervened.

THE METHOD OF CARD INTEGRATION

According to Luhmann the collection is a "combination of disorder and order, of clustering and unpredictable combinations emerging from ad hoc selection."[8] Of course the file collection is not simply a chaotic compilation of notes but an aggregation of a vast number of cards on specific concepts and topics. This order per subject area on a top level is reflected in the first number assigned to the card followed by a comma (first collection) or slash (second collection) that separates it from the rest of the number given each card (see below). The first collection features 108 sections differentiated by subject areas, exploring and reflecting on largely predetermined, fairly detailed fields of knowledge in law, administrative sciences, philosophy and sociology, such as state, equality, planning, power, constitution, revolution, hierarchy, science, role, concept of world, information, and so on. The second collection, by design, is quite more problem-oriented, reflecting the emerging sociological interests of Luhmann: It consists of only eleven top-level subject areas: organizational theory, functionalism, decision theory, office, formal/informal order, sovereignty/state, individual concepts/individual problems, economy, ad hoc notes, archaic societies, advanced civilizations. What this compilation immediately illustrates is that it is not a system of order in the sense of an established taxonomy but a historical product of Luhmann's reading and research interests especially in the 1960s.[9] Following the subject areas defined at the top level are other subsections that revolve around a variety of topics. The relationship between the top-level subject area and the lower-level subjects cannot be described in terms of a strictly hierarchical order; it is rather a form of loose coupling insofar as one can find lower-level subjects which do not fit systematically to the top-level issue but show only marginally connections.

This is a result of the specific system of organization of the notes applied within these sections on a particular subject matter which ensures that the initial decision for a specific topic did not lead to a sequence of cards confined to that one topic: whenever Luhmann came across an interesting idea about a secondary aspect on one of his cards, he pursued this idea by adding additional notes and inserted the respective card at that place in the existing sequence of cards. This method could be applied again to the card that had been inserted and so forth, the result being a sequence of cards leading thematically and conceptually farther and farther away from the initial subject and constituting their own subsection. Furthermore, this technique enabled the collection not only to grow in absolute numbers, but to *grow "inwardly"* without the limitations of a systematic order.[10]

But the positioning of larger subject areas as well as individual cards in the collection was not only the historical product of Luhmann's reading interests and note-taking activities. It also owed to the difficulty of assigning an issue to one and only one single (top-level) subject, which is a *matter of ambiguity* or, so to say, *conceptual indecisiveness.* Luhmann solved this problem by seizing it as an opportunity: instead of subscribing to the idea of a systematic classification system, he opted for organizing entries based on the principle that they must have only some relation to the previous entry without also having to keep some overarching system in mind. One could say: there must be a *local* solution (i.e., connection or internal fit) only. This indicates, accordingly, that the positioning of a special subject within this system of organization reveals nothing about its theoretical importance—for there are *no privileged positions* in this web of notes: there is no top and no bottom.

The decision inherent in this filing technique without a fixed system of order is an essential prerequisite of the creativity of the filing system. In explaining his approach, Luhmann emphasized, with the first steps of computer technology in mind, the benefits of the *principle of "multiple storage"*: in the card index it serves to provide different avenues of accessing a topic or concept since the respective notes may be filed in different places and different contexts. Conversely, embedding a topic in various contexts gives rise to different lines of information by means of opening up different realms of comparison in each case due to the fact that a note is an information only in a web of other notes. Furthermore it was Luhmann's intention to "avoid premature systematization and closure and maintain openness toward the future."[11] His way of organizing the collection allows for it to continuously *adapt to the evolution of his thinking* and his overall theory which as well is not conceptualized in a hierarchical manner but rather in a cybernetical way in which every term or theoretical concept is dependent on the other.

THE SYSTEM OF NUMBERING

Getting the filing system to "speak" requires an additional prerequisite: the possibility of addressing each card individually and hence also of finding it again. Thus, the filing technique does not build on the idea of an order of contents in the first place, but of a fixed order of positioning. This idea is at the root of Luhmann's specific *notational system*: each card is assigned a number and, thus, a fixed position in the file that does not change over time; card 1/1 (or 1,1, as in the first collection)—i.e., the first note in the first section of the collection—is followed by 1/2 (or 1,2), and so on; a card that was created later and pursues an aspect further that is noted on card 1/1 but is not part of the argument followed up on card 1/2 was given the number 1/1a, because the number 1/2 was already assigned, and inserted between card 1/1 and 1/2; at that point, either a card 1/1b on that very same topic could be added or another card 1/1a1 breaking things down further or pursuing other aspects, which would then be inserted between 1/1a and 1/1b, and so forth.

ILLUSTRATION OF THE METHOD OF CARD INTEGRATION AND NUMBERING

1/1 Card with notes referring to a certain topic
1/1a Card containing notes referring to a particular idea from card 1/1
1/1b Continuation of notes from card 1/1a
1/1b1 Card containing notes referring to a particular idea from card 1/1b
1/1b1a Card containing notes referring to a particular idea from card 1/1b1
1/1b1b Continuation of notes from card 1/1b1a
1/1b2 Continuation of notes from card 1/1b1
1/1c Continuation of notes from card 1/1b
1/2 Continuation of notes from card 1/1

In conjunction with the method of card integration outlined above, this rather simple but ingenious numbering system[12] based on the principle of connectivity of arguments results in a complex numbering structure and in cards that bear a combination of numbers and letters with up to 13 digits (e.g., 21/3a1p5c4fB1a on the first card of the subsection "Confidentiality" in the second collection) and thus allows to organize a complex process of inserting a nearly infinite number of cards between what had initially been two consecutive cards created at the same time on a related subject. The numbering structure thus reflects the unique depth of the organization of cards that Luhmann referred to as a "capacity for internal ramifications."[13]

THE SYSTEM OF LINKING

In addition to the notation and numbering system, there is another key feature of the collections that accounts for the creativity of this filing system: a system of referencing or linking. That means that Luhmann on one card noted a number of another card, often thematically and spatially far away, relating the different cards in a specific way. An estimate based on a sample count suggests that the first collection contains approximately 20,000 references and the second about 30,000 references of this kind, that means that there is a reference link on nearly every (first collection) or nearly every second note (second collection) on average.

Three *types of linking* can be distinguished:

a. References in the context of a larger structural outline: When beginning a major line of thought Luhmann sometimes noted on the first card several of the aspects to be addressed and marked them by a capital letter that referred to a card (or set of consecutive cards) that was numbered accordingly and placed at least in relative proximity to the card containing the outline. This structure comes closest to resembling the outline of an article or the table of contents of a book and therefore doesn't really use the potentials of the collection as a web of notes.

b. Collective references: At the beginning of a section devoted to a specific subject area, one can often find a card that refers to a number of other cards in the collection that have some connection with the subject or concept addressed in that section. A card of this kind can list up to 25 references and will typically specify the respective subject or concept in addition to the number. These references can indicate cards that are related by subject matter and in close proximity or to cards that are far apart in other sections of the collection, the latter being the normal case.

c. Single references: At a particular place in a normal note Luhmann often made a reference to another card in the collection that was also relevant to the special argument in question; in most cases the referred card is located at an entirely different place in the file, frequently in the context of a completely different discussion or subject.

Often Luhmann noted the references directly as he created the card but also regularly updated already existing cards by adding references whenever the integration of new cards in other parts of the collection made it necessary. Thus the advantages of the mode of organizing the collection—"The decision where to place what in the file can involve a great deal of randomness as long as I add references linking the other options"[14]—necessitate a *permanent data bank update*. In this way, Luhmann engaged in an ongoing process of tending to his file, which explains why the file, according to him, preoccupied so much of his time and also illustrates how well he really knew it.[15]

Generally speaking, his mode of referencing—developed in the 1950s!—makes use of an idea that would later become the common technology of "hyperlinks" in the computer age. Luhmann himself called his system of references a "web-like system."[16] The metaphor of the web also suggests interpreting it along network-theoretical lines.[17] A key feature explaining the production of serendipity is the potential of the filing system for enabling so-called "short cuts"; i.e., the fact that a reference may lead to a completely different (both in terms of subject and location), distant region in the network (file). The cards containing a collection of references are furthermore of interest because they represent so-called "hubs"; i.e., cards that function as nodes that feature an above-average number of links to other cards so that these few cards provide access points to extensive parts of the file.

The significance of Luhmann's system of referencing cannot be overestimated in the light of the method of integrating new notes into the file described above and the absence of a systematic order. Yet, it must be noted that this method is also fraught with certain risks: a note or a (smaller) subject area that is *not* linked to the web of references becomes lost irretrievably in the bulk of notes. Here the inherent momentum of "*black holes*" applies: parts of the file that are poorly linked with other parts tend to remain isolated later on and hence fade away. This risk is vividly demonstrated by the fact that some smaller parts of the collection seemed to be untouched since their compilation.

THE KEYWORD INDEX AS THE CENTRAL KEY

The structure of the file described so far ultimately provides the backdrop to understanding the function of the keyword index. The absence of a fixed system of order and, in consequence, a table of contents turned the index into the key tool for using the file—how else should one be able to find certain notes again and thus gain access to the system of references? Not wanting to rely on his one memory or pure chance, Luhmann permanently created a keyword index, being able to identify at least one point from which the respective web of references can be *accessed.*

Whereas the index to the first collection was still of fairly manageable size with its 1,250 entries, the continuous updates of the index—as another part of the database maintenance—to the second collection[18] ultimately resulted in 3,200 entries. Contrary to the subject index of a book, the file's keyword index makes no claim to providing a complete list of all cards in the collection that refer to a specific term. Rather, Luhmann typically listed only one to four places where the term could be found in the file, the idea being that all other relevant entries in the collection could be quickly identified via the internal system of references described above. As Luhmann noted,[19] this concept goes back to the general structure of the brain modeled by W. R. Ashby:[20] the capacity of the brain does not derive from a huge number of point-to-point-accesses but on the relations between the nodes (i.e., notes). Therefore, by contrast, the large number of words listed in the keyword index indicates that this list itself was at least intended to meet the standard of (thematic) completeness; i.e., complexity of the index file.

The principles according to which the collections are organized have as a consequence that accessing the file via the keyword index does not limit the search to that term only. Quite to the contrary, the specific method of integrating cards and the system of linking ensure that any search soon opens up a vast web of notes leading away from the original topic to a variety of other subjects that the user initially would not have associated with the first one. If one follows the web of references in detail that are laid down in the file, one constantly encounters new paths leading to new subjects: the decision to pursue or ignore them presupposes that there is a specific research question to be answered within a certain time; otherwise, one risks getting lost in the depths of the file after entering in by using the keyword index.

SUMMARY: THE FILING SYSTEM
AS A THINKING TOOL

It is specifically not (only) the paths that Luhmann tread in his initial readings and note-taking that are constitutive of his filing system
but rather the special filing technique and the (selective) relations
established between his notes by means of his referencing technique
that make it possible to retrieve more in a later query via the pivotal
keyword index than what was intended when the notes were initially
taken. As early as in the 1950s to 1960s, Luhmann simulated a modern
computer-based database system by applying the multiple-storage
principle in filing subjects and utilizing his referencing technique, by
which he anticipated what would become the common technology
of hyperlinking in the era of the World Wide Web. The file's analog
design, however, limited the realization of its potential for technical
reasons since it required the more time-consuming process of physically looking up and taking out the respective card instead of a simple
mouse click.

One must also not lose sight of the fact that Luhmann's filing
system also—and above all—served him as a research or *thinking
tool.* This is not only true in terms of the proposition that the file
acted as a communication partner in the research process[21] but
also in regard to the fact that in Luhmann's mind the process of
writing things down enables disciplined thinking in the first place:
"Underlying the filing technique is the experience that *without
writing, there is no thinking.*"[22] Accordingly, the file also documents the
evolution of important theoretical constructs in Luhmann's thinking.
It contains not only validated knowledge but also reflects the thought
process, including potential mistakes and blind alleys that were later
revised but not (!) removed from the file, as the original cards always
remained in the file and perhaps a new card with revisions was added
if needed. In this sense, the file is more than just an analog database
of Luhmann's theory: it can be seen as—drawing on the words of

Erving Goffman[23]—the *backstage of his theory*, and therefore as Niklas Luhmann's intellectual autobiography.

NOTES

1. Since 1999, a number of more recent monographs and articles have been published posthumously. There are still about 150 other yet unpublished manuscripts in his literary estate, which is now being prepared to make it accessible for research (cf. https://www.uni-bielefeld.de/soz/luhmann-archiv/).

2. In the early 1950s, during his legal clerkship, he was working on his doctoral thesis in law, which he had largely completed in 1955 but did not submit.

3. The following remarks are based on a first insight into Niklas Luhmann's card index, which is a central part of his literary estate. The first part of the card index is now online: http://ds.ub.uni-bielefeld.de/viewer/ppnresolver?id =ZKLuhm. During his lifetime Luhmann himself had published a rudimentary description of its construction principles and how he used it (Luhmann, 1981); in an interview one can find a few remarks concerning the genesis of the collection (Luhmann, 1987).

4. Cf. Cevolini, 2004; Krajewski, 2011.

5. See Merton and Barber, 2004.

6. In 1960–1961, Luhmann spent a year at the Harvard School of Public Administration in Cambridge, MA (USA), where he attended lectures by Talcott Parsons, the leading sociologist in the field of systems theory at the time. There are no documents in the literary estate substantiating the claim that this visit was the trigger to start a new collection of notes, but the chronological sequence seems obvious.

7. Luhmann, 1987:150 (my translation).

8. Luhmann, index card no. 9/8 of the second collection (my translation). In the second collection one can find a small subsection with notes about the card index and its principles.

9. In the literary estate we found a paper with a table of contents for a publication called "*Grundriss einer funktionalen Verwaltungslehre*" ("Outline of a Functional Administrative Theory"). Beside this note there are no other documents which suggest that Luhmann ever really tried to write this book, but the bullets of the elaborate table of contents can be found in the first six subject areas of the second collection of the card index mentioned above. So it might be only a little exaggeration to say that the overall structure of this collection originally is developed "out of the spirit of the administrative sciences."

10. For instance, when we look up the section "functionalism," one finds the following sequence of terms: concept of function—unit of reference of functional analysis—concept of conditions for continued existence—concept of functional problem—concept of expectations—social identity—sincerity—secret (all my translations).

11. Luhmann, index card no. 9/8h in the second collection (my translation).

12. I can't go into too much detail here due to the limitation of space: the example above is of course an idealization. Normally the numbering alternates between numbers and letters, but that was a rule Luhmann sometimes violates (due to an additional insertion of a branch off-card in an existing sequence where the alternation already had taken place); furthermore there was no general rule that the main line of argument is numbered consecutively in numbers or letters, i.e., a sequence 1–1a–1b of mono-thematic cards was also possible. That means that the number *on its own* does not really inform about the relations between different notes. An exception from this is Luhmann's use of capital letters (see below).

13. Luhmann, 1981:224 (my translation of "*innere Verzweigungsfähigkeit*").

14. Luhmann, 1987:143 (my translation).

15. It must be noted that Luhmann never created a detailed table of contents for the collections (which is not really surprising: the compilation of such a survey was just not possible due to the continuous evolution of the collections). A preliminary subject overview in the context of the aforementioned project of making Luhmann's work accessible for research comprises a total of roughly 150 pages.

16. Luhmann, 1987:143 (my translation of "*spinnenartiges System*").

17. For a network model of this kind, see Watts, 2004.

18. The second collection contains four versions of the keyword index: each time the process of continuously adding onto the index resulted in its alphabetical order becoming too messy, Luhmann created an entirely new version of the index.

19. Index card no. 9/8b of the second collection.

20. See Ashby, 1967.

21. See Luhmann's (1981) description of his relationship with the card index.

22. Luhmann, *Zettelkasten II*, index card no. 9/8g (my translation, original emphasis).

23. See Goffman, 1959.

REFERENCES

Ashby, W. Ross. "The Place of the Brain in the Natural World." *Currents in Modern Biology* 1 (1967): 95–104. https://doi.org/10.1016/0303-2647(67)90021-4.

Cevolini, Alberto. "Gelehrsamkeit als Medium des Wissens in der frühen Neuzeit." *Soziale Systeme* 10 (2004): 233–256. https://doi.org/10.1515/sosys-2004-0205.

Goffman, Erving. *The Presentation of Self in Everyday Life*. Garden City, NY: Doubleday, 1959.

Krajewski, Markus. *Paper Machines. About Cards & Catalogs, 1548–1929*. Cambridge, MA: MIT Press, 2011.

Luhmann, Niklas. "Biographie, Attitüden, Zettelkasten." In *Archimedes und Wir. Interviews*, edited by D. Baecker and G. Stanitzek, 125–155. Berlin: Merve, 1987.

Luhmann, Niklas. "Kommunikation mit Zettelkästen: Ein Erfahrungsbericht." In *Öffentliche Meinung und sozialer Wandel. Für Elisabeth Noelle-Neumann*, edited by H. Baier, H. M. Kepplinger, and K. Reumann, 222–228. Wiensbaden, Germany: Westdeutscher Verlag, 1981.

Luhmann, Niklas. *Zettelkasten*. Bielefeld University: Digital Collections, 1951–1996. http://ds.ub.uni-bielefeld.de/viewer/ppnresolver?id=ZKLuhm.

Merton, Robert K., and Elinor G. Barber. *The Travels and Adventures of Serendipity. A Study in Historical Semantics and the Sociology of Science*. Princeton, NJ: Princeton University Press, 2004. Originally published in 1945.

Watts, Duncan J. "The 'New' Science of Networks." *Annual Review of Sociology* 30 (2004): 243–270. https://doi.org/10.1146/annurev.soc.30.020404.104342.

11

OPENINGS

LUCY SUCHMAN

A research project for me occurs at the conjoining of what I could characterize as three intersecting fields. These are (in no particular order, insofar as each is equally important):

- A concern; that is, something in the world that I would like to support and/or in which I hope to intervene;
- A body of scholarship; that is, ways of theorizing the world that feel illuminating, and comprise an ongoing process of thinking together to which I'd like to contribute;
- A location; that is, a place (in multiple senses of that term) from which I'm able and willing to act.

These are fields of thought and action that I am both actively engaged in generating, and that simultaneously capture and compel me in particular (indeterminate) directions at any given time. At the risk of overrationalizing (as retrospective reconstructions invariably do), I can trace the course of my research life to date in these terms, beginning in the United States in the 1960s and 1970s.

The radical politics of those decades in the U.S. circled around concerns of race, war, and increasing concentrations of multinational corporate power. Diffracted through the contemporary anthropological orientations of the University of California at Berkeley, where I was a student, these concerns inspired a turn characterized by Professor Laura Nader as "studying up" (Nader, 1974). This trope urged a shifting of the anthropological gaze from those marginalized by centralizations of power, to the elite institutions and agencies in which political and economic resources were increasingly concentrated. At the same time, my encounters with teachers at UC Berkeley like the great symbolic interactionist Herbert Blumer (1986), along with the expanding fields of ethnomethodology and conversation analysis, opened up the possibilities for what I would now characterize as a performative account of the mundane production of social order. The intersection of these lines led me to the idea of a PhD project that would involve a critical, interactionist analysis of the everyday operations of corporate power.

My search for access to a multinational corporation in the late 1970s took me in an unexpected direction, one that proved highly consequential for my life and work over the ensuing twenty years. My serendipitous arrival at Xerox's Palo Alto Research Center (Xerox PARC) opened the space for a range of collaborations: critical engagement with cognitive and computer scientists around questions of intelligence and interactivity; collaboration with system designers aimed at respecifying central issues for them, including the human-machine interface and usability; extensive studies of work settings oriented to articulating technologies as sociotechnical practice; engagement with an emerging international network of computer scientists and system designers committed to more participatory forms of system development with relevant workers/users; activism within relevant computer research networks to raise awareness of those alternatives; and iterative enactment of an ethnographically informed, participatory design practice within the context of the research center and the wider corporation. Although this extended history of collaborative experimentation and engagement was unquestionably fruitful, it also raised a number of questions for me regarding the politics of design, including the systematic placement of politics beyond the limits of the designer's frame (see Suchman, 2011, 2013).

The end of my tenure at Xerox PARC took me in 2000 to Lancaster University in the UK, and more specifically the Department of Sociology and the Centre for Science Studies. Building on the research enabled by my years at the research center, but freed now from the constraints of that location, I was able to return more directly to the political concerns that had taken me there. More specifically, I began to look for a way that I might enter worlds of critical scholarship and activism aimed at interrupting the trajectories of U.S. militarism in which, as a U.S. citizen, I felt implicated. I hoped to build on the foundations already laid by my previous research, at the intersections of AI/robotics, human-computer interaction, anthropology and STS. My learning curve in relation to military worlds was (and still is) a steep one, having spent my life to this point avoiding any contact with those worlds. The first steps included reading and engagement with the work of others.

My current work in this area is animated by a concern with what geographer of militarism Derek Gregory (2004:20) identifies as the "architectures of enmity"; that is, the sociotechnologies that facilitate enactments of "us" and "them" (see Suchman et al., 2017). A point of contact with my previous work has been the military trope of "situational awareness," which I've engaged both through studies of a project in immersive simulations for military training (Suchman, 2015, 2016a), and in the context of a campaign, led by Human Rights Watch, to "Stop Killer Robots."[1] The campaign is premised on the observation that the threat posed by robotic weapons is not the prospect of a Terminator-style humanoid, but the more mundane progression of increasing automation in military weapon systems. Of particular concern are initiatives to automate the identification of particular categories of humans (those in a designated area, or who fit a specified and machine-readable profile) as legitimate targets for killing. A crucial issue here is that this delegation of "the decision to kill" presupposes the specification, in a computationally tractable way, of algorithms for the discriminatory identification of a legitimate target. The latter, under the Rules of Engagement, International Humanitarian Law, and the Geneva Conventions, is an opponent who is engaged in combat and poses an "imminent threat."

We have ample evidence for the increasing uncertainties involved in differentiating combatants from noncombatants under contemporary conditions of war fighting (even apart from crucial contests over the legitimacy of targeting protocols). And however partial and fragile their reach, the international legal frameworks governing war fighting are our best current hope for articulating limits on killing. The precedent for a ban on lethal autonomous weapons lies in the United Nations Convention on Certain Conventional Weapons (CCW), the body created to prohibit or restrict the use of "certain conventional weapons which may be deemed to be excessively injurious or have indiscriminate effects."[2] Since the launch of the campaign for a ban in 2013, the CCW has put the debate on lethal autonomous weapons onto its agenda. In April of 2016, I presented testimony on the impossibility of automating the capacity of "situational awareness," accepted within military circles as necessary for discrimination between legitimate and illegitimate targets, and as a prerequisite to legal killing (Suchman, 2016b). My ethnomethodological background, and my earlier engagements with artificial intelligence (Suchman, 2007) alerted me to the fact that prescriptive frameworks like the laws of war (or any other human-designated directives) presuppose, rather than specify, the capacities for comprehension and judgment required for their implementation in any actual situation. It is precisely those capacities that artificial intelligences lack, now and for the foreseeable future.

While those of us engaged in thinking through science and technology studies (STS) are preoccupied with the contingent and shifting distributions of agency that comprise complex sociotechnical systems, the hope for calling central human actors to account for the effects of those systems rests on the possibility of articulating relevant normative and legal frameworks (Suchman and Weber, 2016). This means that we need conceptions of agency that recognize the inseparability of humans and technologies, and the always contingent nature of autonomy, in ways that help to reinstate human deliberation at the heart of matters of life, social justice, and death. This concern, informed by rich bodies of relevant scholarship at the intersections of sociology, anthropology, STS, and cultural/political geography (to name only those with which I am most immediately engaged), animates my current efforts to relocate and deepen long-standing heuristics for the articulation of contemporary social formations.

NOTES

1. See https://www.stopkillerrobots.org/, accessed June 29, 2018.
2. https://www.unog.ch/80256EE600585943/(httpPages)/4FoDEF093B4860B4C1257180004B1B30?OpenDocument, accessed June 29, 2018.

REFERENCES

Blumer, Herbert. *Symbolic Interactionism: Perspective and Method*. Berkeley: University of California Press, 1986. Originally published in 1969.

Gregory, Derek. *The Colonial Present*. Oxford: Blackwell, 2004.

Nader, Laura. "Up the Anthropologist: Perspectives Gained from Studying Up." In *Reinventing Anthropology*, edited by D. Hymes, 284–311. New York: Vintage, 1974.

Suchman, Lucy. "Anthropological Relocations and the Limits of Design." *Annual Review of Anthropology* 40 (2011): 1–18. https://doi.org/10.1146/annurev.anthro.041608.105640.

Suchman, Lucy. "Configuring the Other: Sensing War through Immersive Simulation." *Catalyst: Feminism, Theory, Technoscience* 2, no. 1 (2016a): 1–36. https://doi.org/10.28968/cftt.v2i1.28827.

Suchman, Lucy. "Consuming Anthropology." In *Interdisciplinarity: Reconfigurations of the Social and Natural Sciences*, edited by A. Barry and G. Born, 141–160. London: Routledge, 2013.

Suchman, Lucy. *Human-Machine Reconfigurations: Plans and Situated Actions*. Revised ed. New York: Cambridge University Press, 2007.

Suchman, Lucy. "Situational Awareness and Adherence to the Principle of Distinction as a Necessary Condition for Lawful Autonomy." In *Lethal Autonomous Weapon Systems: Technology, Definition, Ethics, Law & Security*, edited by R. Geiss and H. Lahmann, 273–283. Berlin: Federal Foreign Office, Division Conventional Arms Control, 2016b.

Suchman, Lucy. "Situational Awareness: Deadly Bioconvergence at the Boundaries of Bodies and Machines." *Media Tropes* 5, no. 1 (2015): 1–24. https://mediatropes .com/index.php/Mediatropes/article/view/22126.

Suchman, Lucy, Karolina Follis, and Jutta Weber. "Tracking and Targeting: Sociotechnologies of (In)security." *Science. Technology and Human Values* 42, no. 6 (2017): 983–1002. https://doi.org/10.1177/0162243917731524.

Suchman, Lucy. and Jutta Weber. "Human-Machine Autonomies." In *Autonomous Weapons Systems*, edited by N. Bhuta, S. Beck, R. Geis, H.-Y. Liu, and C. Kreis, 75–102. Cambridge: Cambridge University Press, 2016.

II

PUBLISHING

What Is Your Publication Strategy?

12

SHALL I PUBLISH THIS AUF DEUTSCH OR IN ENGLISH?

JENS BECKERT

E nglish is the *lingua franca* of academia. This essay is published in an Italian journal; the authors of the symposium are French, German, Dutch, Danish, Chinese, Canadian, and American. Despite this international reach and the location of the journal in Italy, none of the contributions are written in Italian, French, Dutch, or Chinese. Of course, the editors would have been surprised if a contributor had submitted a manuscript in any other language but English.

What is to be taken for granted in an international collaboration like this symposium, the convention that the conversation takes place in English, is in many other instances a much trickier issue for those whose linguistic competencies go beyond their mother tongue. And in many ways the idea that English would indeed be the lingua franca of sociology is an illusion at best.

I set off from my own experience, but the issues I raise go way beyond personal idiosyncrasies. I am German, studied mainly in Germany, and have always held academic positions at German universities or research institutes. At the same time, I hold a master's degree from an American university and spent altogether four years—first as a student and later as a researcher—at American universities. More recently I have spent several years at academic institutions in France. From the beginning of my academic journey, I published in German as well as in English. Many of my publications have been translated either from English into German or vice versa; other articles are only available in one of the two languages.

ACADEMIC CAREERS

To publish in both languages was a publication strategy recommended to me very early on by my advisers. What is at stake here are the odds of having a successful academic career. But the choices are far from obvious. German is a language spoken in a community of roughly one hundred million people, Germany has one of the most significant traditions in sociology, it has several very reputable sociology journals, a professional association that holds regular meetings, and an academic labor market that has filled the overwhelming majority of positions with Germans. All this speaks for the need of publications in German to succeed in an academic career in Germany. It is by publishing in German that one makes a name for oneself and finds recognition in search committees that consist of German academics who, for the most part, are primarily oriented towards the German academic system with its publications, institutions, and networks. In an evaluation of publication practices in German sociology conducted ten years ago, it was found that only 15.6 percent of publications by sociologists working at German universities or research institutions were published in a non-German-speaking country (Wissenschaftsrat, 2008:36). This may have changed somewhat over the last ten years, but certainly not dramatically. In German economic sociology, for which I have more recent data, 63 percent of publications over the last ten years (2008–2017) have been published in German (270 out of a total of 428 publications).[1] For books the number is 81.1 percent, for journal articles it is 41 percent, and for book chapters in edited volumes it is 74.2 percent. German sociology takes place not only in

Germany but also in German. A career in German sociology makes it necessary to publish in the language of Goethe.

The need to publish in German finds counterfactual proof—though I can give this only in anecdotal form—in German sociologists who published only (or mostly) in English and experienced great difficulties in gaining positions in Germany, but were able to have successful careers outside of Germany. The need to publish in the countries' language holds in similar ways for all large European countries; countries large enough to have developed self-sustaining professional structures in the discipline. France, Italy, and Spain certainly resemble the situation described for Germany. The situation is different in the European countries with smaller language communities, which experience much stronger push factors to publish in English.

At the same time, publishing "only" in German is clearly not enough. Certainly there are many German sociologists who have never published in any other language but German (and for all practical purposes, that means that they have not published in English). But the rhetoric of the internationalization of science offers rewards for showcasing one's ability to also publish in English, especially if such publications appear in highly ranked journals. Publishing in English demonstrates a symbolic capital that increases the author's legitimacy, even if the publications remain largely unnoticed by the "international" sociological community and the community intended to be reached by the author is primarily German sociologists. German sociological institutions buy into a symbolic hierarchy which rewards linguistic reach into the English language and positions American academia at the top.[2]

Just as significantly, "only" publishing in German is not enough if one aims at recognition of one's work beyond German sociology. If you look at citation rankings based on the Social Science Citation Index (SCCI)—which has a global reach but also a bias towards

English-language journals—you see that there are only a very small number of Germans among the most cited sociologists. In fact, only a relatively small number of non-Americans make it onto this list. Among the 195 sociologists most cited between 1956 and today, there are 12 Germans (6.1 percent) (Korom, 2020). Many of them are "classical" authors like Max Weber and Georg Simmel, whose work has been diffused without much active participation on the part of the authors. That Max Weber became known in the U.S. is due to the work of Frank Knight and Talcott Parsons, not to Weber himself. The other authors—examples would be Claus Offe and Hans-Peter Blossfeld—have written large parts of their oeuvre in English and kept very close ties to American sociology, be it through extended stays at American research universities, presence at conferences, or through research cooperations.

Such international reach thus demands a dedicated strategy of participating in conversations that are in many cases detached from the national sociological discourse in Germany; a participation that takes place through publications in English but also through physical presence in the institutions and meeting places of the other country. For any publication—be it in German, French, or any other language—that is not translated into English, the author knows in advance that it will not be recognized outside of the respective language community. When writing in any other language but English, reach is locally restricted. At the same time, as a German sociologist, one cannot take for granted that one's non-German publications are noticed in German sociology. The stronger the institutional integration and the stronger the publication record in the target country, the stronger the recognition of the author's work. The strongest effect is achieved by emigration: many of the sociologists at American universities are not American by birth but are nevertheless fully part of the professional system of American sociology. Some of them were able to also maintain a reputation in their country of origin, mostly by publishing in their mother tongue as well.

SUBSTANTIVE ISSUES

The question of which language to publish in reaches beyond the issues of career and recognition. It also points to substantive issues. One basic observation is that writing in a second language always comes at the cost of subtlety and linguistic precision. Authors are generally best when writing in their mother tongue. Even more importantly, the language of publication has profound implications for sociology as a discipline, if one understands sociology as standing in an enlightenment tradition, seeing its task as contributing to a better understanding of the social forces actors are entangled in. At the bare minimum, this demands that not only other sociologists in the profession, but also experts and laypeople in the public sphere of the community being investigated can read what sociologists find out with their research. That these target publics would read any foreign-language research is wishful thinking at best. Writing in Germany in English about aspects of German society insulates sociological scholarship, which then becomes a project driven by a disconnected elite. Cosmopolitanism easily leads to sociological Globish. Looking at my own publications, I can see that there is one of my research topics, the inheritance of wealth, where my publications are primarily in German. The monograph *Unverdientes Vermögen* has been translated into English, but many of the articles I wrote thereafter on the reform of inheritance law and estate taxation were addressed explicitly to a German audience—the audience I hoped could benefit practically from the insights I could provide. I felt very clearly that if I wrote these articles in English and thus addressed them to a non-German audience, then I would write them differently and the texts would lose much of their significance for the political discourse in Germany.

The rewards coming with publications in English not only have the intended linguistic consequences of increasing the numbers of English-language publications but also unintended substantive consequences. Top English-language journals in terms of status are not equally open to any topic, theory, or method. This is fully understandable because these journals also operate within a cultural and social realm with its specific concerns and priorities. After all, sociology is not a universal science but investigates cultural and institutional particularities. Thus a German author, aiming at success with his or her submission to an American or British journal, will direct his research at topics salient not in Germany but in the U.S. or the UK. The topic will rather be equal opportunities in the U.S., than equal opportunities in Germany or Romania. Or it will be at least a comparative research design including the U.S.

The same holds for theoretical traditions. To find acceptance among reviewers, the work needs to connect to the theoretical and conceptual instruments discussed in the sociological community in which the journal and its reviewers are embedded; contributions that don't meet this criterion run the risk of remaining impenetrable. Sociology is not a universal science. This holds despite the fact that there are authors who are seen to speak universal truths, and their theories are applied to foreign cultural contexts without much thought—Pierre Bourdieu, who is the most cited author in sociology, being the classic example. Some authors have been given this status of a "global ultra elite" (Korom, 2018)—e.g., Bourdieu, Foucault, Weber, and Parsons—who become divorced from the cultural context that informed their work. The aspiration to publish in English makes researchers especially prone to contribute to this cultural decontextualization of theories. It's a kind of sophisticated twist on the classic anthropological problem of going to meet the native in his context and applying one's own cultural frames.

During the last couple of years I spent much time in France, which allowed me the privilege of also learning the language. I wanted to understand French sociology beyond the French authors from the "global ultra elite" whose work has been translated into German and

English. In my observation, French sociology, when compared to German sociology, is even more organized around its own research traditions that primarily take the French intellectual space as its reference point. Some (especially younger) French sociologists regret this and see it as French sociology lagging behind, which should be countered through stronger international openness, including increasing publication in English.[3] To be sure, there is much to be said in favor of this. But it can also not escape one's attention that the reason for the originality of parts of French sociology lies precisely in its embeddedness in intellectual and cultural reference points that are different from American, British, or Polish sociology and that this originality flourishes in a specific language community. Für die Soziologie ist die Sprache der Publikation alles andere als trivial.

NOTES

1. This data is assembled from the website of the economic sociology section of the German Sociological Association (DGS), where authors can have their recent publications listed. See http://wirtsoz-dgs.mpifg.de/neuerscheinungen .asp. It is not a complete set of publications in economic sociology in Germany, but covers a large part of it, and there is no reason to believe that the language ratio would shift with a more complete set of publications.

2. It would be interesting to investigate this more closely, for instance with reference to gender differences. Do German female sociologists pursuing an academic career in Germany need more legitimacy through publications in English than their male peers?

3. Several French sociology journals (*Sociologie du travail* and *Revue Française de Sociologie*) made the move to publish complete or partial English online editions, with translations of the articles published in French. The success of this very costly project in terms of international recognition of the published research is, however, very limited. The reason for this could be that French articles are not only written in French but also use different ways of structuring arguments and order the presentation of information differently. The American standard has not been adopted everywhere. As a result, even the translated text remains difficult to penetrate.

REFERENCES

Korom, Philipp. "The Prestige Elite in Sociology: Toward a Collective Biography of the Most Cited Scholars (1970–2010)." *Sociological Quarterly* 61, no. 1 (2020): 128–163. https://doi.org/10.1080%2F00380253.2019.1581037.

Wissenschaftsrat. *Forschungsleistungen deutscher Universitäten und außeruniversitärer Einrichtungen in der Soziologie. Ergebnisse der Pilotstudie Forschungsrating des Wissenschaftsrats,* April 2008. https://www.wissenschaftsrat.de/download/For schungsrating/Dokumente/Pilotstude_Forschungsrating_Soziologie/pilot _ergeb_sozio.pdf.

13

A PAPER IS LIKE A HORSE—AND
A BOOK IS LIKE A WHALE?

MASSIMIANO BUCCHI

My own experience as author is that there is no straightforward answer to the question of what are the best publishing formats for a scholar in the social sciences.

I started to publish at the end of my PhD, one theoretical paper and some empirical papers based on my doctoral research. My thesis was also published as a book by Routledge. Although at the time I did not fully realize this, I have since then learnt about the importance for a young scholar of publishing a book that captures the essence of your interests and research. It is, in my view, a question of defining your own identity as a scholar, who you are and what you have done so far. My second book was, on the other hand, commissioned directly by the publisher, who wanted an introductory text to social studies of science. It proved much more difficult to try to explain clearly and carefully other scholars' work than presenting my own. I have thereafter edited other volumes, including a textbook in science communication and a 4-volume anthology. My own experience with this kind of work is that it is highly rewarding in terms of international visibility, as well as in terms of the opportunity to learn from coeditors and contributors. However, it can actually be more time consuming and complex than writing your own book.

Since then, the decision about formats mostly came from answering the question: Who do I want to talk to, and what kind of research results do I have? For example, in the early 2000s, natural scientists became interested in science in society and public perception of sciences, also in connection with heated debates about issues like biotechnology. It seemed natural, to me and to my colleagues, to try to engage in a discussion with them: so we targeted top science journals like *Nature* and *Science*, offering empirical results that we thought could help address some of the key questions and further stimulate the debate.

I also continued to write books, i.e., monographs. Quite simply, in my view a paper needs a clear, sharp focus: one central result and some specifications. A book allows one to explore a topic more in depth, analyzing it from different angles. I suppose one could draw an analogy between short stories and novels for fiction writers. In his *Harvard Norton Lectures* (*Lezioni Americane*), Italian writer Italo Calvino (1988) wrote that a short story, or tale, is like a horse: it has to run, trotting or galloping, up to a point.

In my own experience, books are much more demanding to the author in terms of style (I suppose the obvious animal analogy, following Calvino's, would be the whale, particularly for American writers). It is not enough to have a good topic and interesting ideas to have a book: first you have to find your own voice, rather than echoing other people's voices; then you have to find a tone and rhythm for that specific topic. A book is not a collection of papers/ chapters but requires its own structure. If you wish the reader to follow a thread, this thread has first to be clear and exciting to yourself in the first place. Also, a book requires a different discipline in terms of writing. Papers can be written on and off, in between other commitments. Books require more intense dedication and continuity, otherwise the rhythm will be lost. Finally, papers can easily be written with another author, or even as a team. A book, on the other hand, is largely an individual, solitary exercise. I have often wondered how successful twin authors like the brothers Goncourt, Dannay and Lee, and Fruttero and Lucentini could actually write together (apparently Fruttero and Lucentini used to split chapters, to be later revised by the other author).

Perhaps because of these experiences, I became interested in the concept of style in science communication as an interesting bridge between individual experience and collective, normative standards— threads of this concept can be found in the work of great scientists like Galileo or Buffon and of scholars like Alistair Crombie or Ludvik Fleck.

I had an opportunity to reflect on my own experience as author when, in 2016, I became editor of the international journal *Public Understanding of Science*, published by Sage. The journal currently receives approximately 250 submissions each year, with an acceptance rate of 14 percent. One of my first commitments, as editor, was to reduce response time, particularly for those papers that did not have many chances of successfully going through the review process. When we are not sure whether the paper fits the focus of the journal, we now ask a member of the editorial board to do a pre-review. If the response is negative, this at least allows authors to receive a quick feedback and decision and send the paper to another journal. One of the most positive surprises in editing a journal was to discover how much time and energy as scholars we are willing to invest into careful, anonymous peer reviewing.

Overall, the quality of the papers we receive is continuously increasing, as well as the geographical coverage. When the journal *Public Understanding of Science* was founded in 1992, it published mostly papers by authors from English-speaking countries. We now receive an increasing number of papers from Asia, Africa, Latin America. Most of the submissions are based on solid, well-organized empirical research. However, there is a tendency to address consolidated topics and established research lines. For some researchers, the choice seems to be low risk, i.e., getting the research they have done (or been funded for) published in a good journal. It would be important to receive more theoretical papers, or papers that reflect on the increasing body of research produced in our field to provide innovating insights and interpretations.

I am not sure I am in a position to give advice to young scholars, as the editor of this issue asked me. Based on my own experience as author and editor, I would be tempted to encourage them to look for the gaps in literature: do what (almost) nobody else is doing, rather than do what all the others are doing. Perhaps quite naively, I have often written the kind of paper or book that I would have liked to read as a reader.

But of course I realize that young researchers today are exposed to a variety of pressures to publish "safely" and quickly. I sometimes remind my students that Thomas Kuhn took some 15 years to complete *The Structure of Scientific Revolutions* (1962)—a timescale that today would have probably got him into trouble with evaluation bodies.

Another simple advice it is not to take criticism as a sign of failure, but rather be grateful to colleagues who have invested their own time to read and criticize their work. And if they misunderstood, most likely it was your fault for not being clear enough.

In general, my modest experience is that good work always pays. Interesting and innovative ideas, even when rejected in the first place by a specific journal, will find another outlet; well-structured research, rich examples, can be further developed in a number of ways and contexts.

REFERENCES

Calvino, Italo. *Lezioni Americane. Sei Proposte per il Prossimo Millennio*. Milan: Garzanti, 1988.

Kuhn, Thomas. *The Structure of Scientific Revolutions*. Chicago: University of Chicago Press, 1962.

14

WHAT'S GOOD ENOUGH?

WENDY ESPELAND

ACKNOWLEDGMENTS

Thanks to Bruce Carruthers for helpful comments.

One of the most difficult lessons for me to learn about the professional side of academic life was that it is a luxury for me to wait to send something off until I think it is good enough. Left to my own devices, I typically err on the side of "not yet." There are always questions that remain unanswered, some bit of uncollected evidence that could strengthen the argument, another article to read or, the fate of all sociologists, especially those who work on living people, things keep changing. Who knows what explains this proclivity. Perfectionist tendencies? Pigheadedness? What my friends call "girl disease," the disposition of some women to be less confident of their work than they ought to be? Whatever. But "not yet" is, of course, a synonym for "never." Even in graduate school I could see this was self-defeating thinking. So, what to do?

The short answer is, get over it. But, like most advice, that's easier said than done. The longer answer builds on a career of adapting my evaluations of my work, my sense of what is good enough, to a series of professional opportunities, constraints, and experiences. These include things like belonging to workshops or working groups, helping to edit a journal, getting a job, keeping a job, being a reviewer; it includes generous colleagues (especially the one I married), the needs of graduate students and collaborators; and it includes deadlines, whether self-imposed or as institutionalized as tenure. In other words, good enough is always in the context of juggling the multiple roles of writer, teacher, and colleague—the nuts and bolts of our profession.

I have lived a privileged professional life because I have had access to rich and varied professional experiences that people who work in cash-strapped institutions or teach eight classes a year may never have. And these experiences have provided places, resources, and incentives for getting work done and making it better. Having a workshop read your paper and getting comments from a half-dozen smart people should make it better. On the other hand, such richness can amp up expectations. Evaluation, like deprivation, is relative. Learning to mediate expectations, whether it's the voice in your head or the demands of a tight deadline for a conference paper requires judgement honed from experience. For me, this often takes the form of a sooner-or-better calculation.

Like all evaluation, "good enough" is a social process, undergirded by communities, networks, and contexts. Whether it is art worlds (Becker, 1982), Nigerian novels (Griswold, 2000), or finding a good lawyer (Karpik, 2010), our evaluations are always collaborations that are marked by a combination of pragmatic demands, distinctive cultural trajectories, and the kinds of evaluative tools we have at our disposal. Such tools may be as formal as journal prestige or as informal as the disembodied voice of a former advisor. Ideally, all graduate students should have advisors who tell them when a paper is good enough to send off and offer advice about where to send it, and junior colleagues should have senior colleagues who give careful comments on drafts, and we all should have a forum for presenting our work in its various stages of doneness. Whether or not one enjoys those advantages, there are some generic questions that I use when I am deciding if something is "good enough" to send off, broad questions that apply in many contexts.

The first question to ask oneself is "What is the argument?" Good articles make a clear and convincing argument. This entails asking and answering a well-defined question with sections of prose that have logical connections to each other. If you are not able to express verbally the argument in relatively simple language—a sign of mastery—it's more than likely that the written argument is less clear than it should be. Ask yourself, "Can someone who is not me read the piece and summarize my argument?" If someone does read it, ask them to restate your argument. If they can't do it, you have more work to do. Reviewers get frustrated when an argument is buried and they have to work hard to unpack it. Avoid doing this.

The next question to ask is "Why is this argument interesting? Why does knowing this matter?" My colleague, Charles Camic, a former chief editor of the *American Sociological Review* (*ASR*), teaches a wonderful graduate seminar on professional writing. He encourages students to frame their articles around what he calls an "Open Sociological Question" (OSQ). An OSQ is a question that is unresolved. It could be unresolved because no one has studied something before, because current explanations are wrong, because the world has changed and what we thought we knew is out of date, because we have contradictory explanations that should be adjudicated or synthesized, or because new data, methods or theory can unsettle or improve our explanations. The point is to use selectively the existing literature to make a case for why a question remains open and hence why it is interesting or important to know the answer to it. Another way to establish that something is interesting is to say why what is explained in one context is useful to people in other subfields. This is sometimes a matter of identifying mechanisms that apply in many situations. One challenge in assessing whether something is interesting or not is that sheer familiarity can blunt what is original or interesting about something. Especially in long research projects, something that seems obvious to you, and therefore uninteresting, may be news to someone who has not been grappling with the same issue for years. This is another reason why readers of drafts are so helpful.

An equally important part of "good enough" is to ask "Is my answer convincing? How might one argue with my answer?" I try to imagine what objections reviewers might have. For example, are there other ways to interpret the evidence? Am I making a claim that is too broad for my evidence? How might other kinds of evidence challenge my findings? What alternative explanations might there be? By trying to anticipate objections, it is sometimes possible to counter them in advance. It is at this point in my self-evaluations that I have to manage my expectations carefully. I can always find flaws in my explanations that can lead to my failing to submit something.

Another question I find useful is to ask is, "Who is the intended (or aspirational) audience for this article?" What is good enough depends on where it is going and for whom one is writing. One important distinction is whether something is for a generalist or specialized audience. Making things accessible and interesting to a general audience usually takes more work than when one can assume that readers share more knowledge; however, specialists may be more likely to find technical mistakes.

The prestige and rejection rates of a journal also matter in determining quality. For a journal like the *ASR* or the *American Journal of Sociology* (*AJS*), where rejection rates hover in the 90 percent range, space is tight, and multiple revise and resubmits are the norm, "good enough" means something different than it does for a chapter in an edited volume. Not that quality always correlates with the reputation of a journal—we all know of great pieces in obscure places and mediocre pieces in high-profile ones; nevertheless, if one is aiming for a more selective journal, it's worth getting as much feedback on a piece as possible. And it may be worth perusing the latest issues of the journal to see if there are articles related to your topic that you can include in the framing of your OSQ.

The type of journal one writes for also shapes what is good enough. Space is rarely the same constraint in a law review as it is for other journals, so writing can be more leisurely than for a journal where every word matters. Writers are generally allowed a more distinctive voice and informal style in essays or book chapters than in mainstream journals. And if one is writing for a journal that is oriented to the layperson as, for example, *Context* is, then clarity and vivid prose are even more important than these are for other publications.

Until now, I have talked about "good enough" in relation to articles. The questions raised about articles pertain for books as well. Writing a book is more like solving a giant puzzle in that fitting the pieces together, the structure and order of the book, is a bigger task. The luxury of more space and the capacity for greater complexity and detail are accompanied by the challenge of order and sequence. The question of what readers need to know first before they can understand what comes next is key. The overarching framework for a book often takes one of several forms. Chapters can be organized chronologically, over time. They can be organized around the substantive themes of the book as these are defined by theory or by evidence. Chapters might also be organized spatially, according to various locations, or according to different social groups if that is an important part of the argument. Part of what is "good enough" about a book is how well the pieces contribute to the whole, its flow.

What is "good enough" depends on the particular job a paper is supposed to do. It depends on its intended audience. It depends on genre and publication. Sending in an article or a book manuscript is making oneself vulnerable to reviewers and, one hopes, to an audience of readers. For me, good enough is always a compromise between what I imagine is possible and what is demanded, when. The trick is, of course, to get the right balance. I can still hear the voice of my former advisor, Wendy Griswold, telling me that "Perfect is the enemy of the good." That's not a bad thing to remember.

REFERENCES

Becker, Howard S. *Art Worlds*. Berkeley: University of California Press, 1982.

Griswold, Wendy. *Bearing Witness: Readers, Writers, and the Novel in Nigeria*. Princeton, NJ: Princeton University Press, 2000.

Karpik, Lucien. *Valuing the Unique: The Economics of Singularities*. Princeton, NJ: Princeton University Press, 2010.

15

PUBLISHING IN MODERN TIMES

NEIL D. FLIGSTEIN

T he good thing about the modern era of publishing is that there are many outlets for publication. There are many journals, with new ones appearing all of the time. The possibility to publish in edited volumes, often gathered from a conference, is also a siren song that is sometimes hard to ignore. The bad thing is that the proliferation of these outlets means that having others find your work becomes harder. After putting in hundreds or even thousands of hours, your published work can go completely ignored if it appears somewhere where audiences are sparse. Given this problem, it is important for young scholars to find their way into the best outlets they can. Journals like the *American Sociological Review* have over ten thousand potential viewers while edited volumes may sell as few as 300 copies that mostly end up in libraries. It, of course, is harder to publish in the top outlets than place a paper in an edited volume. But in terms of the impact for your work, it matters a lot.

This is not just a matter of increasing your visibility to other scholars. Most universities value publications in refereed journals in their promotion to tenure. It is no surprise that junior scholars dominate such journals. There is empirical evidence that when people get tenure, they are more likely to publish in specialty venues or edited volumes where they can avoid the slow and capricious review processes that can produce aggravation. But, as most established scholars will tell you, their publications in the most important outlets are the ones that are the most cited. Established scholars can occasionally get a paper that is more hidden to become part of the discussion in a particular literature, but that is often because their reputation helps find readers. My advice is that it is ok to publish in lesser outlets or edited volumes, but your finding an audience for your work will be aided by working to raise your work to the highest levels. So, if you are a junior scholar, how can you maximize the chance to get your work published in the best possible place?

We spend a huge part of our time worrying about our research and trying to find and define research problems, figure out how to engage them empirically, and produce new and definitive knowledge. If we are lucky at the end of the process, we have something interesting to share. But it is equally challenging to find an audience for our work. My basic idea here is that thinking about research and publication without thinking about audiences is a mistake. It is important when you do your research to have a particular audience in mind for your work and preferably a debate to enter into. If you want to generate new knowledge and engage others, this cannot be done without foresight. Who are you talking to; what do you have to say; why is it important to those scholars? Pragmatically, if you don't have a sense of who the work is for, your reviewers will scratch their heads and wonder what the paper is about and be inclined to reject your paper.

Some of us solve this problem by joining ongoing research programs where our work is already recognizable by a group of scholars. Here, one finds a natural audience for what one has to say and the framing of the work is made easier by having a known corpus of concepts. The trick is to use those concepts to suggest a new or novel puzzle for the research program and offering your work as a solution to that problem. While this is by no means easy, it does imply that the question of who might be interested is pre-solved. An audience exists, and as long as we have something to say, our work will find a home. Finding a home for the project means going to outlets where scholars have previously published and referring to the work that has already been presented.

But for many of us, the problem of finding audiences is more difficult. We have found something we think is really interesting and important, but we are not sure how to find people who will agree. The biggest mistake graduate students make in picking projects is to fall in love with a research site and fail at the beginning to have an idea about what their site is a case of. This raises the problem of "framing." This can be done after the work is done, but it is way harder to do, as one must figure out for whom to frame the project. This problem has other implications. How you frame a paper or book will determine who the reviewers are and, in the end, what readers might find their way to what you have to say. Given that it is so much work to accomplish anything, one wants a good framing, one that will be sensible, not straw man anyone's argument, and hopefully define the broadest possible audience at the beginning of the project. It is this challenge that is so daunting to most young scholars. After working so hard and long to do anything, you now must confront the world of reviewers and audiences, none of whom have to like or pay attention to a word you say. One device that scholars use to make this easier at the beginning of a project is to set up their project as a "theory contest." By pitting two perspectives against one another, whatever your empirical case shows can be news. Using your empirical case to illustrate what is right or wrong about the perspectives instantly interests an audience. If your goal is to show why both have it wrong, your results can lead to a third way to think about the problem. This gives you a chance to try to set up your own research program.

These problems are quite different for junior and senior scholars. Senior scholars have done a lot of work and have lots of intuition of who might be interested in what they are doing. They are somewhat used to being treated rudely, either through rejection by reviewers or by other scholars who ignore what they have done. You learn to have thick skin if you stay in the research world. If someone does not like what you are doing, you just move on down the road to see if you can find someone else who does. I often tell students that we are like peddlers going from town to town with our wares. In some places we sell a lot and in others, not so good. You've got to get used to that kind of rejection and learn to move on. Interpreting the signals the world sends you is often difficult. Reviewers can be capricious or vague and most of us are unprepared to take criticism. It is hard to not take it personally when you get a harsh review that dismisses our hard work. How you deal with such rejection goes a long way towards how you will do as a scholar. There are things you can do to make sure your work is ready for prime time before it goes out. My best advice is to seek out advice from people who have experience. While they are not always right, their experience will help you learn about short cuts you can take to make sure your work has the best chance to get published.

It is here that the capriciousness of the review process enters into our work. It is my experience that reviewers and editors can frequently be random. About half of what they say shows they did not read the paper carefully or alternatively reject the premises of the paper out of hand. If you are unfortunate enough to be working in a field where there are multiple research programs, which in sociology is nearly every field, you can be guaranteed that if your paper is sent to someone from one of the other programs, it will certainly be rejected. If you do not include a citation of the person who is reading the paper, you can be guaranteed to get a tougher review. What having someone with experience does is to alert you to the pitfalls of your paper. They can help you figure out if the main protagonists are fairly represented in the paper and if the relevant literature is covered. While you can't control who the reviewers are, you can protect yourself from making mistakes that can engender rejection.

But sometimes the problems in the paper are not just framing or failure to mention someone that might be a reviewer, but instead there is a real problem with the paper that you can fix. I review at least a dozen papers a year and I can tell you that the basic problem of most of the papers I reject is that the theory and literature review and often the conclusion have little or nothing to do with the empirical act. For example, when I review quantitative papers, I start by looking at the tables to figure out what is going on. Then, I read the paper to see if the story from the paper is consistent with the results. I can tell you that frequently it is not and that if I decide to reject the paper, it is most often motivated by this disconnect.

It is here that having people read and discuss your work before submitting it for review is most important. The biggest mistake younger scholars make is to submit their papers for review before they are ready. You should make sure to present or workshop your paper at least once, and three or four times if possible. You should work hard to get people who you know to read it if they will and give comments. You should work to incorporate their comments and listen to what they have to say. If someone points out logical problems with what you have done, you should fix them before sending the paper out. Going the extra mile to get it right or to consider any obvious problems with what you are doing makes it more likely that your work will get a better reception once it is under review.

I love to get a chance to present work in progress. When I go in front of an audience I will always get really good ideas. These ideas will make the paper better, make it more impactful, and increase the chances of acceptance by a journal. Win-win-win. When reviews come in, and a paper needs rewriting, you should listen to what the reviewer proposes and try to do what they want. If you get a rejection, it is ok to get mad and depressed. But when you get over it, you should try hard to listen. You can reject some of what a reviewer says as being out of hand, but you need to be able to read reviews carefully enough to know when to respond. There are no shortcuts here.

As someone who has written both books and articles, I can say that they are different art forms. A given project and its character determine whether or not I am writing a book or a paper. Often I write papers as a backdrop to doing a book. This is usually because

I am still exploring a larger theme and have not yet figured out what it will be. This can be helped by taking bites at the apple to see how things actually worked. Papers allow me to fill in details and figure out sub-themes that will appear in the book. The book operates as being synthetic, as a place to draw together a larger story. It is natural for the overarching message to emerge from the writing.

I liken a paper to a pop song. At the core of a pop song is the line you can't forget, what music writers call the "hook." A great paper is like a great pop song, in that it has one message captured by the hook that you don't forget. The best papers stick in your mind because you can sum them up in a sentence or two and their result is provocative and memorable. A book is more like a symphony. It comes in acts (chapters) and rises and falls, often telling a story. In a book, just like in a symphony, there are multiple themes that swirl around, ebbing and flowing in the text. The decision to write a book should not be made lightly. They are a lot of work and require a different skill set. It is not surprising that some scholars are article people and others book people. Figuring out your style is important to your growth as a scholar.

Books can be purely theoretical. Ethnography also can lend itself to books when they aid the scholar in presenting an in-depth understanding of a way of life. The book form makes the most sense where the topic is historical or comparative. In terms of historical work, if you are writing about the emergence of some new feature of social life or the rise and fall of something important, then the chapters of a book build on each other. They go from period to period establishing how something previously changed into something new. Comparative work considers why it is that some phenomena appear differently in different times and places. This kind of work illustrates what is common about such occurrences and what is different.

There are many challenges for young scholars in publishing in sociology. We are currently living with a mode of publication whose rules have changed very little since World War II. Peer-reviewed journals still are the gold standard for sociological work. But the competition to appear in those journals has increased dramatically as the number of young scholars who need to publish has increased. This has been met by journals with long waiting times and uncertain outcomes. The fragmentation of the discipline means that finding a significant audience is harder and harder. My advice is directed to help you control what you can control. Making your work fit into the literature by placing it in real debates, making sure your work answers potential criticisms and tries to meet those criticisms before the review process, all work to make your chance of publishing significant work higher. Since the goal is to make new knowledge, going the extra steps not only works to make your contribution better, but also makes it more visible.

16

HABITS, CANVASES, AND CONVERSATIONS

How I Think about Publishing

SHAMUS RAHMAN KHAN

INTRODUCTION

I have written in a wide range of formats: for example, books (Khan, 2011), shorter versions of those books (Khan and Jerolmack, 2013), long articles (Accominotti, Khan, and Storer, 2018), short articles (Khan et al., 2018), long-form "journalism" (Khan, 2015), long op-eds (Khan, 2012, 2013), short op-eds (Khan, 2016), and even, some time ago, regularly on a blog. I've also spent the last four years editing the journal *Public Culture*, and have edited special issues of other journals (Cousin et al., 2018; Tahir and Khan, 2019). And I've written using a wide range of methods, from experiments (Schneiderhan and Khan, 2008), to historical analysis (Abu-Odeh et al., 2020), to ethnography (Khan et al., 2018), to quantitative analysis (Mellins et al., 2018). The first, rather sobering realization I had upon being asked to write this piece was that I don't have a publication strategy. At best my approach might be called "pragmatic." But in practice and upon reflection it is far more experimental. I've never been terribly good at predicting how something is going to work until I try it. I have tried lots of different kinds of writing and in the process learned a good bit about how I think (writing is thinking for me). I have learned a lot about how to write and publish by doing it with others; most of my academic writing is coauthored. While the editors who solicited this piece of writing are, no doubt, most interested in my strategy for academic publishing, it also occurred to me that I could not make sense of my writing independent of the work I'd done writing for a non-academic audience. In this reflection I provide short bits of practical advice, divided by theme, which I hope will be useful for those just starting out in our profession, and those who have far more experience than I.

BEFORE YOU STRATEGIZE: WRITE HABITUALLY

Before you can strategize on how to publish you have to actually have words on a page. This is the subject of a wonderfully helpful previous issue (*Sociologica*, 1, 2018), but I want to return to it for a brief moment. Because in my experience the greatest challenge with publishing is not getting something published, it is writing something at all. My first bit of advice, then, is to write habitually. I find I can't think very seriously or intelligently for very long, and writing requires deep thinking. As a consequence, writing days are a waste of time. I can't think in that way for more than three hours, much less eight. My habit is to do two, maybe three 45-minute chunks of writing five days week. The greater the gap between the days the harder it is to write. That's because for me writing is in the rewriting. So the shorter the intervals between coming back to my text, again and again (I often write upwards of 100 drafts), the easier it is for me to remember what I was trying to do and then try to do it better. My first bit of advice, then, is not to write a lot. It's to write frequently. I get up early and write for a little under two hours, and if I'm in a grove, two and a half. But that's it. I take a 10-minute break between the 45-minute intervals where I usually pace around. I try not to lose my focus by looking at email or the internet during this time. A wonderful consequence to this morning routine is that my day is done before I walk into my office.

That is wonderfully liberating for the rest of the day. But how do I know what to write?

RECOGNIZE CANVASES

Just as I was finishing my PhD, my doctoral supervisor, Mustafa Emirbayer, advised me to ask myself a simple question: "What is your canvas?" His career had been spent mostly writing articles. He had honed his skills through practicing within this canvas again and again, until he could reasonably be considered a master. His focusing on this particular kind of canvas wasn't rare. Indeed, we often think of "book writers" and "article writers." The form of an article had a size that made certain kinds of arguments possible. Thinking of an argument as a "form" and recognizing that the structure of such forms allow for certain kinds of arguments has been a bit of a revelation. More so than the more pedestrian quip that there are book people and article people. Yes, people tended to write things of a particular size. Books are relatively big canvases (60,000–200,000 words); articles have a similar kind of size range (2,000–20,000 words). We might even add to this opinion pieces, which typically have canvases of around 750–1,500 words. In the decade since I've completed my PhD, I've found this question of my canvas enormously useful. To paint the *Sistine Chapel* is very different than to paint *View of Delft*. Both contain entire worlds, are masterpieces of detail and subtly and of many things left unpainted, and yet they are able to accomplish something similar in very different ways on radically different scales.

Yet as the example of painting indicates, the question of different canvases isn't a question of how much detail is allowed. In fact, articles are often far more detailed than books. They require, for example, more systematic coverage of the relevant literature and deployed methodology. Such details are (typically) "distracting" in books, and such in depth discussions are often avoided. There is, of course, a lot of variation we could point to. Some book canvases are densely packed with details. Others have a more relaxed, open feel to them. The distinction, then, is not so much the details as it is the potential set of forms that fit within articles as opposed to books.

The problem is that you don't know what your canvas is until try it out. At first I thought the canvas was the "size of the idea." But this isn't correct. My first book has three main points in it. I've written papers with far more (Hirsch et al., 2018). Instead of how "big" the idea is, you should think about it in geographic terms: "What is the space I need for that particular idea to be understood?" In order to figure that out, I suggest you think less about your own ideas, and more about others and what they need to receive your ideas. This brings me to my second recommendation.

DON'T REINVENT THE WHEEL

The best way to figure out your canvas is to see how someone else has done it. While we often think of outlines as things we do before we write, I tend to do them after I have something written. It's difficult to see the structure of a work that's longer than about 1,000 words, and the things we write are often at least ten times this length. I turn text into outlines, rather than outlines into text.

But this practice generates a realization: you can also do this for someone else's writing. This is a frequent exercise I give to my students, and that I continue to do myself. I think to myself, "I wish I could have written this paper," or, "I wish this terrible paper of mine were like this wonderful paper I love." When I feel this way, I reverse outline that other paper by that other author, to see its basic structure. It's like an analytic dissection which reveals something the whole body of text somehow obscures. After I've done this exercise, I ask myself, "could I restructure my work to look like this?" This is a general writing strategy, but it's also a publishing one. It's often hard to imagine what your paper could be. But it's easy to see what an actual already published paper is. Find one that's closely tied to your own work, reverse outline it, and then see if you can restructure your own work to mirror this successful model. Once you've done this, send it to where that paper was published.

BE PART OF A CONVERSATION

Your job as a scholar is to contribute to general knowledge. Take that word seriously. Contribute. This is not the same as critiquing. You should have far more citations to friends than to enemies. You're not entering a shouting match. If you can avoid it, don't have enemies at all. Think, for a moment, about a dinner party. Imagine that you invited me and I told you that your home was poorly decorated, your food subpar, your other guests boring, and your outfit old and tired. Or imagine instead, if I told you that you had a lovely home, that you looked wonderful, that it was a joy to be part of the conversation, and that I had a lovely side dish recipe I'd like to give you that would pair well with the lovely dinner you served. Which contribution to the evening would you appreciate and want to hear more from, perhaps even invite again? The one that insulted you, or the one that sought to build upon and be part of your community?

What I'm suggesting is not that you be fake. Instead, it's that you focus on the more positive aspects of community and seek to add to its conversations not by telling everyone every problem you see, but instead, providing something that might improve the community overall. Other scholars work very hard trying to develop understandings of the world and contribute to conversations about those understandings. Your job is to join rather than ruin the conversation.

Conversations have different characters. My dinner parties with my queer community in New York tend to be a little more raucous than those with my colleagues. Neither community would particularly appreciate my bringing the conversation style from the other to the dinner table. What does this long analogy mean? Recognize the conversation you want to join. Be generous with the existing conversation. Recognize and appreciate the voices of others.

I have written one set of papers that were rather critical of conversation (Jerolmack and Khan, 2014a, 2014b). But it was a conversation I'd been a part of for some time. And I would not recommend making a habit of this style of writing; it should be used sparingly, and I would suggest, after you've already made a few contributions to the conversation on its own terms. Most of all, joining a conversation means not just thinking about what you want to say. It means thinking about what others have said, and what is useful for them to hear. Your aim in publishing is not to monologue. It is to dialogue. And that means that as you write, you should think as much about how people will hear what you're saying as what it is you want to say. More prosaically, write for your reader, not for yourself. Your reader is a community. That community tends to have a space where they work. Recognize those spaces, what the conversations are there, what the kind of dialogue looks like, and try to publish by mirroring this. The best way to do this is to say something that constructively helps them do what they're trying to do (rather than something that tears them down).

RESPONDING TO CRITICISM

First let's get this out there: most of my submissions are rejected. I'd say I have to send work to 2–3 journals before it's published. My "hit rate" is probably around 30–40 percent. We're not in the publication business; we're in the rejection business. And you have to try and try again to get things published. That's life for pretty much all of this.

Rejection or revision, I hate getting reviews back. They always make me angry. First at the reviewers. Next at the editor. And finally, if I'm being honest, at myself. The first big step for me when dealing with a revision is managing my emotional response. I usually read the reviews. Get angry. Put them aside. Read them again. Get angry. Put them aside. And then get to work. The first thing I do is create a chart with three columns. Each row corresponds to a statement the editor or reviewer made. The first column is small. It's just where a comment came from: the editor, reviewer A, reviewer B, etc. The second is bigger. It's the text of what the person said. I arrange these by theme, and usually color-code those themes (I highlight these themes in response memos, and often have one theme, "miscellaneous," for things I couldn't categorize). The third column is initially for me. It's the steps I've taken to address the reviewer comments. This includes where my addressing them appears in the manuscript with a bit of text about what I've said, or, a short justification as to why I don't address the comment. I always address the vast majority of the comments. The first purpose of this chart is to make sure I deal with all the comments.

What gets me over my irrational and/or emotional reactions to reviews is the recognition that reviewers are doing massive amounts of unpaid work to make our scholarship better. Add to that my drive to publish the work I've spent so long writing, and I typically revise within a month or so. In my experience the most important part of the revision is the response (not the new text). The response should do three things. First, the response memo should rearticulate the main argument of the paper, pointing to additional clarity provided through the review process. Second, the response memo should acknowledge and appreciate the work of the reviewers, and do the job of categorizing that work by theme, instead of responding point by point. I also highlight the specific passages where the manuscript has changed given the themes of the reviews. This is where the chart I make comes in. The memo graciously hits on the big points; the chart gets into the gritty details. Finally, when responding to reviewers, don't do things you don't want to just to get published.

This foreshadows one of the things I suggest you avoid. Your job is not to get something published. It is to say something useful for a group of scholars involved in a conversation. Responding to reviewers doesn't mean doing what they want. It means asking yourself why someone read your paper in the way that they did, and exploring ways you might avoid having future readers getting caught up on the same issues. The privilege of my position may allow me to be naively Weberian in thinking of our enterprise as a vocation. But I tend to avoid changes just to get published. It's not about sticking to your guns. It's about staying true to the contribution you want to make. I sometimes point that out in my memos: that there remains some disagreement between myself and the reviewer, and this is fine. Healthy communities feel comfortable disagreeing with respect, and do future work to resolve those disagreements.

THINGS TO AVOID

I end with the five perils of publishing. There are, no doubt, more than five. But if I could stamp things out, these five would be high on my list.

1. LPUs

"What is an LPU?" you might ask? It's the "least publishable unit." And it is a horrible way to write. For some it's a strategy, "How do I divide this project into the least publishable units so that I can publish as much as possible from it?" This might be good for you, but it's not good for a conversation, because it means that insights happen in fragments. Publish what's logically coherent, not what is likely to produce the most lines on your CV.

2. Not Every Paper Needs a New Theory of the World

If every paper has a new theory, theory can't advance. Instead, papers can be "just" description, helping us better understand the world with the theories we already have. A different way of putting this is that you should think less about your theory, and more about your findings—presenting them clearly and getting them right. Few of us will ever have a field-changing idea. And if we do, we probably aren't aware of it. It's not the idea that changes the field; it's what others do with it. Lots of field-changing ideas are never realized, and some ideas that aren't that radical are mobilized by others to make them revolutionary. You will never have an important idea; others will make it so. There's an important consequence of this: when you read the papers of others, please, stop writing reviews that ask for new theory. As I've said before, we're a discipline that could benefit from, "Less Theory. More Description" (Besbris and Khan, 2018).

3. Perfection

You'll never write the perfect paper. Instead of trying to do this, highlight your own weaknesses. It defangs reviewers and liberates you from the necessity of feeling like every bit has to be tied off perfectly. You have responsibility to a community, not to your own interest in publishing. And so instead of burying your failures—trying to hide them—raise them up. This has three major benefits. It will free you of the feeling that every paper has to be perfect. It will eliminate those annoying "gotcha" moments of review writers and critics. And it will help your readers better understand your own ideas—not just their strengths, but their limits. This allows readers to see where they might join your conversation to improve upon the weaknesses you highlight in your own work.

4. Cleverness

Resist the temptation to prioritize cleverness over correctness. There's nothing worse than scholarly work that would rather be clever than right. The scholarly enterprise should be fun. It should excite. But it is also of enormous consequence. There's a responsibility to produce ideas that improve our capacity for human understanding. "Cuteness" can be a happy consequence of a project, but it shouldn't take precedence over the drive to be correct.

5. Self-Serving Strategies

Never publish anything you aren't convinced is correct. You can later change your mind. But in the moment, you must believe what you're saying. A variant of this is never publish anything because you can.

All of this is to say that you should only deploy a publication strategy after you've done what is necessary for any and all projects: earnestly, sincerely, and honestly tried to make sense of something in the world, and join a conversation of people who will be interested in hearing about that.

REFERENCES

Abu-Odeh, Desiree, Shamus Khan, and Constance A. Nathanson. "From Crime to Gender: The Construction of Campus Assault as a Social Problem." *Social Science History* 44, no. 2 (2020): 355–379. https://doi.org/10.1017/ssh.2019.49.

Accominotti, Fabien, Shamus Khan, and Adam Storer. "How Cultural Capital Emerged in Gilded Age America: Musical Purification and Cross-Class Inclusion at the New York Philharmonic." *American Journal of Sociology* 123, no. 6 (2018): 1743–1783. https://doi.org/10.1086/696938.

Besbris, Max, and Shamus Khan. "Less Theory. More Description." *Sociological Theory* 35, no. 2 (2017): 147–153. https://doi.org/10.1177/0735275117709776.

Cousin, Bruno, Shamus Khan, and Ashley Mears. "Theoretical and Methodological Pathways for Research on Elites." *Socio-Economic Review* 16, no. 2 (2018): 225–249. https://doi.org/10.1093/ser/mwy019.

Hirsch, Jennifer S., Leigh Reardon, Shamus Khan, John S. Santelli, Patrick A. Wilson, Louisa Gilbert, Melanie Wall, and Claude A. Mellins. "Transforming the Campus Climate: Research on the Social and Cultural Roots of Sexual Assault on a College Campus." *Voices: Journal of the Association for Feminist Anthropology* 13, no. 1 (2018): 23–54. https://doi.org/10.1111/voic.12003.

Jerolmack, Colin, and Shamus Khan. "Talk Is Cheap: Ethnography and the Attitudinal Fallacy." *Sociological Methods and Research* 43, no. 2 (2014a): 178–209. https://doi.org/10.1177/0049124114523396.

Jerolmack, Colin, and Shamus Khan. "Toward an Understanding of the Relationship between Accounts and Action." *Sociological Methods and Research* 43, no. 2 (2014b): 236–247. https://doi.org/10.1177/0049124114523397.

Khan, Shamus. "The Allure of Equality." *New Yorker*, June 5, 2016. http://www.newyorker.com/tech/elements/when-does-equality-flourish.

Khan, Shamus. "The New Elitists." *New York Times*, July 7, 2012. https://www.nytimes.com/2012/07/08/opinion/sunday/the-new-elitists.html.

Khan, Shamus. *Privilege: The Making of an Adolescent Elite at St. Paul's School*. Princeton, NJ: Princeton University Press, 2011.

Khan, Shamus. "We Are Not All in This Together." *New York Times*, December 14, 2013. https://opinionator.blogs.nytimes.com/2013/12/14/we-are-not-all-in-this-together/.

Khan, Shamus. "You Weren't Born That Way." *Aeon Magazine*, July 23, 2015. https://aeon.co/essays/why-should-gay-rights-depend-on-being-born-this-way.

Khan, Shamus, Jennifer Hirsch, Alexander Wamboldt, and Claude A. Mellins. "I Didn't Want to Be 'That Girl': The Social Risks of Labeling, Telling, and Reporting Sexual Assault." *Sociological Science* 5 (2018): 432–460. http://dx.doi.org/10.15195/v5.a19.

Khan, Shamus, and Colin Jerolmack. "Saying Meritocracy and Doing Privilege." *Sociological Quarterly* 54, no. 1 (2013): 9–19. https://doi.org/10.1111/tsq.12008.

Mellins, Claude A., Kate Walsh, Aaron L. Sarvet, Melanie Wall, Louisa Gilbert, John S. Santelli, Martie Thompson, Patrick A. Wilson, Shamus Khan, Stephanie Benson, Karimata Bah, Kathy A. Kaufman, Leigh Reardon, and Jennifer S. Hirsch. "Sexual Assault Incidents among College Undergraduates: Prevalence and Factors Associated with Risk." *PLOS ONE* 13, no. 1 (2017). https://doi.org/10.1371/journal.pone.0186471.

Schneiderhan, Erik, and Shamus Khan. "Reasons and Inclusion: The Foundation of Deliberation." *Sociological Theory* 26, no. 1 (2008): 1–24. https://doi.org/10.1111/j.1467-9558.2008.00316.x.

Tahir, Madiha, and Shamus Khan. "Special Issue: Violence and Policing." *Public Culture* 31, no. 3 (2019). https://read.dukeupress.edu/public-culture/issue/31/1.

17
ON PUBLICATION STRATEGIES

KRISTIAN KREINER

*In an email message responding to my request for a contribution,
Kristian Kreiner explained why he was declining the invitation. Like
the reply from Andrew Abbott, published in this book as chapter 1,
I found his reasons so eloquent and compelling that we have
excerpted his message and are publishing it with Professor Kreiner's
permission. I am grateful to Professor Kreiner for providing the
bibliographic references.*

—The editor

I have searched my soul and picked my brain and concluded that
the only publishing strategy I can imagine for myself is never
to submit a paper that I wouldn't want to read in print myself,
immediately and 30 years later.

I began to put some thoughts on paper, but what I have written
in response to your call doesn't meet that criterion. I have elaborated
on strategizing in architectural competitions as an analogy (Kreiner,
2012, 2013, 2020); I have played and amused myself writing about the
role of the Just-World hypothesis in academic management; I have
produced arguments to convince myself that we (I) should be careful
to project our strategies onto young aspiring scholars without a strong
"situational awareness" (a concept I picked up in Lucy Suchman's [2018]
nice response to your earlier call [published in this book as chapter 11]);

and I have relativized our learning from history by treating success as a by-product. The baseline is that none of us—not the architects and even less academics—are the architect of our own fortune.

However, none of this reflects my own publishing experience (limited, as it is). I could perhaps find a pattern in my publication record: I have published much "by invitation" (and thereby often ending up publishing in edited volumes and special issues), but to suggest that this is a strategy—good or viable—I would never do. The fact that I have survived career-wise would suggest to most people that I'm old, unambitious, or otherwise privileged (i.e., beyond competition and therefore irrelevant to the concerns of most academics).

I think you can tell that I have had a great time searching for a response to your call—and that I painfully recognize the distinction between searching and finding (Ryle, 1979). The few answers I found were not answers to your call, and the answers to your call that I could find, I either didn't like or didn't believe.

I apologize for not submitting a contribution.

REFERENCES

Kreiner, Kristian. "Constructing the Client in Architectural Competitions: An Ethnographic Study of Architects' Practices and the Strategies They Reveal." In *Architectural Competitions: Histories and Practice*, edited by J. E. Andersson, G. Bloxham Zettersten, and M. Rönn, 217–245. Fjällbacka, Sweden: Rio Kulturkooperativ, 2013.

Kreiner, Kristian. "Organizational Decision Mechanisms in an Architectural Competition." In *The Garbage Can Model of Organizational Choice: Looking Forward at Forty (Research in the Sociology of Organizations, Volume 36)*, edited by A. Lomi and J. R. Harrison, 399–429. Bingley: Emerald Group, 2012.

Kreiner, Kristian. "Pick the Winner, So You Can Then Choose the Reasons: Epistemic Dissonance in Architecture Competitions." In *The Performance Complex: Competition and Competitions in Social Life*, edited by D. Stark, 31–54. Oxford: Oxford University Press, 2020.

Ryle, Gilbert. *On Thinking*, edited by K. Kolenda. Oxford: Blackwell, 1979.

Suchman, Lucy. "Openings." *Sociologica* 12, no. 1 (2018): 61–64. https://doi.org/10.6092/issn.1971-8853/8351.

18

HOW TO PUBLISH, BUT MOST IMPORTANTLY, WHY

MICHÈLE LAMONT

FIRST, HOW DO YOU KNOW WHEN A MANUSCRIPT IS READY TO GO?

I am anal-retentive. I think on paper, which means that I go through a great many passes that (in my mind at least) lead to qualitative shifts in the elaboration and clarity of my argument and in its insertion in the literature. I aim to do this until the deadline hits. I feel quite anxious about meeting deadlines.

AN OBVIOUS SECOND QUESTION IS ABOUT BOOKS VERSUS ARTICLES OR CHAPTERS IN EDITED VOLUMES

I far prefer writing monographs because they allow me to set the terms of the discussion and I am less likely to be the victim of capricious reviewers than I would be if I submitted articles. But most importantly, I get a lot of satisfaction from developing book-length arguments. One can go deeper in elaborating an explanation with a book. There is nothing like it in terms of sheer intellectual joy.

BUT ALSO, WHAT ABOUT PUBLISHING IN ESTABLISHED OUTLETS VERSUS NEW JOURNAL VENTURES?

I have generally preferred writing what I want to write and placing papers in journals that may be less finicky over publishing in the top two journals. This has allowed me to develop an intellectual agenda that is more cohesive than it would be had I spent much of my time pleasing random reviewers. I have very rarely sent papers out to *ASR* and *AJS*, perhaps because I did not want to spend years pushing a single paper. But I have also gone for leading specialty journals such as *Social Science & Medicine* and *Socio-Economic Review* to engage in a conversation with new audiences.

HAVE YOU EDITED A VOLUME OR SPECIAL ISSUE OF A JOURNAL?

I have done both. I have been very lucky with some of my collective volumes (e.g., Lamont and Thevenot, 2000; Lamont and Fournier, 1992). At this time, I am not interested in editing volumes anymore (even when I have splendid material, as was the case recently with a conference on the middle class in comparative perspective that I organized in fall 2018). This is because edited volumes don't circulate enough. They easily go unnoticed. I would rather do a special issue of a journal as these can be promoted digitally, and indeed I edit issues regularly. It's stimulating to bring colleagues together around a specific topic. For instance, I have coedited with Paul Pierson (2019) an issue of *Daedalus* on "Inequality as a Multidimensional Process," which will come out this summer. It brings together leading political scientists, psychologists, and sociologists to bridge the micro, meso, and macro levels in the study of inequality. This came out of the meetings of the Canadian Institute for Advanced

Research's Successful Societies program, which I have codirected since 2002. It is our last act . . .

IN GENERAL, ABOUT PUBLICATION STRATEGY, WHAT ADVICE WOULD YOU GIVE TO A YOUNG ASPIRING SOCIOLOGIST?

At the start of a career, you have no choice; if you want to be a part of the disciplinary conversation you have to go for the journals that have the most visibility. I was extremely lucky that my very first paper in English, "How to Become a Dominant French Philosopher: The Case of Jacques Derrida," came out in the *American Journal of Sociology*. It was a tongue-in-cheek article, and it became famous quite rapidly.

But young scholars should keep in mind that what truly matters is not where you publish but what you publish: the work should be original, daring, stimulating. Otherwise, it is not worth doing . . . and it is unlikely to interest others. Doing exciting work opens all doors. This is in part why one should aim to publish . . . it keeps the creative juices flowing, may influence how we understand the world, and may even contribute to shaping it . . .

ADDITIONALLY, YOU MIGHT WANT TO COMMENT ON THE CURRENT STATE OF ACADEMIC PUBLISHING IN SOCIOLOGY

The situation in sociology is not that bad, all things considered: there is a good market for nonfiction books, and we have strong editors at several university presses. The interest from trade publishers is growing, especially in this Trumpian moment. We have a number of good journals. Of course, some of the top journals are much too slow, and this has clearly had a detrimental effect on the careers of some of our excellent qualitative, comparative-historical, culture types—which is absolutely unacceptable. I can't wait for such journals to get their act together!

REFERENCES

Lamont, Michèle. "How to Become a Dominant French Philosopher: The Case of Jacques Derrida." *American Journal of Sociology* 93, no. 3 (1987): 584–622. https://doi.org/10.1086/228790.

Lamont, Michèle, and Marcel Fournier (eds.). *Cultivating Differences: Symbolic Boundaries and the Making of Inequality*. Chicago: University of Chicago Press, 1992.

Lamont, Michèle, and Paul Pierson (eds.). "Inequality as a Multidimensional Process." *Dædalus* 148, no. 3 (2019).

Lamont, Michèle, and Laurent Thévenot (eds.). *Rethinking Comparative Cultural Sociology: Repertoires of Evaluation in France and the United States*. London: Cambridge University Press; Paris: Presses de la Maison des sciences de l'homme, 2000.

19

FROM PUBLIC ENGAGEMENT
TO PUBLICATION

JENNIFER LEE

INTRODUCTION

In *Nothing Ever Dies: Vietnam and the Memory of War*, Pulitzer Prize–winning author Viet Thanh Nguyen (2016) claims that all wars are fought twice—the first time on the battlefield, and the second, in our collective memory. Our collective memory of the Vietnam War is constructed from manifold narratives, but most are told from the point of view of the majority—in this case, white Americans. Nguyen points out that that the majority enjoys narrative plentitude; most of the stories focus on them, and they are told from their perspective. Minorities, by contrast, experience narrative scarcity. Relatively few stories are told about us, and even fewer are told from our perspective.

Minority groups want narrative plentitude, but we can only achieve this when we have influence over all levels of narrative production. Nguyen has stated that individual writers and artists cannot achieve narrative plentitude on their own, but I would add that, as social scientists, we can work toward narrative plentitude by contributing to narrative production. This involves all facets of social science research, from designing projects to collecting accurate data to publishing our findings in the top journals and university presses.

I would add another component to narrative production—public engagement—which entails publishing beyond the boundaries of academia, and writing for and engaging with a broader, more diverse, and more inclusive audience. It involves a willingness to make one's research accessible and relevant beyond the gatekeepers of academic publishing: book and journal editors, editorial board members, reviewers, and our academic peers. This is especially germane for minority groups who must not only fight to relay our narratives, but also fight against the narratives that distort us.

Public engagement is a skill that I never formally learned nor was encouraged to develop, yet I have found, quite serendipitously, that it has enhanced my academic research and writing. This came as a surprise because I often heard the opposite—that public engagement and rigorous research and writing are incompatible—so I never sought public engagement. Nevertheless, public engagement found me.

The narrative scarcity of Asian Americans—exacerbated by popularly held myths and misconceptions about them—propelled me to override my reticence and fear and embark on a path for which I felt woefully unprepared.

DECLAWING THE TIGER MOM

In February 2014, I received an inquiry from *CBS News*, inviting me to appear on a segment featuring Amy Chua (better known as the "Tiger Mom") and her husband, Jed Rubenfeld. The network wanted a social scientist to provide expert commentary on their highly anticipated book, *The Triple Package: How Three Unlikely Traits Explain the Rise and Fall of Cultural Groups in America* (Chua and Rubenfeld, 2014), which had yet to be publicly released. My research was cited by the authors, so the producers contacted me. The central argument in *The Triple Package* is simple: certain groups are successful because they possess a "triple package" of cultural traits, including a superiority complex, insecurity, and impulse control.

After reading the advance copy given to me by the producer, I found glaring flaws with their argument, the most obvious of which is by reducing success to a trio of cultural traits, the authors simply reframed the "culture of poverty" thesis into a "culture of success" anti-thesis. Cultural traits are touted as both the dependent and independent variables to explain the success of ethnic groups like Chinese and Jews—who happen to be the groups with which Chua and Rubenfeld identify, respectively.

Armed with a slew of "talking points," I arrived at the *CBS* studio fully prepared for the interview. When the segment aired the following day, I was stunned to find that my hour-long detailed critique was reduced to a single quote: "It's certainly not social science. The traits in themselves don't explain group success" (CBS Los Angeles, 2014). The first lesson I learned about public engagement was a brutal one: hours of judicious preparation can be reduced to a few seconds of airtime.

The few seconds on air, however, caught the attention of an editor, who invited me to write an op-ed about *The Triple Package*, which I approached with a renewed purpose and clearer direction. Rather than focus on a critique of Chua and Rubenfeld, I would highlight social science research. And rather than offering a slew of detailed critiques, I would focus on two: *starting points* and *hyperselectivity*.

REFRAMING SUCCESS: STARTING POINTS AND HYPERSELECTIVITY

I began with a question: "Who is more successful: a second-generation Mexican whose parents immigrated to the United States with less than an elementary school education, and who now works as a dental hygienist; or a second-generation Chinese whose immigrant parents have PhD degrees, and who now works as a doctor?"

Chua and Rubenfeld would claim it is the latter. They argue that certain American groups (including Chinese, Jews, Cubans, and Nigerians) are more successful and have risen further than others because they share certain cultural traits. The couple bolsters their argument by comparing these groups' median household income, test scores, educational attainment, and occupational status to those of the rest of the country.

But what happens if you measure success not just by where people end up—the cars in their garages, the degrees on their walls—but by taking into account where they started? Comparing second-generation Chinese, Vietnamese, and Mexicans in Los Angeles, I came to a conclusion that flies in the face of the Tiger couple: Mexicans are LA's most successful immigrant group (Lee, 2014a).

Like Chua and Rubenfeld, I found that the children of Chinese immigrants exhibit exceptional educational outcomes that exceed those of other groups, including native-born whites. In Los Angeles, 64 percent of Chinese immigrants' children graduated from college, and of this group 22 percent also attained a graduate degree. By contrast, 46 percent of native-born Anglos in LA graduated from college, and of this group, just 14 percent attained graduate degrees. Moreover, none of the Chinese dropped out of high school. These figures are impressive but not surprising. Chinese immigrant parents are not only the most highly educated, but they are also "hyperselected" (meaning that they are doubly positively selected). They are more likely to have graduated from college than their nonmigrant counterparts in China, and also more highly educated than the U.S. mean. About half of Chinese immigrants in the United States have a BA or higher, compared to only 4 percent in China, and 28 percent of the U.S. population. In other words, Chinese immigrants in the United States are twelve times as likely to have graduated from college than their nonmigrant counterparts in China, and nearly twice as likely as the U.S. mean.

In Los Angeles, over 60 percent of Chinese immigrant fathers and over 40 percent of Chinese immigrant mothers have a BA or higher. The children of Chinese immigrants begin their quest to get ahead from more favorable "starting points" than other immigrants because they benefit from their parents' human and financial capital, giving them a boost in their quest to get ahead. This boost—which includes resources like after-school programs, SAT prep courses, and tutoring—is not limited to the middle class. The children of working-class Chinese parents employed in restaurants and factories benefit from capital and resources that are made widely available to other Chinese Americans.

At what seems to be the other end of the spectrum, the children of Mexican immigrants had the lowest levels of educational attainment of any of the groups in our study. Only 86 percent graduated from high school—compared to 100 percent of Chinese and 96 percent of native-born whites—and only 17 percent of graduated from college. But their high school graduation rate was more than double that of their immigrant parents, only 40 percent of whom earned diplomas. And the college graduation rate of second-generation Mexicans more than doubles that of their fathers (7 percent) and triples that of their mothers (5 percent).

Parental legal status is key. On average, the children of Mexican immigrants whose parents are undocumented attain 11 years of education. Those whose parents migrated here legally or entered the country as undocumented migrants but later legalized their status attain 13 years of education on average. This two-year difference is critical in the U.S. education system because it divides high school graduates from high school dropouts, making undocumented status alone a significant impediment to social mobility. But even accounting for this additional obstacle for children of undocumented parents, there is no question that, when we measure success as intergenerational mobility, second-generation Mexicans come out ahead.

Yet this point is often lost on many Americans who rely on status markers like our college degrees, jobs, cars, homes, zip codes, and (if you live in Los Angeles) area codes to measure success. Americans also like to believe that those who are successful earned it through hard work, cultural traits, and grit. After all, this is how we justify why some people and groups are more successful than others.

But many Americans work hard, are smart, and exhibit grit in spades. In spite of this, we do not graduate from college at the same rates because we begin the race at different "starting points." Moreover, some get extra boosts during the race to help them speed across the finish line, including members of "hyperselected" immigrant groups. So, before we measure someone's success by their diplomas, jobs, or zip codes, we should first ask about the diplomas, jobs, and zip codes that came before them.

FROM PUBLIC ENGAGEMENT TO PUBLICATION

The editorial and others that followed became the basis of the introduction of the book manuscript, which was published in the following year as *The Asian American Achievement Paradox* (2015). The exercise of writing this and subsequent editorials (Lee, 2015) pushed me to convey my central arguments clearly, convincingly, and succinctly in under 800 words—a challenge for academics (myself included) who often bemoan having to trim our manuscripts to under 10,000 words.

Soon after, I would engage with other reporters, do radio interviews, and appear on television again, and each opportunity presented an occasion to be clearer, more thoughtful, more convincing, and more succinct. While public engagement never came easily nor naturally to me, knowing that I was armed with social science research helped me to overcome my fear, doubt, and insecurity, and also exercise my growth mindset (Dweck, 2006).

Public engagement also helped me to complete my book manuscript in a timely manner. By writing editorials, doing interviews, and giving public talks, I quickly learned what points resonated most strongly, and how to deliver those points most powerfully. My media "talking points" became the bases of book chapters, and the feedback from the public engagement was immediately incorporated into the revisions of the book manuscript. Without question, I became a more effective writer, researcher, speaker, mentor, and instructor because I engaged with a more diverse audience, and pushed myself to lay bare my arguments without shrouding them in the academic lingo that often makes our writing more elusive than need be. In the process, I helped to place the study of Asian Americans as a central research problematic in the discipline of sociology, which is especially meaningful in light of the narrative scarcity of Asian Americans.

The synergy between public engagement and publication continues in my current research, including a timely project on Asian Americans' attitudes of affirmative action—a hot-button issue that is fueled by myths, misconceptions, stereotypes, and narrative scarcity. Presumed competent, Asian Americans are also presumed to uniformly oppose affirmative action, but this myth is a far cry from reality.

Dismantling the misperception in steps through a variety of editorials, radio interviews, and public lectures (Lee, 2018a, 2018b, 2018c) has helped me to craft a compelling and nuanced narrative based on novel survey research that forms the basis of several published papers (Lee 2021a, 2021b). In these papers, I show that there is no single, uniform stance on affirmative action, and, surprisingly, there is more diversity in opinion among Asian Americans than between Asians and other racial groups. Moreover, I unveil how Asian Americans' perceptions of who is morally deserving shifts their attitudes, underscoring their malleability in opinion. And again, not only has public engagement helped to frame this research project, but it is also contributing to narrative production and narrative plentitude in the process.

CODA

I would be remiss if I did not mention that regardless of the medium in which you aim to publish, you will get rejected. Many times. No matter how prolific the author, she, too, has been rejected many times. Keep in mind to divorce the substance of comments from the tone of the criticism. Take what you need, and leave the rest. Make your work better, and try again. Persistence is key to publishing.

REFERENCES

CBS Los Angeles. "Authors of Controversial New Book Try to Pinpoint What Makes Certain Ethnic Groups Successful." February 14, 2014. http://losangeles .cbslocal.com/2014/02/14/only-on-cbs2-married-couple-pen-controversial -book-on-what-makes-certain-ethnic-groups-successful/.

Chua, Amy, and Jed Rubenfeld. *The Triple Package: How Three Unlikely Traits Explain the Rise and Fall of Cultural Groups in America.* New York: Penguin, 2014.

Dweck, Carol S. *Mindset: The New Psychology of Success.* New York: Ballatine, 2006.

Lee, Jennifer. "Asian-American Plaintiffs Are 'Pawns' in Affirmative Action Lawsuit, Says Professor." *CBC Radio, As It Happens,* September 3, 2018a. https://www.cbc .ca/radio/asithappens/as-it-happens-friday-edition-1.4731087/asian-american -plaintiffs-are-pawns-in-affirmative-action-lawsuit-says-professor-1.4808856.

Lee, Jennifer. "Asian Americans, Affirmative Action, and the Rise in Anti-Asian Hate." *Dædalus* 150, no. 2 (2021a): 180–198. https://doi.org/10.1162/DAED_a_01854.

Lee, Jennifer. "Don't Tell Amy Chua: Mexicans Are the Most Successful Immigrants." *Time,* February 25, 2014a. http://ideas.time.com/2014/02/25/dont-tell -amy-chua-mexicans-are-the-most-successful-immigrants/.

Lee, Jennifer. "Harvard May Discriminate against Asian Americans, But Its Preference for Legacy Students Is the Bigger Problem." *Los Angeles Times,* June 22, 2018b. http://www.latimes.com/opinion/op-ed/la-oe-lee-harvard-legacy-student -advantage-20180622-story.html.

Lee, Jennifer. "Race, Affirmative Action, and Social Inequality." *The Tavis Smiley Show,* June 23, 2014b. http://www.pbs.org/wnet/tavissmiley/interviews/jennifer -lee/.

Lee, Jennifer. "Reckoning with Asian America and the New Culture War on Affirmative Action." *Sociological Forum* 36, no. 4 (2021b): 863–888. https://doi.org /10.1111/socf.12751.

Lee, Jennifer. "The Truth about Asian Americans' Success (It's Not What You Think)." *CNN*, August 4, 2015. http://www.cnn.com/2015/08/03/opinions/lee -immigration-ethnic-capital/.

Lee, Jennifer. "Understanding SFFA v. Harvard: Asian Americans and Affirmative Action." Presentation at Columbia Law School, 2018c.

Lee, Jennifer, and Min Zhou. *The Asian American Achievement Paradox*. New York: Russell Sage Foundation, 2015.

Nguyen, Viet T. *Nothing Ever Dies: Vietnam and the Memory of War*. Cambridge, MA: Harvard University Press, 2016.

20

NOT HAVING A PUBLICATION STRATEGY IS MY STRATEGY

CELIA LURY

've been asked to reflect on my publication strategy. But I don't have a publication strategy, other than: try to make sure you publish (otherwise you will lose your job!). If pushed, I would say not having a publication strategy is my strategy. Having been pushed by the editors, I would also say that just as I don't find thinking of publishing—or more or less any activity in my life—as a strategy, I also don't find it helpful to think of publishing separately from a whole host of other academic activities. These activities include writing, of course, but also giving papers (performing papers?) which may or may not involve PowerPoint presentations, that may or may not combine text and image, arguing, disagreeing, agreeing, collaborating, editing, teaching, and talking—with colleagues but also anyone outside the world of the university who is willing to talk with me about whatever it is that is the subject of the publication. My best advice is to make sure that doing and reflecting on all these activities feeds into your publications.

Why do I say this? For three reasons: process, form and audience, and authorship and collectivity.

PROCESS

One of the reasons I am wary of focusing on publishing alone—as in having a publishing strategy—is that a publication is a stopping point. But, actively situated in a flow of other academic activities, it can be seen as a pause, and not a final stopping point. And this pause can be shorter or longer: I understand what I am trying to say differently when asked a question in a seminar than I do when I respond to reviewers of what I write. This variety of temporal stagings of ideas is important to me, in that ideas, arguments, debates—the life of the mind, if we are being grand—don't have a natural stopping point. So, the stopping point of publication is, in my head, arbitrary, and not to be considered an end in itself.

FORM AND AUDIENCE

On the other hand, that arbitrary stopping is also a way of holding something, caring, through the fixing of a form. And form is also important to me: how something is said—and to whom—is constitutive of what is said. I could go on about form, in particular my frustration that it seems harder and harder to publish what I would call essays as articles in the highly ranked sociology journals. This is a great loss; it contributes to blind empiricism, diminishes the sociological imagination, and obscures an understanding of sociology as a discipline in-between science and the humanities. But maybe this is the topic for a different discussion. One other point to make about form is that it draws attention to the medium of publication. While I shudder at the use of the word "output" to describe academic work in exercises such as the Research Excellence Framework (REF), at least it has the merit of reminding us that academic work—like art work—does not operate in one medium alone. There is more to academic work than print (although even print can be used as an expressive medium).

AUTHORSHIP, CITATION, AND COLLECTIVITY

No one would deny that thought is collective, however that statement is understood, but the politics of authorship and citation indices have made some kinds of collectivity more visible than others. I have been told to include references to publications authored by the editor of the journal to which I submitted my article. I've been told to change titles of essays (articles); to think carefully about key words as these will increase the visibility of my work; and so on. Now all of these (except perhaps the first) can be understood as good advice—ensuring that my work is communicable. But I resist, in part because I believe that the communicability of an idea, a finding, an argument, should not outweigh other principles of academic work. Sometimes it may be that making an idea communicable—at least in an academic world beset with ordinal technologies of communication—does not serve the idea well.

21

A BALANCED PUBLICATION STRATEGY

CHRISTINE MUSSELIN

A WHAT? A PUBLICATION STRATEGY?

This might seem curious to many of our readers—especially the younger ones—but when I was a PhD student with Michel Crozier and Erhard Friedberg in the mid-1980s, nobody would have used the expression "publication strategy" or have spoken about it. In order to have a chance to get a position at the CNRS (largest French national research institution), it was advised to have at least one paper published in one of the main French sociological journals (*Revue Française de Sociologie* or *Sociologie du Travail*, for instance), but there was no "publication strategy" to imagine and to adopt. It was also rather evident that when a research project or a PhD was over, a monograph should be published. On top of this, some papers could also be issued, but a monograph was the rule. Furthermore, writing with a colleague was possible but not so frequent and if you wanted to have a chance to get a position, solo papers or books should also appear in your résumé.

After I got a position at the CNRS, regularly publishing has always been expected for the every-two-year individual evaluation of my records by the CNRS. I tried to write papers or books and I edited some special issues, but I first of all followed my own preferences, or grasped an opportunity to publish, or accepted an invitation from a colleague to write a chapter in a book, with no further consideration. I also regularly published in English but not by pure strategy. My field of study was almost inexistent in France and therefore I have been very early engaged in international networks in order to find colleagues with whom to exchange on my research. Publishing in English was thus a necessity.

I happened to first see a publication strategy "in action" by the beginning of the 2000s, when I led a research on gender bias in the access of French academics to professorships, with a colleague in management studies. When we got the first results of our study, he opened his computer and said: "Let's see in which journal we publish them. . . . I suggest this one. Its impact factor is very high." It was, of course, a journal published in English. For him, writing a monograph for a French audience on research led in France was not an option. He clearly expressed it: "I do not need it for my CV." And if he was to write a paper, it could only be for a journal with a high impact factor. He therefore had access to a ranking of journals recognized in its discipline with their respective impact factors on his computer.

I am still not that far. When I think I have a good idea and decide to publish it, I still do not choose a journal because of its impact factor. I know which journals are considered as relevant by my colleagues and I also know what kind of papers they publish by reading some of these papers. Depending on the idea and on the material (qualitative or quantitative data for instance) I have, I will first send it to a journal for which I think it may be of interest but I will also read the recent publications of this journal to check whether it could fit with it and in order to cope with the style of the journal when I start writing. As one can see, the relative lack of concern for a publication strategy that characterized the first part of my career is not possible any longer. Writing a paper is somewhat like hiring: one has to adapt one's paper (candidature) to the style (the profile) of the journal (the position).

Furthermore, because the administrative responsibilities I took over during the last decade left me less time, but also because the requirements for recognition in the world and in France have become more precise, more formalized, and more standardized, I have become more selective in my publication choices. I less and less agree to publishing chapters unless there is a strong editorial project for the edited book or if the editors are well-known scholars in the field or in the discipline, and I refrain from accepting to publish papers in non-peer-reviewed journals or in professional journals.

This being said, many choices still have to be made, and even if it is not a very calculated and long and well-thought-out decision, I intentionally try to manage the following alternatives in a quite balanced way.

PAPERS OR BOOKS? PAPERS AND BOOKS!

Only in books can the complexity and the systemic character of social facts be tackled. It is almost impossible in papers, and it is more and more impossible as journal reviewers expect papers to be focused on one idea, one mechanism, one issue. Therefore, no paper can replace a book. I always warn PhD candidates to resist the temptation of trying to write a paper summarizing their thesis. It never works and can never be published. Either they transform their PhD into a book, or they slice it into different papers. But a PhD is (hopefully) too rich, too complex to be summed up into one paper.

I nevertheless do not consider that books and papers are contradictory. They are complementary. Books tell the whole story, give room for details, and above all, allow for linking mechanisms together. When I for instance wrote the French version of the book translated as *The Market for Academics* (2009), it was important for me to be able to put in the same piece the analysis of the different phases of academic hiring: decision to (re)open a position, definition of the position's profile, selection of the candidates and academic judgment, negotiation of the "price" of the selected candidate. And then, to show

how these phases are more or less articulated and to insert this specific moment of hiring within a wider understanding of academic labor markets in the three countries under study in the last chapter. But a series of papers on related issues preceded and followed this book on more specific aspects and more focused arguments: academic labor markets as an economy of quality; comparative analysis of European academic labor markets; the paradox of pricing in higher education; a comparison between the market for musicians and the market for academics . . .

Some could say that I am the only one seeing the coherence and interactions between all these publications as I am the only one who read them all; that only very few people, if any, read the whole book; and that most readers focused on the chapter(s) they were interested in and did not look at the others, thus losing the systematic character I mentioned above. This is probably true, but I think the book and the papers would have been very different if I had not been able to develop this broader perspective. And for that very reason, I am not in favor of article-based PhD. The ones I read never completely convinced me and I mostly found the synthetic introduction and conclusion trying to bring the different papers together rather poor. And it can hardly be different. If you ever transform a chapter of a book into a paper or the inverse, you probably know that it means quite a lot of work for the chapter to be detached from the logic of the book and to become a piece in itself, or for the paper to be integrated in the logic of the book and to become part of it. Papers stand alone and cannot easily be articulated one with another. Or if they are, it means that they are too close and too similar.

I know this position is not shared by some colleagues in the discipline but I really think that we will lose the richness and the complexity of the content and of social facts if we were to just publish papers. Some years ago, a mainstream economist explained to me that he was not interested in the results of the papers he reads but first of all in the beauty, the robustness, and the novelty of the method leading to the results. I really hope that sociology will not be reached by such rationales and that publications in our discipline should first provide new evidence and analysis.

But the capacity to still publish books is also linked to funding issues. Publishing books based on a research program implies that ambitious multisided research programs are funded and not, or not only, one-question-based research projects. It also implies that one does not run from one funded project to another but has the time to sit, to think, and find a way to describe and analyze in a relevant and understandable way the complexity of what one has studied. Conditions that are not always provided nowadays.

ENGLISH OR FRENCH?
ENGLISH AND FRENCH!

This is a crucial issue when you work in a non-Anglophone country, even if today almost all of my colleagues read English. My concern is about managing two different goals. A first goal consists in being read by as many colleagues as possible, and the only chance to reach that goal is to be published in English—and in a journal that is not invisible. We are also pushed in this direction by the objectives set by all higher-education institutions nowadays. Some offer specific funding for the translation or for the editing of texts in order to encourage the publication of papers in non-French journals. Having published in a respectful non-French journal has almost become a condition to get a CNRS position nowadays. That was not the case when I applied thirty years ago.

It is revealing to observe that non-francophone journals are called "international" journals. As if French journals were only read by French people and had no international outreach. As if not being written in French was a synonym of quality. As if Anglophone journals were "international" by definition. These three assumptions are taken for granted in my home country but all can be contested. As for the last one, some years ago, I collected data on the institutions of the authors of all the papers published between 2001 and 2010 in the *American Journal of Sociology (AJS)*, *American Sociological Review (ASR)*, *American Journal of Political Science (AJPS)*, and *American Political Science Review (APSR)*. These four journals are considered in France as top international journals, and publishing in one of them is highly regarded in CVs. But I observed that the percentage of papers written by authors affiliated to U.S. universities reaches more than 82 percent in all of them: it is even almost 90 percent for *AJPS* (89.5 percent). The percentage of papers with at least one author affiliated to a U.S. university reaches 92 percent for *AJS* and 94 percent for *ASR* but almost 95 percent for *AJPS* and over 95 percent for *APSR*.

This is not the case in top field journals—generally less prestigious than the former ones—as they are more often entrusted to non-U.S.-based editors in chief. It is also different for journals that have been created in Europe or that are linked to a discipline that is more internationalized (economics or management for instance) than sociology or political science. But the international character and the assumed quality of journals published in English should be more often questioned and at least checked out by evaluators.

But even if we are more and more encouraged to publish in English, I maintain another strategy related to my second goal. I think it is important to maintain the French tradition of writing sociology, i.e., writing a paper that tells a story in order to demonstrate an idea (and sometimes two); writing papers for which each outline is different and deviates from the "state of the art—method—results—discussion" standard of many "international" journals; writing papers with long sentences; writing papers with some paragraphs that are not completely useful for the demonstration but introduce nuances and make detours; and also writing more literary papers where my vocabulary will be richer and more precise because it is my native language.

I generally choose French when I write more empirical papers, based on French data only, or when I think that the argument of the paper would be difficult to "sell" to a non-Francophone audience (for instance if it is related to a rather French debate, a typically French institution, or to recent French publications). I also choose French if I have not published in French on a specific research project. In recent years, I have limited the publication of papers in French to what I considered as the top sociology or political science journals in France. It is also what I advise the PhD candidates I supervise and suggested my colleagues of Sciences Po to do, when I was the vice-president for research of this university specialized in humanities and social sciences. "Publishing in French is fine, but it must be in the most respected journals of our disciplines." I nevertheless never convinced my colleagues of the department of economics to publish in French . . .

ALONE OR WITH COLLEAGUES? ALONE AND WITH COLLEAGUES!

As explained at the beginning of the paper, coauthorship was not always well considered in the 1980s. It is much more encouraged nowadays, especially if one publishes with authors located outside France. The opportunity for coauthorship is also more frequent than it was before. This is linked to the fact that French and European research funding schemes promote networking and collaborative research. Papers with more than two authors have become more frequent. But this kind of collaboration is easier with some disciplines than with others. In a research project led with an economist and a colleague in management sciences, we accepted that the economist publishes alone in economics journals in order for her work to be recognized by her peers. She nevertheless also publishes a paper in a journal of social sciences with my colleague in management sciences, but she knows it will not be considered by her peers as a "normal" publication, i.e., a publication to be taken into account.

Furthermore, even if it has become more frequent and if I appreciated and found very productive and rich the collaborations I experienced recently or in the past, I still like developing my own ideas by myself and being confronted with myself and my computer. Coauthorship also raises concerns about how to proceed to individual evaluation. Because it is difficult to assess the autonomy of a colleague who only publishes with coauthors and to identify his or her individual contribution, coauthorships might lead to relying on the reputation of the journals or reputation of the coauthors rather than on the contribution of the papers themselves. For that very reason, individual publications should still be encouraged and required.

OPEN SCIENCE OR PRIVATE PUBLISHERS? NOT AN ISSUE YET . . . BUT

In a final point, I would like to stress that open science issues are becoming more and more crucial. France contributed to the European "Plan S" and the mobile barrier has been reduced to one year for French private editors according to the 2016 law for a digital Republic.

Up to now I never chose to publish here or there in relation to open science policy. I never agreed to pay for my paper to become freely available when it is published by a private publisher, but such questions will probably become more and more accurate in a near future. Free access to the data on which the paper relies will also become an issue. This might impact the publication strategy of all of us in the very near future.

REFERENCES

Musselin, Christine. *The Markets for Academics*. London: Routledge, 2019.

III

REVISING

How Do You Improve a Manuscript
for Publication?

22

ON SECOND THOUGHT

Re Revising

BRUCE G. CARRUTHERS

To "revise" is to re-examine and make alterations to written material; literally it is to re-vision. It includes the process whereby authors re-visit their own arguments, but it is also a distinctive phase in the formal publication process. Let me consider these two separately, starting with the first and drawing on my own experience.

As you will see from reading this, nothing that I have ever written, or ever will write, is perfect. Far, far from it. It can all be improved, and so potentially I could revise forever, progressing towards perfection but never achieving it (Zeno's paradox for writers). But my need for revision is even more basic, because putting my ideas into writing is in large measure how I think. It isn't so much that I form thoughts in my mind and then find a way to express them using external media. Rather, expressing them is how I think my thoughts, and revision is how I re-think them once I've learned what my thoughts look like. So in effect I perform a personal and usually iterative form of distributed cognition that involves my brain, fingers, books, software, computer screen, and/or printed page. And I always have second thoughts (and third, and fourth, and so on). It would be nice to imagine that revision brings progress, and sometimes it does, but occasionally I digress (and regress). At times, I have written myself into a dead end, for example, and can only escape by reversing direction and backing out. And, of course, to be "revisionist" is to end badly.

At the very start of my career, revision was costly and involved manually retyping a paper manuscript (thank god I didn't live before the invention of the typewriter). In that era, I and everyone else would "think hard" before modifying their prose. My college essays went through two complete drafts, maximum, because of how much time and effort retyping a clean copy required. Does anyone else remember Liquid Paper? Now, endless tinkering is facilitated by text editing software that spell-checks, auto-completes, offers menus of synonyms and antonyms (and fonts), and evaluates grammar. It can even translate into other languages, if one wishes to provide to readers the frisson of multilingual prose, or the scholarly patina of a dead language, i.e., et cetera. Such toys invite further play, but this potentially infinite process usually stops when I decide that what I have fashioned is now "good enough," or when I face a hard deadline imposed by someone else. And the "good enough" standard is best gauged after a suitable pause: a break in which I stop writing and stop thinking about my argument. After that break (which can range from a day or two to several months), I bring a pair of fresh eyes to my own argument and often see flaws and gaps that had previously escaped me. Showing prose to a friendly reader can also produce sage advice (fortunately, I'm married to one and so can always access my in-house critic). There is a final set of revisions, and then I'm ready for the next phase.

Time gives me a bit of distance and affords a more critical perspective on my own prose. It is always tempting to view writing as a deeply personal form of expression, wherein one's most beautiful and insightful thoughts are laid out on the page. Words that become like adorable children are impossible not to love, just as they are. But such adoration gets in the way of revision, because it prevents authors from recognizing all the non sequiturs, tangents, mixed metaphors, verbosities, awkward transitions, and excessive detail in their arguments. One might, for example, be excessively fond of long lists. Authors should be ruthless about their own prose: if it doesn't work, fix it, replace it, or ditch it. Don't treat your words like beloved family members. Be instrumental.

After authors have finished writing and rewriting, they usually try to publish, and so a second form of revision occurs. I have a few old manuscripts mouldering in my desk, but mostly I attempt to get things published somewhere. After all, my annual raise depends on it. But to enter into the formal publication process is, in effect, to invite someone else to help revise the paper. With a proper double-blind peer review process, neither I nor any other author gets to pick their new coauthors (the journal or press editor does), but these people will play a key role in the revision process. Reviewers read the written analysis and offer feedback. Sometimes their comments are useful, and sometimes they are ill-informed. Sometimes they are so stupid that you wonder if the reviewer actually read your paper. But you are stuck with them because their judgment of your writing, communicated to the editor and later to you, determines your chances of publication. And if you survive the reviewing process and eventually pass muster, your reviewers' fingerprints will be all over the footnotes you included, the citations and caveats you added, the analyses you conducted, and sometimes even the conclusions that you drew. You may suspect that they forced you to cite their own work ("Carruthers 1996 is obviously relevant here"), or made you criticize their enemies ("The limitations of Carruthers 1996 have long been obvious"). Ritually, one thanks anonymous reviewers even if the revisions they imposed feel to you like base compromises and cheap concessions. Your name is on the publication, after all, but standing beside you are the invisible coauthors who were foisted on you by an editor. You may never know who they were, and sometimes it is better that way.

Peer reviewers seldom think your initial submission is perfect. That is, they will typically indicate to editors a number of ways in which your argument can be improved. They may also believe your paper to be so flawed as to be unsalvageable, in which case they recommend rejection. If you are rejected outright, then a post-mortem is advisable: Were any of the reviewers' comments useful? Did reviewers identify critical flaws? Are there new literatures you can productively engage? Is there a better way to manage readers' expectations so that they perceive your findings to be insightful, as opposed to merely obvious? Is your case study, lovingly elaborated in such detail, really necessary after all? Answers to these questions can provide a road map for revision, and then one sends the manuscript to a different venue. Hopefully, you won't run into the same unhappy reviewers again, but it happens. Particularly if your argument fits into a well-defined academic niche or stream of research, then quite likely you will run into the same reviewers multiple times. If you find yourself confronting hostile responses over and over, then it makes sense to reframe your argument substantially enough that editors will deem a different group to be the relevant judges. Either that, or put your manuscript back in your desk and forget about it.

Suppose, however, that the editor invites you to revise-and-resubmit your manuscript. Then it is your job to surmount the reviewers' concerns and change for the better their assessment of your work. Different reviewers may push you in different directions ("cut section 3" vs. "elaborate section 3"), but editors will sometimes offer guidance for how to reconcile conflicting advice. Otherwise, you are on your own. Whatever the recommendations, it is important to make (or at least to appear to make) a "good faith effort" in your revisions. If you think that the reviewers were complete idiots, kindly keep that opinion to yourself. Calm yourself down, let your indignation subside, and see if there isn't a way to be responsive even to foolish comments. If some of their suggestions are unreasonable or infeasible, explain to the editor why you will not, or cannot, follow their advice, in as respectful a manner as you can manage. If possible, ensure that your response mixes some compliance with your defiance. In other words, pick your battles and avoid playing chicken games with reviewers.

Once your revisions have satisfied the reviewers and the editor, and your manuscript is accepted for publication, your writing is back in your hands. Take another break, then look at your prose again. It won't be perfect, but is it now good enough? If yes, then the time has arrived to send it off to the publisher and be done with it. On rare occasions (like the second edition of a book), you may have the opportunity to revise something you wrote years ago. But mostly, publications simply age in place. And if we wish to revise our thinking on some topic, we will use a fresh piece of writing to make a new or updated statement rather than fiddling with old prose. Most people prefer not to recant in public or otherwise explicitly criticize their earlier formulations, but if you have really changed your mind about something, or possess a very different perspective, then it is best to be up front about it. There is no shame in admitting you've learned something and have revised your thinking.

And now, because I have revised this paper several times, received the advice of a friendly reader, and followed my own advice about the importance of pauses, I declare it "good enough." Done.

23

WORKING AT WRITING

JAMES M. JASPER

Anyone can learn to write well. This is not some innate skill like perfect pitch. Solid, even elegant writing is an ability we acquire little by little, learning the proper uses of one verb or preposition at a time, mastering long sentences, then short ones—and then figuring out how to combine the two. We learn to compensate for our own stylistic idiosyncrasies, whether these are an excessive use of adverbs or logical connectors or a tendency to write one paragraph after another of exactly the same length. Anyone can improve their writing, but they have to work at it.

The problem is, at some point in each academic's career she stops worrying about writing. She concludes that she writes well enough. Complacency blocks improvement. No one sets out to be a mediocre writer; we just end up that way out of self-satisfaction. And why not? There are precious few incentives for good writing in the academy.

Another reason we stop working at our writing is this crazy idea that some people are natural writers, and most are not. This is like telling Isiah Thomas that he is a natural athlete (a few readers may remember the hullabaloo about his comments on this point in the early 1990s). To say this is to downplay all the hard work, intelligence, and other attributes that go into success in sports. In that case, it also implied that Black players are lazy compared to players like Larry

Bird. Of course NBA players have natural talent, but they need a lot more than that.

Writing is similar. To write graceful prose requires some intelligence, but not at a level the average academic does not have. (To write poetically or humorously may require skills that few of us can master, but they are still not as rare as we think.) Much more, it requires continual work at improvement, at honing the relevant skills. Most of us give up.

A related error is to think of a draft as either good or bad. Every version of a book or paper can be improved; it is raw material waiting for the next round of editing, revising, proofing. Call it what you will: it can be a small or large transformation, but in the direction of more effective prose, table layouts, images, and their captions. As well as better titles for chapters and subheads (often an opportunity for a bit of poetic imagery or memorable turn of phrase).

The natural place to start becoming a better writer is learning how to revise.

TEACH STUDENTS TO CARE ABOUT WRITING

It is easier to explain why academics don't care about writing than to figure out how to inspire our students to care. And if we write badly, what hope is there for teaching them? Occasional lip service is given to good writing, as to a liberal education generally, but what gets done about it?

In the United States, writing is usually taught in colleges as a distinct endeavor, divorced from regular courses and subjects. Most often it is the subject of a dull semester-long class required of first-year students. Required courses face an uphill battle to start with. Those about skills like writing, often taught by adjuncts, are impossible. (Expository writing classes replaced public speaking a generation or two ago.) This is an artificial approach, as though writing is something you can learn in short order, then use subsequently as you need to, like long division.

If we are going to teach our students to write, we must persuade them that writing is important. And to do that we must talk about it in regular classes from time to time, rather than restricting it to a student's first-semester initiation. If nothing else, talking about writing in a class, even once in a semester, at least signals to students that we think it's important. Important enough to interrupt the regular subject matter.

In undergraduate classes, I discuss simple usage problems and, more importantly, how to structure a paper: how to make an argument, how to adduce evidence, how to open and close. Even the best undergrads rarely understand the functions of paragraphs, of sentences.

Graduate-student writing can also be improved. The trick here is usually persuading them that there is room for improvement. They are usually adequate writers and have been told at various stages in their education that they are good writers. For them, I usually concentrate on the desirability of going through many revisions, in order to break them from the undergraduate one-shot, all-night approach to writing papers (as though papers were aptitude exams). To learn to write professionally is to learn to edit and revise.

Writing is a broadly useful skill. If you can't write well, you are probably not thinking well either. Writing clearly helps students become better readers, too, as they are more aware of style. No other skill we teach them is so certain to be helpful later. It will stick with graduates long after they have forgotten the effects of Protestantism on early capitalism. What's fundamental is to show them that writing matters, that we care how they (and we) write.

BE ALERT TO SUGGESTIONS

I've been lucky. Over the years a series of advisors, coauthors, and editors have shown me tricks, pointed out my writing tics, and given me various kinds of feedback about my writing. Hal Wilensky, my PhD advisor, went through drafts of my grant applications, marking them up with the crazy multicolored Bic pen that he always carried; by the time of my thesis, I had learned to do the same kind of editing. When I submitted it to Princeton University Press, reviewer Chick Perrow called my writing style "unobtrusive," a word that annoyed me at the time but which I have come to understand and appreciate in the years since.

On my second book, my coauthor Dot Nelkin taught me to write short, punchy sentences. Unfortunately, that was the only kind she wrote, leading one acquisitions editor to criticize our prose as "breathless." I taught myself to vary the lengths of sentences, and also paragraphs, as well as to vary their structures. (Bruce Ross-Larson's *Stunning Sentences*, 1999, was useful.) We were lucky to publish this book, on the animal rights movement, with one of the large trade presses, which offer authors (or impose upon them, if they are too dense to appreciate it) intense line editing of multiple drafts. I learned a huge amount, from when a reader will need an example to how to build suspense.

With my next book I had the experience—increasingly rare—of having an excellent copy editor, Nick Murray. The most memorable thing he taught me, among many, was how to stick with a root metaphor in a paragraph. If you start with a verb such as "built," don't switch later in the paragraph to an evolutionary verb such as "evolved" or an organic one like "grew." Verbs are mini-metaphors, and should cohere, so I learned to remain with words like "crafted" or "constructed" if I had begun with "built." In other words, to take seriously the embedded meanings of words.

In helping other sociologists write better, when Jeff Goodwin and I edited *Contexts* magazine, I learned even more about different kinds of styles, different uses of words. I also learned that many sociologists think of themselves as having a distinctive writing style. In most cases "distinctive" was synonymous with "bad." I never said that to an author, since we had enough trouble filling the magazine four times a year, but I did inflict my frustrations on grad students who claimed that my editing did not respect their style. If you have a style, I would say, you need to be able to explain what choices you make to deploy it and what impacts you want the style to have on readers. If you have a style by default, it is probably not a style at all.

WORD ELIMINATION

My favorite editing exercise in seminars is the Word Elimination Game. Everyone brings the first page of the best paper they've written, enough copies for all of us. We pick several. We spend five minutes going through the first paragraph individually, trying to eliminate words without changing the meaning. Then we do the same thing together, combining our deletions. In many cases we can get rid of not only words, but entire sentences, occasionally the entire paragraph! We think about every word and what it contributes to the meaning. (I teach them to be especially suspicious of adverbs, because I myself am forever sticking "very" and the like into first drafts.) As Mark Twain advised, "Substitute damn every time you're inclined to write very; your editor will delete it and the writing will be just as it should be."

I'll share a few common examples of unnecessarily wordy construction, some of which I hope will sound familiar. These are the kind of things I look for in the Elimination Game. (The ASA Style Guide provides a good list of examples.)

There is the obsessive use of logical connectors, like "however," or "thus." If the relationship between two successive sentences isn't clear without these, from their internal substance, you're already in trouble. (I could have said, "then you're already in trouble," or "thus you're already in trouble.") There are also phrases that mean nothing at all, like "In this regard . . ."

Here's an example: "Young people long to experience participating in something like consciousness-raising groups." Here we see a doubling of the verbs, "experience participating in." It's much better—in reality and writing—to experience something, or to participate in something, than to experience participating in something. As with this gerund, nouns are often put in sentences to do the work of a verb, which is fine if they replace the verb, less so if they just duplicate it. For instance: "Race and class were not simply added on as an afterthought." Well, an afterthought IS something added on, so we can just say, "Race and class were not simply an afterthought." Or more simply, "were not an afterthought." Adverbs like "simply" (or "very") should always raise suspicions.

Another way of complicating our prose is to create a clause where a participle would do: "Young and old people who are today actively working for human rights . . ." need only be, "Young and old people actively working for human rights . . ." A relatively smooth participle replaces a whole awkward clause.

On the other hand, some verbs can simplify the work of a gob of nouns and prepositions. "They worked to implement laws against pretrial detention" easily becomes, "They worked to ban pretrial detention." Three words become one. We could even write, "They fought pretrial detention."

The principle in all these cases is the elimination of unnecessary words and phrases. I ask of each word, would the meaning change if it were removed?

The result is a kind of spare, Strunk-and-White style. And unless you're a poet-turned-sociologist, I can almost guarantee this is the style that will be best for you. You avoid the embarrassment of a pseudo-literary effort that falls flat, while serving your readers in getting your argument across in the least painful way. You keep them reading.

GOOD WRITING IS NOT OVERWRITING

When Jeff and I edited *Contexts* magazine, I dealt with sociologists trying to break out of their normal writing habits. When sociologists try to reach broader audiences, they tend to overwrite, adding similes and descriptions they think are "literary." They know that novelists observe details, and they think they should do the same thing, without really being able to distinguish a new trope from a hackneyed one, a unique trait from a demographic fact.

So when they switch from talking about, say, "39 percent of the females in our sample" (admittedly a deadly construction), to talking about an actual woman, she becomes a "tall woman," or a "tall, Black woman." Now, being Black, or being a woman may be an important demographic variable, but it is dull prose.

Another kind of overwriting comes from the abuse of the thesaurus. I use my word processor's thesaurus all the time. But you need to have a writer's sense of which word on the list has the right nuances, something you get mostly from years of reading English novels from the nineteenth century. (That was my version of a misspent youth, which I should have spent playing pool and chasing girls.) You shouldn't use it just to vary the words you use, as you can easily pick a synonym that jars the reader rather than imparts nuanced (often subconscious) information. This is a special challenge for nonnative speakers of a language.

In the end, there is no reason we cannot improve our writing. It takes work, like everything else, and it may not always be worth the effort. I understand that many younger scholars are engaging editors to improve their prose. I think that is great, a sign that they care and can acknowledge room for improvement. This has always gone on, but not always out in the open, as though there were something wrong with trying to improve your prose. A final word of advice: don't just hire others to edit your prose. Also study how they do it, so you can learn how to do it yourself and pass it on to others.

REFERENCES

Ross-Larson, Bruce. *Stunning Sentences* (The Effective Writing Series). New York: W. W. Norton, 1999.

24

WHEN REVISING A TEXT CAN TRANSFORM YOUR RESEARCH

MIGNON R. MOORE

I n the "Heuristics of Discovery" special issue of *Sociologica*, Andy Abbott (2018) shared the following rumination: "The art of research is knowing how to recognize when it is that you have run into something that you ought to have wanted to look for" (4). Over the course of my career, I have found that my most significant research projects have tended to include such a revelation, the discovery of which has often occurred during the manuscript revision process. I will share one example of this experience.

In the 2010s I began a pilot study to assess the medical and social support needs of racialized sexual minority elders in order to determine the ways community institutions could best serve them. My prior research concerned a younger population of African American sexual minorities, so although I had not previously studied health, the award was based in a center in the medical school and pulled me in the direction of studying health and aging for LGBT groups. I collected oral histories with about 25 black respondents, and added an ethnographic component to the data collection because the lives of the people I was interviewing were sociologically interesting in ways that fell outside of the aims of the pilot award.

In addition to examining health and social support, I also wanted to study my respondents' coming of age experiences to understand what it was like for black sexual minorities during the 1950s, 1960s, and 1970s to act on their same sex desires in the context of the social movements of those time periods, and as many were advocating for basic civil rights. I had just finished writing a book on family formation and identity development among black lesbian women who were born during these time periods (Moore, 2011), and was curious to know more about those who had been adults during that time. I thought I would write a second book about this previous generation, this time interviewing women as well as sexual minority men. It was a nice, neat study design, and I created a great codebook that I used to analyze the qualitative interviews. Overall, I felt satisfied with where the project was heading.

However, as I began to write and rewrite, I kept hitting a brick wall. I was having a hard time understanding the full life stories of my interlocutors, and this was affecting the quality of the arguments I was able to make. As I worked with the oral histories and used them to write, I began to see that important gaps in my knowledge remained. I realized that there were silences in the data. My narrators were reluctant to fully share about personal experiences that involved sex work, homosexual relationships they formed with others in church congregations, or behaviors they participated in that went against discourses of respectability. While I was able to write about health challenges as they approached older age, it was only through the writing and revision process that I began to see the limitations of the data I had collected in its ability to answer deeper, more pressing sociological questions.

My solution to this dilemma was to supplement my interviews and ethnographic field notes with archival materials on African American sexual minorities who had also come of age during the period I was studying. I scoured African American historical collections and LGBTQ collections across the country and found letters, personal memorabilia, news clippings, lesbian organization meeting minutes, and other matter. It took some time to transcribe, code, and analyze data from these new sources, but I was eventually able to piece together in-depth interviews with 29 black, sexual minority women that originated from ten different archival collections, and incorporate them into my study. While many of the questions these new narrators were asked differed from the queries in my original interview protocol, they all came of age during a similar period as the one in which I am writing, and their experiences fit well together. This new material filled in many of the gaps from my initial data, resulting in a richer, more complex story about the lives of this population.

With archival materials in hand, I now had a new context for understanding my interview data. The goals of the book project began to manifest themselves in a new and clearer way. In earlier drafts of the book proposal, my intention was to write about how black sexual minorities understood themselves and their multiple identities in the context of the social movement of the mid-twentieth century. However, I was now writing a more foundational story about the ways community developed around sexual orientation for black sexual minorities in the period before the LGBT rights movement, and the importance of the Second Great Migration as well as gender and race discrimination in employment, for the development of sexual communities that were bounded in particular ways by race and gender. Moreover, I was now emphasizing the experiences of African American sexual minority women. The writing and revision process had helped me see what was lacking in my own data, in my own thinking, and in the larger set of literatures around sexual community, migration, and the underdeveloped story of black women's involvement in mid-twentieth-century formal and informal labor markets.

Revising, I have learned, is not only about revising a text (editing, reworking, even rewriting a manuscript). If you are open to the process, it can launch a search that transforms your research project.

Careful thinking and revising at particular stages of the writing process can unearth meaningful ideas. You may begin thinking you are saying or intending to express one idea, and that idea shifts and changes, you learn how to communicate it more deeply, and/or you learn how to express it in a more expansive way. We strive for these revelatory moments, but in order to get to them it can take many drafts of writing, thinking, and discussion. We have to be willing to take that time (if we are so fortunate as to have time), because it is the repeated dismantling and reconstruction of the argument that can lead us to innovation. In the "Heuristics" issue, Peter Bearman (2018) muses that when he writes, he understands that his papers are waiting for him to "understand what their contribution could be. And that takes a long time to see" (14). The revision process helps us attain such a discovery if we let it.

REFERENCES

Abbott, Andrew. "The Art of Recognizing What You Ought to Have Wanted to Look For." *Sociologica* 12, no. 1 (2018): 3–4. https://doi.org/10.6092/issn.1971-8853 /8219.

Bearman, Peter. "Notes for 'Heuristics of Discovery.'" *Sociologica* 12, no. 1 (2018): 13–19. https://doi.org/10.6092/issn.1971-8853/8334.

Moore, Mignon R. *Invisible Families: Gay Identities, Relationships, and Motherhood among Black Women*. Berkeley: University of California Press, 2011.

25

REVISIONS AS A COMPLEX INTELLECTUAL JOURNEY

AMALYA L. OLIVER

ACKNOWLEDGMENTS

I wish to thank my dearest friend and colleague—Kathleen Montgomery—for her critical and thoughtful comments on this text and on many others.

A STORY AND AN INSIGHT

Revisions are always hard and many times painful . . .

Let me start with a real story: I was a freshman student at the department of philosophy and took a course in the philosophy of science. The professor was well known for his scholarly work in philosophy of science, yet notorious for his intolerance of students and for being very idiosyncratic. After seeing how he offended and teased the students, I decided to stay in the class as a free listening student and enjoyed the topics the class discussed on science and ethics. There were a few students who chose to formally enroll. Some students realized that the semester was moving on, yet the professor did not discuss the final assignments in class. Some students approached him at the end the class, as he was walking out of the classroom, and we all could overhear the conversation (the professor did not ask them to come to his office hours, and this was before the Internet period, so everything was in the classroom where all students were around listening):

STUDENT: Can I ask about the final assignment?
PROFESSOR: What do you mean?
STUDENT: You know—what I need to do in order to get a grade in class.
PROFESSOR: How should I know? What do you think you need to do?
STUDENT: Well, I guess I need to write a paper?
PROFESSOR: Okay. What do you want to write about?
STUDENT: Well, I thought, maybe, on XXXX.
PROFESSOR: Okay—then go write the paper.

The students went on to write a final paper on a topic they chose, and after a couple of weeks, at the end of the class, they handed the papers to the professor, again at the end of the class . . .

STUDENT: Professor X—here is the paper I wrote.
PROFESSOR: What do you want me to do with it?
STUDENT: Hmmm . . . Read it, give me comments . . .
PROFESSOR: No, I do not need to read it. Take it back and correct it—rewrite it.
STUDENT: Why??? How do you know I need to rewrite it?
PROFESSOR: I do not need to read the assignment in order to know it is not good enough and needs to be rewritten.

And these interactions went on a few times.

Despite the professor's idiosyncratic behavior, I realized that there was an important lesson in his (albeit rude) response to the students. Any work is never good enough after the first round. One needs to write and rewrite a paper many times before it can be considered good. It is also common, in our intense and demanding careers where publications are key elements in the promotion process, that we send our papers out before they are good enough (Espeland, 2019), knowing that there is need for further revisions.

REVISING OUR OWN WORK

So, back to the issue of revisions of a paper or a book manuscript. My first claim is that no work submitted for review after a first round is good enough. However, the process of getting back to the same paper again and again and to revise it can generate a love-hate relationship with the paper. This is when I start to make up excuses for not getting back to the paper, giving it a low level of priority in my mind. Yet, this should be a wake-up call for me that it is time to move on to the next stage of rewriting and revision.

In general, when first writing a paper, I have an *imagined reader* in my mind, someone who I hope will appreciate and learn from the paper. At this stage, I need to replace the imagined reader with two kinds of *concrete readers*. First, I try to send it out to a close colleague. There are two advantages to this stage of revision: one is that I can rely on my close and trusted colleague to be critical on all levels—on the language used, the flow of the text, the logic of arguments, the literature reviewed, the research question, the hypotheses, the data used, the description of the data, the findings (including the title of the tables or graphs), the conclusion and the discussion. These rough criticisms can be painful, but they are highly important and valuable.

The second advantage is that the review from my close colleague allows me to distance myself from the paper. This step gives me time to see the paper afresh, place myself in the role of a second *concrete reader* and to read it as if I were an external reviewer. While I wait for my colleague's review, I usually shift my attention to another project or on revising another paper. I've found that there can be unexpected new learning and synergism between different papers

I am working on. Therefore, having a pipeline of papers, even on different topics, can allow for vicarious ideas that can be fruitful for more than one paper.

REVISIONS AS A PART OF THE FORMAL REVIEW PROCESS

Reacting to external reviewers after a journal submission creates its own dynamics. Obviously, an external critical review is highly important, with the potential to improve any paper. However, we also know that the review process does not always operate ideally and there are some built-in deficiencies. First, the review process can be political and arbitrary (Gove, 1979), suffering from judgment biases (Teplitskiy et al., 2018). Studies have found that the coefficients measuring inter-rater reliability among reviewers fall in the range of 0.2 to 0.4 (Bornmann, 2008), and this lack of consensus shows that luck can be an important factor in the review process.

In my experience, editors can vary greatly in how they will assign reviewers or integrate the different reviews in order to provide helpful guidelines for revisions. Some editors take on the responsibility of summarizing the reviews and clarifying where important revisions are needed. Highly ranked journals with high rejection rates generally assure this level of feedback. Even a very detailed and demanding request for revision from such a journal may lead to more requests for revisions and may even end up with rejection after a few revision rounds. At the other end of the spectrum are those editors who are less helpful, simply writing a boilerplate paragraph and referring the author to the comments of the reviewers to sort out with little guidance.

That said, while having a thoughtful set of requested detailed revisions is better than the other extreme, it is never pleasant to receive a request for heavy revisions. It is obviously better than a rejection letter, but it often feels like an insult or a sense of frustration about a lack of understanding of what we were trying to say. When I receive such feedback, I usually quickly scan the editor's letter and the reviewers' comments, just to get a sense of the general direction of the feedback. Then, I wait for a few days before going back and carefully rereading the letter in order to react in a nonemotional, instrumental, and technical way.

HOW I DEAL WITH REVISIONS

The first moment when an e-mail from the editor arrives, I can feel my heartbeat . . . I hope for an R&R rather than a rejection. We all get rejections—this is a secret that every newcomer to the field of publishing should know. When I started my tenure-track position, I heard from a colleague that, "Everyone gets rejections— even the advanced and well known scholars get rejections." This was very helpful to hear as a socializing practice to the "publish or perish" world.

When I am fortunate to get an R&R, I start by creating a response file that has two columns. The first column contains the suggestions/ requests of the editor and the reviewers, and the second column contains my responses. I begin by tackling technical and minor issues, such as requests for additional description of the findings, changes in the sequence of the arguments, or adding references. This gives me a sense of progress and starts the process with the easy part.

Next, I deal with what I classify as "main issues" in revisions, such as changes in the statistical analysis, or in case of a qualitative paper, changes in the presentation of the data, the themes, the model, or the findings. In addition, there may be requests for changes in discussion and implications.

Finally, there may be requests for more complex revisions, such as changes of theory and major changes in the focus of the literature review. That is, in some cases, a reviewer might suggest that I reconstruct the whole paper around a new theoretical framing or that I develop a different approach to the literature review. This calls for me to bring a creative and open mind to rewriting and can require substantial reworking within the sections of the findings and the discussion. This remapping of the paper is neither a simple matter, nor is it clear at first reading. It requires rereading of the paper several times, in a distant manner that will enable the detection of weak parts that need reframing. Fortunately, I have not needed to undertake such a fundamental restructuring and revision in most of my papers, but it can be a highly rewarding process, encouraging me to let go of older theoretical framings and bringing innovative framing with fresh insights to my work.

WHAT WAS MY BEST EXPERIENCE WITH AN EXTERNAL REVIEW?

My best experience with reviews began with a high level of anxiety over one of my first papers. It took me the longest time to write the first draft, worrying that it would never be good enough. After finally deciding to send it out, I received an R&R based on five reviewers. I initially felt paralyzed when one of the reviewers suggested that I replace the theoretical framing I had used (based on a very central and popular theory at that time) with something different. "Use another theory, something fresh and innovative . . ." she suggested. To my surprise, this reviewer shared her identity with me and suggested that I should feel free to consult with her directly.

This was then, and is now, a very unusual gesture, especially coming from a well-known scholar. It was a huge learning experience for me. This expressed challenge and simultaneous support spurred me to enter a new intellectually daring phase. Although it was a scary and complex journey for me, I felt empowered and energized by this gesture. I ended up enjoying the creative process that enabled an exploratory scholarly revision of the paper and freed me from my anxieties. Despite the opportunity to consult with the generous reviewer, I decided to explore the options by myself. However, I have adopted this approach, and whenever possible when reviewing dissertations or manuscripts, I disclose my identity, with the offer to consult with the authors should they wish to.

There are, however, many bad stories about editors and reviewers that provide less than professional work. There are reviewers that offer unclear suggestions or insulting comments. There are also editors that do not offer constructive feedback, do not add their comments in their summary letter, or conduct unjust review processes where new reviewers are invited after one or two rounds, and based on their critical comments, decide on rejection. It is important that new scholars be aware that they may encounter editors and reviewers who do not take their responsibilities seriously enough. We rely on editors to conduct a fair and transparent review process. We expect them to monitor their reviewers carefully and to dismiss those who do not deliver comprehensive reviews, and we rely on reviewers to offer serious and thoughtful reviews for our papers. When we encounter a less-than-professional reviewing experience, we must not let these intimidate us; instead, we need to take a deep breath and to move on to another journal, with the hope for a more professional and supportive review process.

Obviously, this responsibility for fair and helpful reviews extends to ourselves as well, when we are asked to serve as reviewers or editors. We should always remember to think about how the author/s will feel upon receiving our review and to make sure to offer supportive comments, even if we are critical. Such supportive culture will improve the quality of our scholarly contributions and do good to all our scholarly community.

REFERENCES

Bornmann, Lutz. "Scientific Peer Review: An Analysis of the Peer Review Process from the Perspective of Sociology of Science Theories." *Human Architecture: Journal of the Sociology of Self-Knowledge* 6, no. 2 (2008): 23–38.

Espeland, Wendy. "What's Good Enough?" *Sociologica* 13, no. 1 (2019): 13–16. https://doi.org/10.6092/issn.1971-8853/9380.

Gove, Walter R. "The Review Process and Its Consequences in the Major Sociology Journals." *Contemporary Sociology* 8, no. 6 (1979): 799–804. https://doi.org/10.2307/2064432.

Teplitskiy, Misha, Daniel Acuna, Aïda Elamrani-Raoult, Konrad Körding, and James Evans. "The Sociology of Scientific Validity: How Professional Networks Shape Judgment in Peer Review." *Research Policy* 47, no. 9 (2018): 1825–1841. https://doi.org/10.1016/j.respol.2018.06.014.

26

AUTHOR, EDITOR, AUDIENCE

ERIC I. SCHWARTZ

ACKNOWLEDGMENTS

Thank you to Marielle Poss, Director of Editing, Design, and Production at Columbia University Press, for your copy edits and to David Stark for inviting me to participate in this special issue and for your insightful suggestions.

There is a saying in book publishing, attributed to the late Roger Straus of Farrar, Straus, & Giroux, that "we publish authors, not books" (Alter, 2018). Unlike journal editors who rely on review and revision for gate keeping and triage, book editors make initial decisions about what to publish based on the author's potential to contribute to the press's short- and long-term mission, message, and brand identity. An example of what publishers call list-building, this choice is made by an editor before any review takes place.

Book publishing is a relational business. It is less about a specific work than about maintaining connections with authors over time and developing their body of work. A book editor wants to deepen their understanding of who the author is and what they want to do with their work in order to expand the scope and size of the author's readership. This affords the author an opportunity to increase the influence of their ideas in a way that they could not accomplish on their own, while the publisher seeks to improve their reputation for publishing meaningful and important work (and sell a few copies along the way in order to keep the lights on).

What this means is that authors and editors share the mutual objective of cultivating audience, but this doesn't always materialize.[1] One reason is that authors fail to take advantage of the opportunity that this relationship offers, settling instead for a transactional dynamic afforded by the necessity of peer review and revision familiar in article publishing. A relationship that should be triadic between an author and editor working together to engage an audience becomes dyadic, between an author and editor directed towards getting a manuscript through a bureaucratic approval process, with book readers and buyers left largely as an afterthought.

Too often, authors set their expectations low and settle for a baseline of editor engagement. What does this look like? Insofar as all university press books undergo peer review, an editor's role in the details of revision can and should be fairly limited. Since the assessment of content is largely outsourced to the professionals in the field, the editor's role is to advise the author, as necessary, how to parse, manage, and incorporate the information they've received from the reviewers, some of which may be contradictory. With some experience, the editor should be able to accomplish this task with little difficulty, as consistent patterns for text revision appear regularly.

Take the advice from Reader 1, take the advice from Reader 2, find the overlap in the spaces in which they disagree, and commit to one direction or the other. Add more explanation where needed, and reduce the explanation when it gets repetitive. Begin the introduction with a strong, relatable example that readers can connect with. State the book's motivating question and its answer clearly and early. Ensure that there is a narrative arc intended to change the reader's view on the subject from beginning to end and a chapter structure that contributes to its development. Find the balance between the theoretical contribution and the descriptive examples so that the lesson of the book can be applicable to other cases but without minimizing the details. Situate the book within a scholarly discourse without reviewing the literature, as all work builds on what has come before it. Use the conclusion both as a summation of what has been covered as well as an opportunity to suggest the future of the subject which others might use as a point of departure.

From a process standpoint, this is all sound advice that I give routinely, but it doesn't really get to the more difficult personal and market-oriented aspects of cultivating readership, mentioned earlier, which peer review is not suited to support. What should an author be aware of beyond the changes suggested during peer review as they revise their manuscript for production and publication? How can an editor help an author publish their book to maximum effect?

A book editor's job, first and foremost at any type of press, is to help an author make their book a success. What counts as success is subjective from publisher to publisher and may even be subjective for publishing staff, depending on their departmental and individual responsibilities. From an editor's perspective, a successful book is one in which the publisher has accomplished something with the author that the author could not have accomplished on their own.[2]

There are two unique ways an editor helps an author improve their book. The first is individual and the second social. The individual way is to help the author to understand what it would mean to fulfill their personal goal for the book. What would have to happen for the author to meet or, better yet, exceed the goal they have set for themselves? The social way concerns the book's audience. Who are the book's readers and what does the author need to do to get them to buy and read their book? A truly successful book is one for which the author has achieved their goal for the book while, at the same time, the book has found a readership, effectively meeting or exceeding their individual and social expectations. For career academic authors, this is by no means an easy task on either front for reasons that are endemic to the profession.

Professional expectations can intrude upon and eclipse an author's individual goals. Books are instrumental to careers, and meeting professional expectations and obligations can overshadow and even overtake the author's personal aims. A book can secure a job, tenure, or promotion, and these are meaningful accomplishments, but they are not about intellectual self-expression. Further, the ultimate judgment of worth and determination of professional progress does not fall to the author but to their colleagues. Academics are particularly attuned to and accomplished at meeting the expectations of others for occupational progression. A good editor is a helpful mediator, a voice of external validation that allows the author to balance their full set of needs. Ideally an editor will lead the author to a place in which they can meet their professional obligations, contribute to worldly knowledge, and at the same time, communicate their ideas in a way that the author finds personally fulfilling.

Though it is by no means guaranteed, the individual success of the book is the easier of the two goals. For starters, social success requires satisfying more than one person. There is no person more invested in a book than its author. True, not all authors have realistic expectations, and some people are never satisfied with anything, but this is rare. In my experience, the bigger challenge is that plenty of very good books don't find a readership for all kinds of reasons beyond the control of the author and publisher. Fortunately, unlike commercial nonfiction, scholarly books are insulated from the pure whims of the market and the news cycle. The book is part of a discourse that began before its publication and will continue long after it. Unfortunately, the potential audience size for academic books, even ones that have some commercial market, is limited to those readers interested and aware of the topic and capable of engaging with it at the level and depth that the author is. In more esoteric scholarly subjects, this reader pool is potentially only a few hundred people in the first year.[3] Academic books have a predictable floor and limitations on ceiling in terms of audience size.

With this in mind, an editor can provide an author with a market perspective. What are the right expectations and what needs to be done to meet them? Anecdotally, authors tend to overestimate the number of peers in their field who will buy and read their book as well as the capacity and interests of the generalist reader. Understandably, authors are close to their subjects and have difficulty understanding what someone unfamiliar with their book's topic needs to know before it could interest them. Beyond this, there is a baseline level of knowledge across academia that even smart, college-educated people simply don't have. At the same time, authors tend to underestimate the number of potential readers in adjacent fields and, more importantly, students as potential readers in their own field. A publisher's sales are generally 30 percent frontlist and 70 percent backlist, meaning that most of a publisher's sales come from books that are more than a year old, and many of those older books sell routinely, year after year, through course adoptions. An editor can work with an author to make their book more appealing for teaching. At the same time, while a readership of professionals within a field may be limited, there is always the possibility of scholars and students just outside the field who may be interested in the book's topic.

The key to having a good perspective on a book's market potential is to think in concentric circles from subdiscipline outward. An author needs to establish the audience they wish to reach and work with their editor on the kinds of textual revision that will help to reach that group. As a rule of thumb, an editor should be able to help an author move their text to the next wider circle, all while affirming that successful academic books are measured by decade, not season, and that an audience that appreciates a work for its contribution to scholarship in their field, no matter how small it may be, is still an important, incremental addition to the body of human knowledge.

In sum, whether or not a book is improved by an editor's work, is truly known only by the author and publisher. A seemingly successful book—one that received positive reviews or sold many copies—can end up a disappointment if it fails to live up to the author's personal expectations or if the publisher miscalculated the book's market size. A book that has seemingly made no apparent mark on the world may still leave an author unexpectedly pleased because, in the end, they were able to say exactly what they wanted to say in a way that was better than they had hoped. The best sellers on a publisher's backlist are rarely obvious to outsiders. They are the books that continue to sell year after year with little to no new attention.

Were a book's revisions successful? It is ultimately the author who decides if they truly improved the book and to what degree. From the start, a good editor knows this to be true, listens, and offers advice accordingly. But the end results—if the book was successful—are only knowable if the conversation between author and editor continues and deepens, and this relational dynamic is precisely what Roger Straus meant when he said, "we publish authors, not books."

NOTES

1. Some publishers and editors are better suited to cultivating relationships than others. The fewer books a publisher works on at a time, the more individual attention an author should receive.
2. By "editor," I mean the acquiring editor. There are various other people associated with book publishing who have "editor" in their title, including the copyeditor, production editor, and developmental editor, all responsible for a specific aspect of the publishing process.
3. It should come as no surprise then that university press book publishing is a deficit-producing business model, reliant on institutional subsidies, revenue gap closing endowments, diversified yet complimentary portfolio of revenue streams like journals or business-to-business services, or some combination of all that cover for book publishing losses.

REFERENCES

Alter, Alexandra. "A New Publisher for Farrar, Straus, & Giroux." *New York Times*, March 8, 2018. https://www.nytimes.com/2018/03/08/books/mitzi-angel-new -publisher-farrar-straus-giroux-replaces-jonathan-galassi.html.

27

WHY I REWRITE

MARIO L. SMALL

ACKNOWLEDGMENTS

I thank Tara García Mathewson for comments that have improved this paper.

1

At some point in junior high school, back in Panama City, Panama, I first heard of, but did not quite learn, the importance of revising. Professor Betancourt, who taught us math and physics for several years, implored us to revise our homework, and exams, before turning them in. "Everyone makes mistakes," he said in Spanish, "and we make mistakes repeatedly." As an adolescent, I was sure I was an exception, sure that if I focused enough, I could turn in bullet-proof assignments without the drudgery of revising. But in truth it was impossible to complete those long problem sets—to recall formulas, to apply old solutions to new tasks, to solve that many puzzles, to do so much arithmetic by hand—without making mistakes. Everyone made them. Revision was a simple way to ensure that my submission matched my learning, my progress, and my ability. "Revisa, Mario, revisa." And that is how I first understood revision: as a correction mechanism.

2

In my first year in college, during an English class, I first learned of something deeper. The course required writing a few short papers on the American novels we had read, and the professor, Gregory Blake Smith, implored us "to rewrite, not just revise but to really stop, rethink, and rewrite" our papers before submitting them. Revising and rewriting, he insisted, were different things. It was a small revelation. Until then, to the extent I revised my essays—which, at age 17, I did not always do—I did so with a mind similar to that in my math assignments, to check for and correct errors. Revisions were tweaks. But now I came to see that with a deeper form of revision, one through which I approached the project anew, I could in fact produce a better essay, one clearer than the one I had first drafted. And, thus, through rewriting, I came to understand revision as an entirely different thing: as a clarification mechanism.

3

In my third year in college, I learned something important that I had missed. I had decided I wanted to be a writer of one or another sort. I studied many books on writing, from simple guides such as William Strunk and E. B. White's (1999) *The Elements of Style* to elaborate handbooks such as Joseph Williams's (1981) *Style: Ten Lessons in Clarity and Grace*. But none of them had a bigger impact on my view of revision than William Zinsser's (2006) *On Writing Well*, which included something I had never seen before. At the end of chapter 2, Zinsser included the last two pages of that very chapter's first manuscript version. The inclusion was a photocopy of the typewritten pages, complete with the author's handwritten editorial changes. The image was eye-opening. Zinsser made vivid what others had not. I saw how he changed "any number of different forms" to "any number of forms," and how he rearranged and even removed entire passages. Most importantly, I saw that the final two pages of that chapter—the ones he actually published—looked nothing like even the edited version of the manuscript he first drafted. They expressed a similar notion, but with greater cogency and sophistication. He had rewritten the pages not just once or twice but multiple times. And the published version was so completely different from the earlier ones that through rewriting, he was self-evidently not just clarifying his ideas; he was in fact producing them. And, thus, I came to understand revision as not only a clarification mechanism but in fact something more important— a production mechanism.

4

In my last year in graduate school, I learned that rewriting for production could entail an additional, and much more radical, act. I was writing my dissertation, eager to be finished. Having done fieldwork in a housing complex in Boston, I was writing a dissertation on neighborhood poverty. I spent many months writing what I had determined would be the dissertation's signal chapter, one that brought fundamental ontological questions to bear on a literature— the research on neighborhood poverty—that was, and remains, less theoretical than empirical. After many months of writing and revising, including a few top-to-bottom rewrites of the entire chapter, I submitted the theoretical exegesis to my committee. One of the members, Katherine Newman, was usually the first to write back, and this was no exception. Her comments were supportive but unambiguous—there was a core flaw, she thought, in my approach to the chapter. I first spent hours thinking through all the reasons she had to be wrong. After all, I had devoted more months to this single chapter than I would spend on the majority of the remaining chapters combined. I read and reread; I studied and took notes; I tossed and turned, most of it in frustration that she could not see what I thought was my creative conceptual leap. In the end, though, I concluded she was right—the chapter had a major flaw. But there was more. I realized that the chapter's entire conceit was wrong, not just flawed but unsalvageable. So, I chucked it. To my surprise, this defenestration was not, after I had actually executed it, that painful. If anything, it was liberating, because I could see the rest of the dissertation with far more clarity, unburdened as it was now without the heavy, and misguided, theoretical baggage. And, thus, I came to understand fully the importance, in the process of production, of removal. Rewriting is a means to get out of our own way, to drop ideas we have needlessly become attached to. But I realized that cutting could be radical, as sizeable to a work as losing a leg is to the body. But unlike the painful loss of a limb, this process of removal could immediately and self-evidently change things for the better.

5

While writing my last book, many years after I had learned, multiple times, that true revising is rewriting, that only by writing do one's thoughts become clear, that one writes not to report but to produce, and that production requires creation and removal—that revision is, therefore, central to the act of doing social science—I still uncovered something more about revision. In *Someone to Talk to* (Small, 2017), I was reporting a discovery: that, when it comes to trusting others, while we see ourselves as inherently cautious, we nonetheless willingly, and routinely, confide deeply personal problems to people we are not close to. I had discovered that social fact early in the process, and devoted a book to examining its implications. As part of the process, I revised all of the chapters several times, including refining ideas many times over, rearranging paragraphs, and cutting entire sections. Much of what I had learned about revising—about rewriting—I applied. The reviewers were happy with the final manuscript, and the press was just waiting for me to submit the final version for copyediting. I was nearly done. I set it aside.

Then, over the course of a six-hour flight, I reflected, with some distance in time and space, on the manuscript. Somewhere over the Sierra Nevada, I realized I was wrong. I was not nearly done; regardless of what the reviewers, the editors, and anyone else thought, two of the chapters, and most of a third, needed to be rewritten from scratch. The reasons why were not quite clear at the end of that flight. At the time, I could not yet articulate that the argument lacked coherence; that the chapters needed restructuring; that the arc of the book was flawed. It was not yet obvious to me that several important ideas were not fully developed. I had not yet understood that the tone was inconsistent; that there were tangents. All I knew at the end of the flight was that, for somewhat nebulous reasons, those chapters were not what I wanted, and that the book, as a result, did not represent who I was. So, I deleted all of them and started over—much happier. And that happiness, saddled as it was with the anxiety and self-doubt that burdens any project, came from the expectation that, by figuring out exactly what *I* believed was wrong with a book that others had nonetheless approved, I would discover something new about myself—that because my unease would not cease until I wrote a draft that no longer felt untrue to me, I would learn one way or the other what dissatisfied me, and, by extension, what I wanted to see in a work that represented me. I would come to learn, for example, that the arc of a book mattered much more to my own work than I might have previously expressed as necessary to a piece of sociology. And thus I came to see clearly what lurked beneath the surface all along: that rewriting is, ultimately, a mechanism for self-discovery.

REFERENCES

Small, Mario L. *Someone to Talk to*. New York: Oxford University Press, 2017.

Strunk Jr., William, and Elwyn B. White. *The Elements of Style*, 4th ed. Boston: Allyn & Bacon, 1999.

Williams, Joseph M. *Style: Ten Lessons in Clarity and Grace*. Glenview, IL: Scott, Foresman, 1981.

Zinsser, William. *On Writing Well*, 7th ed. New York: Harper Collins, 2006.

28

TO REVISE OR REWRITE ANEW

That Is the Question

MARTA TIENDA

ACKNOWLEDGMENTS

Rachel E. Goldberg and Dawn Koffman provided helpful suggestions on earlier versions of this manuscript.

> Writing is thinking. To write well is to think clearly. That's why it's so hard.
>
> MCCULLOUGH (2002)

Writing was my greatest weakness in graduate school. Only part of this limitation was due to my shift from humanities to social science as a graduate student. Drawing on my background in literature to interpret social science led to more creative if not well-written papers, but lack of training in research methods and data analysis made the transition difficult. Despite the appeal of objectivity in social science, I was clueless how to write about numbers when I began my first empirical paper about women's labor force participation in Mexico. Jane Miller had not yet published her excellent primer, *The Chicago Guide to Writing about Numbers* (2004), but it would have saved me endless revisions. This volume became a staple of my undergraduate methods seminars and still sits in my home library. That several research seminars required research proposals rather than literature reviews for final projects was fortuitous because it helped structure my thinking from topics to research questions. Then came the test—conceptualizing and writing a master's thesis using newly published Mexican census data. Using Friden desktop calculators to generate descriptive statistics from hand-coded data and IBM punch cards to program regressions were minor feats compared with the goal of interpreting and summarizing results in concise prose. The first draft probably read like a stream of consciousness.

My readers—a demographer and a labor economist—agreed that the findings were promising but advised that the analyses and writing needed "tightening." It was a polite way of saying that a major overhaul was in order: data reanalysis, new tables, and a sharp storyline aligned with the research questions. And tables should always be self-contained so that readers do not need to read the text to understand them.[1] With the benefit of my advisor's strong editorial hand and guidance about what to modify and how, I produced a stronger thesis. Both empirical chapters were accepted for publication before I began the dissertation project. The life lesson was clear enough: publication required a willingness to embrace constructive criticism, discard, or revise drafts, and repeat the process until a deadline. Note I did not say until perfect.

Word-processing software has certainly facilitated manuscript revision, but only authors must decide when sections of a manuscript are superfluous. In my experience introductions and background sections often qualify, particularly when I am trespassing disciplines or beginning a new project. The sputtering introduction to the chapter I coauthored for the *Urban Underclass* volume edited by Sandy Jencks and Paul Peterson (1991) was largely "throat-clearing," according to commentary on the first draft. The two seasoned editors were correct, of course, and their message guides critical reviews of my own writing and that of others. I revise introductions several times as I write, often scrapping and starting anew, as I did for this essay. I also advise students to write their introductions last, once both key arguments and evidence are clear.

Legal writing is replete with throat-clearing, but so is the world of academic scholarship. Jonathan Wallace (2014), expert copy editor for *The Future of Children* volumes, warned volume authors against throat clearing, which he illustrated using Princeton University Library's 2018 mission statement.

> In this era of rapid technological change, it is the goal of the Library to address the information needs of each group among its diverse set of users—faculty, undergraduates, graduate students, staff and the general public. With this goal in mind, the Library endeavors to continually review and update its collections and resources to ensure that it is providing access to those tools and materials—both in print and electronically—that best meet the University's evolving mission of scholarship. (83 words)

Restated in plain English:

> The library strives to give all its users the tools and materials they need. (14 words)

Wallace's (2014) pithy reformulation may oversimplify, but the message is accurate and his point about unnecessary wordiness in academic writing is warranted. Important ideas do not require more words, but rather succinct exposition. Clarify, explain, avoid jargon, and eliminate wordiness. These principles guide my approach to revision both in my own writing and that of students and collaborators. I confess to more success with others' manuscripts than my own.

Partly because I was driven to improve my writing and partly because I had access to editorial assistance and word-processing support in my early career, I revised manuscripts relentlessly. As a newcomer to sociology and demography, I often delivered muddled prose laced with jargon, which Jamie Whyte (2004) defines as "the substitution of bizarre, large and opaque words for ordinary, small and well-understood words" (117). Harley Browning, my dissertation director, despised jargon as much as he appreciated clear, crisp text. I still have a copy of Strunk and White's (1972) paperback edition of *The Elements of Style*, with a handwritten dedication, "For Marta, Best wishes on the eternal quest." On completing my dissertation, he gifted me a dictionary to assist my "quest for the right word."

Browning had an uncanny ability to identify confused ideas cloaked in jargon and garbled prose for lack of clear thinking, and he always called me out with a simple question: "What IS the question?" Rather than more or different words, revision first required rethinking or sharpening the question, which often meant a restart. Even as marginal comments praised promising ideas in later drafts, his sharp pencil left extensive editorial "track changes" on dissertation chapters that rivaled those received by nonnative English speakers. I embraced his pointed, but always fair criticisms. Professional editors at the University of Wisconsin–Madison further improved my writing for clarity and conciseness. Their mark-up drafts became study guides as I edited my writing and learned to "test" whether ideas made sense at various stages of incubation. Over time I became an obsessive editor of my own manuscripts and those of collaborators and students, although not everyone appreciates my heavy-handed word smithing.[2] Currently external reviewers and journal editors structure my approach to revision, but in different ways.

REVISE AND RESUBMIT:
A TALE OF THREE MANUSCRIPTS

My scholarship has benefitted immeasurably from peer review partly because revisions often resulted in better alignment between writing and thinking. Only a handful of my papers were accepted conditionally or with optional revisions on first submission, and I have had my share of outright rejections that required makeovers before seeking new venues. Early in my career, manuscripts typically required one revision and resubmission (R&R), usually accompanied by a cover letter summarizing key changes.

Over time, R&R decisions became repeating events, with most manuscripts subjected to two, and occasionally three, rounds of review, revision, and resubmission. The revision ritual involved making marginal comments on the referee reports, charting new analyses, and multiple rounds of rewriting. Responses to referee reports also have become more comprehensive and laborious because editors now request, and referees expect, detailed responses to their reports. Preparation of responses to reviewers presents another opportunity to realign thinking with writing by finding common themes in the comments, consulting new studies, and crafting diplomatic replies when the referee is dead wrong. Revision usually entails switching back and forth between the manuscript and the responses, tightening prose in both directions.

Decisions to subject a manuscript to a second (or third) round of review presume a high degree of confidence that the manuscript will be accepted. For this reason, journal editors are cautious about inviting revised resubmissions. Because invitations to revise manuscripts explicitly acknowledge that publication is not guaranteed, R&R decisions motivate authors to address referee reports comprehensively. Whether and how editors participate in the decision process varies appreciably and yet is quite important when referee reports conflict. A strong "editorial hand" can prevent response memos from becoming a discussion between authors and referees, can influence the odds that revised submissions succeed, and can also bring promising ideas to fruition, as the following cases illustrate.

CASE 1

How many reviews are required to fairly adjudicate the scientific merit of a social science manuscript? In my experience, two to three

independent referee reports typically accompanied editorial decisions, but occasionally an additional late review followed the editor's
decision to accept, reject, or invite a revision. I was surprised to receive
an invitation to revise and resubmit a manuscript, accompanied by six
lengthy referee reports in the first round of review of a coauthored
manuscript. The lead author, a graduate student for whom a publication in a top journal carries considerable weight in the job market,
was undaunted by the pages and pages of comments. Addressing the
critiques required re-estimation of complex models along with several
robustness checks, rewriting large sections of the text, and preparation
of extensive supplementary appendix material. Revisions in response
to the first round of reviews improved the clarity of the arguments
and the exposition of technical results, but neither additional analysis
nor robustness checks changed the main findings. The revised manuscript was resubmitted along with several appendices and a 17-page
point-by-point response to referee comments that connected specific
comments to the revised text. The second round involved two original and one new referee. All three praised the responsiveness of the
revision to the six referee reports, and yet requested more analyses.
Revisions in response to the second round of review involved more
robustness checks with supporting text and different supplementary
materials. The editor was silent in the exchange between authors and
referees, never indicating which should be addressed.

Did the peer review process improve the manuscript? Yes, especially on the first round. Was a second round of revision required?
Perhaps, but editorial guidance would have benefitted the revision
process. Adding a new referee in addition to the two most critical referees from the first round required reversing modifications made in
response to prior suggestions. Through both major revisions, results
proved robust to alternative specifications and seemingly endless sen-
sitivity tests to verify or disprove counterfactuals the reviewers proposed. Modifications in response to the second round largely involved
rewriting text, adding a new "current study" section, eliminating

appendices requested in the first-round review, then cutting 900 words to stay within the allowable word count. The editor's hand was largely invisible in the adjudication process, which was relegated to iterative consensus among reviewers.

CASE 2

While the prior manuscript toggled between revisions and resubmissions, a second coauthored manuscript had a very different revision journey—one guided by a strong editorial hand. Within four weeks of submission, we received two reviews and a "soft" rejection letter. Based on the referee reports, the editor had every reason to decline the manuscript yet saw promise in both the originality and timeliness of the study. Rather than render a typical reject verdict, the editor served as the third reviewer and left the door open for revision and resubmission, inviting a response to the referee reports before rendering a final decision:

> I would like to receive general thoughts on how you would address key concerns (just to reduce the chances of a negative editorial decision after having spent so much energy revising). . . . I desk reject the vast majority of submissions, indicating that if I sent it out for review in the first place, I am quite interested in supporting it.

The last sentence reveals an engaged and active editor who willingly encouraged promising ideas that were underdeveloped. There was no commitment to reconsider a revised manuscript, but we accepted the challenge. With support from my coauthor, I drafted and revised several times a three-page memo that addressed referee reports and mapped a clear revision plan. The exercise was critical in forcing an alignment between thinking and writing. We acknowledged the constructive critiques, set forth plans to revise analyses, yet diplomatically noted which comments were ill-advised.

It was not a point-by-point response, but rather a revision strategy. It was successful:

> Well, if ever there was a well-crafted response, yours is it! Substantively, I do think your intended responses are moving in the right direction for our journal.

The response from a veteran editor was especially reassuring, but also illustrates how to use the peer review process to shape social science research. Encouraged that the manuscript could be salvaged, he provided detailed guidance about requirements for a successful resubmission.

I now appreciate why the revision strategy memo succeeded in converting the rejection decision to an invitation to revise. Although the guiding research questions remained unchanged, the original manuscript lacked a clear storyline. One referee rightly called out the "background" section, which I realized was throat clearing because it contained extraneous information that deflected attention from the core questions. The revision replaced the background section with a succinct literature review that situated the study theoretically and substantively. A new "current study" paragraph framed the research gap and emphasized the novel contributions. In addition to tipping the editorial decision from reject to R&R, the strategy memo guided the revision from theoretical reframing through empirical execution. The memo also served as a template for the detailed response to reviewers. No additional review was required. I credit the success of the revision to a seasoned editor who saw promise in an idea and used editorial discretion to bring it to fruition.

CASE 3

The final example is from my term as editor of the *American Journal of Sociology* when I exercised editorial discretion to avoid rejecting a manuscript about differential fertility and the distribution of IQ by Samuel Preston and Cameron Campbell (1993a). In the early 1990s the proliferating literature about the urban underclass often invoked intergenerational transmission to explain persisting poverty, but seldom provided rigorous empirical evidence. This manuscript was an important exception. I recruited James Coleman, a distinguished social theorist and mathematical sociologist, and David Lam, an economic demographer with expertise in differential fertility and theories of population change, to serve as referees. I recall that at least one recommended outright rejection and the other likely requested a substantial revision. Had I followed typical protocol, the article would have been declined without further consideration. But that decision seemed unreasonable given the limited rigorous literature about intergenerational transmission processes at the time and the novelty of the submitted manuscript.

I approached Coleman and asked to speak about his critical review. His response was just what I needed: he had been thinking about the manuscript since he wrote the critique and thought it deserved further consideration. I invited him and Lam to participate in a symposium that elaborated their referee reports into self-standing responses to the article and would invite Preston and Campbell to prepare a short rejoinder (1993b). Both invited responses were subjected to peer review. It was one of the rare moments when, with support of the associate editors and always deft guidance from the managing editor, Susan Allan, I exercised editorial discretion to showcase the value of interdisciplinary approaches in the study of inequality and social change. The original submission along with the two peer-reviewed comments and authors' rejoinder were published as a "Symposium on Intergenerational Transmission" in volume 98, no. 5 of the *American Journal of Sociology* (Preston and Campbell, 1993a, 1993b; Coleman, 1993; Lam, 1993). In this instance, peer review broadened the conversation about intergenerational transmission processes, exposing the need for rigorous theoretical formulations and genuine multigenerational data.

EPILOGUE

I was invited to write this short essay about revision as a process of improving a book or an article just as I was finishing revisions of the two articles described above and was excited about the opportunity to describe the painstaking process of editing, revising, and rewriting. Two days into the essay I started anew because I was writing about how technology modified manuscript processing and peer review, rather than on the process of "revising, reviewing, and editing," as requested. This is the eighth revision of the essay, not counting the numerous rewrites of the introduction or the restart. A four-day hiatus provided a needed refresh that allowed me to see that a paragraph I had revised several times was a digression—a remnant from the false start. I excised it on the seventh revision.

The key take-away message is that revision is a repeat process that relies heavily on both critics and editors. The three cases feature distinct approaches to the exercise of editorial influence in both reviews and revisions. I added the *AJS* symposium to bolster my argument about the importance of active "editorial hands" in shaping which ideas appear in print by drawing on their expertise and by purposefully using peer review as a tool to improve academic scholarship. Reviewers play an important part in screening and improving social science, but editors also can exert outsized influence when they actively guide promising manuscripts. Few editors allow authors to challenge editorial decisions even when reviewers offer misguided criticisms. Preparing revision strategy memos can guide manuscript revisions more effectively than segmented responses to specific critiques, but the latter are often required to satisfy referees. Authors should embrace constructive criticism, revise text for clarity and conciseness, and repeat the process as needed until deadline.

NOTES

1. As a reviewer I always study the tables before reading an empirical paper.
2. A former undergraduate thesis advisee expressed her appreciation for my heavy-handed "editorial guidance" with a gift of three red pens to partly replace the red ink I spilled on her thesis drafts. Graduate students who are not native speakers are always grateful.

REFERENCES

Coleman, James S. "Comment on Preston and Campbell's 'Differential Fertility and the Distribution of Traits.'" *American Journal of Sociology* 98, no. 5 (1993): 1020–1032. https://doi.org/10.1086/230136.

Jencks, Christopher S., and Paul E. Peterson (eds.). *The Urban Underclass.* Washington, DC: Brookings Institution Press, 1991.

Lam, David. "Comment on Preston and Campbell's 'Differential Fertility and the Distribution of Traits.'" *American Journal of Sociology* 98, no. 5 (1993): 1033–1039. https://doi.org/10.1086/230137.

McCullough, David. "Interview with NEH Chairman Bruce Cole." *Humanities* 23, no. 4 (2002).

Miller, Jane E. *The Chicago Guide to Writing about Numbers.* Chicago: University of Chicago Press, 2004.

Preston, Samuel H., and Cameron Campbell. "Differential Fertility and the Distribution of Traits: The Case of I.Q." *American Journal of Sociology* 98, no. 5 (1993a): 997–1019. https://doi.org/10.1086/230135.

Preston, Samuel H., and Cameron Campbell. "Reply to Coleman and Lam." *American Journal of Sociology* 98, no. 5 (1993b): 1039–1043. https://doi.org/10.1086/230138.

Strunk Jr., William, and Elwyn B. White. *The Elements of Style,* 2nd ed. New York: Macmillan, 1972.

Wallace, Jon. "Writing for Future of Children Readers." [PowerPoint slides] 2014. Slidetodoc. https://slidetodoc.com/writing-for-future-of-children-readers-authors-conference/.

Whyte, Jamie. *Crimes against Logic: Exposing the Bogus Arguments of Politicians, Priests, Journalists, and Other Serial Offenders.* New York: McGraw-Hill, 2004.

29

THANK YOU, REVIEWER 2

Revising as an Underappreciated Process of Data Analysis

STEFAN TIMMERMANS AND IDDO TAVORY

Qualitative data-analysis is considered finished after the researcher writes up the analysis for publication. However, if we compare the text as initially submitted to a journal with what has been published, we often find great discrepancies because of the way reviewers push authors to revise their article during the review process. We show how reviewers may initiate a new round of data analysis by focusing their comments on three areas: the fit between observations and theoretical claims, the plausibility of the theoretical framing or explanation compared to other possible explanations, and the issue of relevance or the contribution to scholarships. The result is that reviewers as representatives of a community of inquiry help shape data analysis.

Qualitative data analysis books extensively discuss making sense of observations as a process of gaining theoretical closure. The texts give advice on looking for places to start analyzing in the mess of observations by singling out luminous data (Katz, 2001), conduct open coding of fragments to get a sense of their theoretical or conceptual heft (Charmaz, 2014), look for patterns by coding along a conceptual axis (axial coding) (Corbin and Strauss, 2008), map the data in a two-dimensional space (Clarke, 2005), and then settle upon a promising theme (Glaser and Strauss, 1967). Once a theme has been singled out, the researcher is encouraged to explore its manifestations across the dataset and examine variations, negative cases, consequences, and causes (Tavory and Timmermans, 2013) by focused coding, spinning off memos, and gather additional materials until data saturation has been reached (Small, 2009). The goal of theory-driven data analysis is to draw a theme out of observations and, at the same time, transcend the immediacy of the observations to speak to a broader theoretical concern.

The qualitative data analysis process starts thus in an open-ended way and gradually homes in on an analytical theme. The different data analysis approaches differ on when existing theory and scholarship becomes relevant: grounded theory saw existing theory as potentially corrupting data analysis and recommended that scholars only consult the literature after they worked through their observations (Glaser, 1992), while extensive case method adherents skirted closer to a deductive approach where researchers update or extend their "favorite" theory (Burawoy, 2009). A new approach grounded in pragmatism, abductive analysis (Tavory and Timmermans, 2014), encourages the researcher to theorize surprising findings in light of existing theories, advancing a recursive dynamic between data and scholarship.

Whether the literature is present throughout the research project, is already guiding research from the get-go, or consulted at the end, the qualitative researcher then writes up an article (or book, but we focus on articles here). If the researcher has followed the steps of data analysis, this last step to submission should happen smoothly. The analytical memos articulating theoretical insights based on observations form the foundation of the data analysis section of the article (Corbin and Strauss, 2008). Writing up qualitative research at that stage is then a matter of articulating a compelling argument that ties memos, maps, and luminous data together. Format the references in the journal-required format and press "submit."

Except that's not usually where the analysis ends. If you were to compare a researcher's data analysis at initial submission with what ends up being published, the difference is often astounding.

The original analysis occasionally offers a bare-bones outline that was further refined and elaborated in the writing process but often there is even less continuity: the published analysis is completely different. Obviously, tremendously important analytical work is done during the review and revision stage of publishing, but it falls outside the purview of most methodology books.[1] While authors thank reviewers for helpful comments during the review process in their acknowledgments, no methods section explains how reviewers shaped what was published.

If the article is not desk-rejected or rejected after reviews, most manuscripts will come back with a "revise and resubmit." Here is the dilemma: reviewers and editors are the gatekeepers to your work getting published. Ignore them, and they may get upset and take it out on your manuscript. Few editors will give you another chance if the reviewer thinks you did not respond sufficiently to the initial round of suggestions. Also, even if you think the reviewer is misguided, it is always wise to accept that your writing may have played a role in the misreading and give the reviewer's reading the benefit of the doubt. At a minimum, some clarification is warranted to avoid further misinterpretations. But seeing it in this way still makes reviewers seem like foes rather than allies. Even while we compliment them for their "wonderful insights" and resist misguided requests, we "capitulate" to their demands. And yet, often begrudgingly, responding to reviewers often takes the analysis in a new, positive, direction: the analysis needs to be reframed, the data needs realigning, the concepts need rethinking, and sometimes the entire argument requires overhauling.

Most often, more analytical work is needed because the reviewers take issue with the data interpretation and the theoretical contributions. In her observations of grant panels, Michèle Lamont (2009) found that 75 percent of the panelists mentioned that the connection between theory and data analysis is an important aspect of grant proposals (182). In a study of the role of peer review in published quantitative papers, Teplitskiy (2015) compared papers presented at the American Sociological Association meetings and their publication in two major general sociology journals: *American Sociological Review* and *Social Forces*. She found that the nature of the data analysis altered modestly while the theoretical framing changed substantively. "This finding suggests that a chief achievement of peer review may be to provoke authors to adjust their theoretical framing while leaving the bulk of the data analysis intact" (Teplitskiy, 2015:266). In other words, the theoretical framing for quantitative papers is collectively negotiated during peer review.

Qualitative researchers aspire to convince readers of the observed facts: the I-was-here textual effect that Atkinson (1990), drawing from literary theory, refers to as *verisimilitude*. These eyewitness reports depend on the utilization and obfuscation of discursive conventions to give the impression that the text conforms to an observed reality. Qualitative research persuades through a combination of demonstration (e.g., excerpts of field notes or interview transcripts) and analytical commentary, with the proviso that the observations are always already analytically infused (Atkinson, 1990). This verisimilitude renders an analysis transparent but also invites reviewers to take issue with the presented interpretation.

Verisimilitude is a necessary starting point. Yet, it only convinces readers that we were, in one way or another, *there*, that our data is valid, systematic, sufficient, and reliable. Focusing on the relationship between data and theoretical claims requires us to think more deeply about the different ways in which readers assess our argument as a trustworthy contribution to scholarship. Following a proposed set of evaluation criteria for qualitative analysis (Tavory and Timmermans, 2014, chapter 7), we can divide reviewer comments that push an analysis into three categories. These considerations, of course, should be contended with even before authors submit their work: they form the backbone of comments from colleagues, advisors, or conference participants. And yet, they are also crucially important during the review and revision process where under the cloak of anonymity reviewers may offer pointed criticisms.

First, reviewers may question the *fit* between the evidence and the researcher's claims. The researcher offers data to back up a claim but the reviewer is not convinced that the claims really provide an accurate analysis of the data, even if they are convinced that the researcher indeed collected the data appropriately. The fit between data and claims is too loose: the researcher argues relationships that a reader just doesn't see in the quoted examples. Too close a fit between data and claim is also problematic: a strong argument transcends the immediacy of the observations. Simply summarizing the data adds little value. A second group of criticisms are directed to the *plausibility* of the explanation. The author argues in favor of a set of connections, a causal relationship, or consequences, but the reviewer offers an alternative explanation that is already described in the literature. Then there is the criterion of *relevance* or the dreaded "so what?" question: even if your analysis is correct, how does it matter for social science scholarship. As pragmatism holds, a theory needs to be evaluated for its practical effects, commitments, and consequences. The problem here is that the analysis might be accurate but doesn't offer any novel insights. The authors only address narrow substantive concerns, repeat what others have said before, don't move the analysis forward (e.g., introduction and conclusion are interchangeable), or add negligible nuances to scholarship (Healy, 2017).

In what follows we offer illustrative examples of reviewers who pushed authors on these three criteria and we examine how the analysis was affected. Our contention is that exposure to peer review changed the initial analysis, and often for the better. Authors tightened the links between their data and claims, weeded out alternative explanations, and participated in broader theoretical debates. Much of this work is hidden in a private dialogue between reviewers-editors and authors during the review process. However, we draw on our roles as current editors of social science journals (senior medical sociology editor of *Social Science and Medicine* and editor-in-chief of *Sociological Theory*, respectively). We picked examples that have been published and of which the authors are publicly known. For the examples we used, we asked permission of the authors (because of double-blind peer review we did not approach the reviewers for permission but we do not provide identifying information about them). The authors of the articles also had an opportunity to make changes to our write-up.

FIT: DOES THE EVIDENCE STATE WHAT YOU CLAIM?

One reviewer put the crux of *fit* eloquently: "I question if some of the conclusions were really 'earned'? . . . I question if this concern about some of the conclusions is an outcome of findings that are presented in a rather cursory and superficial manner?" Such concerns are a challenge to rethink the analysis and play to the data's strengths.

Manuela Perrotta and Alina Geampana (2020) submitted a manuscript to *Social Science and Medicine* that analyzed the proliferation of add-on technologies in fertility medicine. These technologies are promoted on the websites of fertility clinics as improving IVF success rates, which hovered around a low 22 percent. The add-on technologies were aimed at patients with repeated implantation or IVF failures. A British TV program, however, had exposed these technologies as having little evidentiary backup for their effectiveness, even though they greatly added to the cost of treatment. In their research project, the researchers asked fertility specialists about the benefits and drawbacks of one such add-on technology: time-lapse imaging. These are laboratory incubators with integrated cameras that continuously take pictures of embryos during their development. The technology was promoted as a promising way to improve the live birth rate of embryos.

Based on their interviews, the authors argued in their initial analysis that the fertility specialists were not bothered by the lack of clinical trial evidence for the technology. Instead, the researchers reported that respondents embraced orthodox views of evidence and highlighted additional benefits of the technology (such as allowing to monitor fertilization, deselect some embryos, and managing the expectations of patients). While both reviewers were enthusiastic about the submitted manuscript, reviewer two made a couple of critical points. First, the authors reported that they had conducted observations and interviews in five UK clinics, but they only drew from interviews. The reviewer argued that the analysis would be strengthened with observational data. This recommendation questioned the fit between data and claims, or more precisely how best to empirically support the manuscript's claims. Second, drawing from the work of Karin Knorr-Cetina (1999), the reviewer encouraged the authors to pay attention to the forms of knowledge offered *by* the technology, and not simply at the evidence *for* the technology. Given the positive reviews, Perrotta and Geampana did not comprehensively rewrite the manuscript or reanalyze the data. Instead, they drew out some themes already present in the manuscript and gave them more prominence. Doing so, however, changed the analysis. Prompted by the second reviewer, the authors thought carefully about the kinds of interactions that spoke to the strength of their interview data. They decided to limit the analysis for the *SSM* paper to the interview data but that required them to address how interview data could speak to the lack of evidence for the add-on technology and capture the broad range of other reasons their respondents offered for using time-lapse imaging. They added a section on *narrative legitimation*, a concept social scientists have used to analyze other areas of medicine (e.g., alternative medicine and midwifery) to show how actors deviate from prevailing evidentiary standards in medicine. This literature predicts that health professionals either accept the customary standards of scientific evidence, rely on lower forms of evidence to support decisions, or question customary standards of evidence. This new theoretical setup allowed the authors to emphasize that fertility specialists agreed with orthodox views of evidence and acknowledged that time-lapsing imaging did not meet those criteria, but brought up other reasons for using the new technology. While the fertility specialists could not prove that time-lapse imaging improved live births, for instance, the film of the fertilization process as it occurred over time allowed them to discard some embryos with three rather than two viable pronuclei.

This invigorated analysis opened a new theoretical front in the analysis where the authors could contrast external knowledge and evidence criteria with the persuasive power of accumulated clinical experience, in the process expanding the range of treatment benefits beyond traditional effectiveness endpoints. This also increased the relevance of the manuscript because it allowed the authors to engage the literature on the hegemony of evidence-based criteria to evaluate new technologies at the expense of other, more practice-based forms of knowledge.

As with the other evaluation criteria, it is not surprising that our exemplar is of a more gradual analytical modification. If the reviewer found the analysis inadequate—usually telling the editor that the data is "under-analyzed"—the reviewer would likely have rejected the paper rather than asking for a major revision. It is one issue to miss some analytical leads; it is a more profound problem to comprehensively ignore the interpretive potential of observations. In our experience as journals editors, unfortunately, this systematic underplaying of the data happens more with some analytical approaches than others. Some researchers have (mis)interpreted grounded theory as a license for searching for themes without bothering with a theoretical argument. The result is an exercise in coding and classification. The abstract announces that the authors found four or five themes and the manuscript's analytical section lists these themes without connecting them in a theoretical way. While a list of themes may initiate, they do not constitute a compelling analysis. Grounded theory may tell you what's in your data with its useful coding paradigms, but it does not necessary tell you what the theoretical relevance is of the observations. For that, you need to closely engage the existing literature and figure out what's surprising or novel, and therefore analytically relevant. Deductive qualitative research papers, using extended case method analysis or a similar approach, are rare. Their weakness may be that the author ignores the richness of the data due to a strong precommitment to theoretical precepts. Different analytical approaches then produce different challenges around fit and some of these challenges may lead to a premature end in the review process.

PLAUSIBILITY: WHAT ARE ALTERNATIVE EXPLANATIONS?

If *fit* focuses on the relationship between the theoretical claim and the data, *plausibility* focuses on alternative explanations of the empirical pattern. If we see any writing as enmeshed in a conversation with a particular disciplinary community of inquiry, reviewers may well ask whether there aren't alternative existing theoretical tools that would do the job just as well. This is, for many manuscripts, a make-or-break question because it questions the entire theoretical construct the author created and suggests that there is a different, often simpler and more familiar, explanation for the data. Even if the data fits the theoretical claim, it may fit other claims just as well—making the theoretical intervention tenuous.

To take one example, this time culled from the pages of *Sociological Theory*, we turn to Sourabh Singh's (2022) "Can Habitus Explain Individual Particularities?" The question animating the manuscript was interesting: sociologists have increasingly used Pierre Bourdieu's notion of *habitus* to explain actors' actions. Since a *habitus* is defined as the tastes, and (mostly) class-based "principles of vision and division," it operates as a conservative force, reproducing positions and inequalities within the social field. Yet, can we explain any particular actor's actions by recourse to such a theory? This question, dubbed the "problem of particularity," remained a sticking point in post-Bourdieusian sociology. The analytic claim made by Singh was that part of the supposed Bourdieusian problem to account for actions stems from the fact that Bourdieu's theories of habitus and of capital have been analyzed as separate from his analysis of fields. Without accounting for field structure, including the possible shifts of actors within fields, among fields, and of the fields themselves, the problem of particularity seems more intractable than it otherwise might be within the Bourdieusian framework. Put otherwise, we often treat the problem of particularity as intractable because people change the course of their actions over time. But, argues Singh, part of the reason we consider this a problem is that we forget that habitus is always located within a field's structure, and as people move within a field, and as the field itself changes, we should, in fact expect to see changes in actors' strategies of action. Singh then exemplified this problem by detailing the biographies of two important leaders in Indian national history—Jawaharlal Nehru and Indira Gandhi—over their political careers. Singh argued that understanding their habitus in conjunction to their movement within the political field (and the changing political field itself) provides a strong key for understanding their actions. While the reviewers generally liked what Singh did in his manuscript, they weren't completely sanguine. Even within the world of Bourdieusian scholars, there were other ways to account for the problem of particularity. There were, in other words, other explanatory alternatives.

Summarizing reviewers' concerns in his decision letter, Tavory wrote:

> Within the Bourdieusian literature there seem to be basically four reactions to the problem of particularity: (a) most common: implicitly denying that there is a problem at all. (b) arguing that the notion of habitus is not intended to capture each particularity, but a kind of "zone"—that it is sociology, and sociology trades in generalities. Bourdieu explicitly says this in a number of places; (c) Bernard Lahire's

solution: which the author completely ignores, in what is currently the most significant omission in the manuscript—that habitus are themselves complex and discontinuous. That the context(s) of transmission involves multiple actors, and modes of being-in-the-world, located in relation to specific practices and situations. Thus, to get at "sociology at the level of the individual" we need to go account for the such complexity; (d) the solution provided by Atkinson, Crossley and some others: that sedimentation occurs throughout, and that taking phenomenology seriously (whether Schutz or Merleau-Ponty) means that we account for a living, changing, personhood.

The author considers mostly the first and the last of these. I think that in revising this work, the other alternatives need to be accounted for. I think, especially, that they need to take on Lahire's solution, which is, probably, the most concerted and sophisticated effort to account for the problem of particularity within a Bourdieusian framework. I am also surprised that the author did not delve more deeply into Bourdieu's (2008) own *Sketch for a Self-Analysis*, which is very much about crafting a sociology on the level of the individual. At its core, the author ran into a theoretical issue with empirical implications. Although Singh paid attention to some solutions presented in the literature to the problem of particularity, he didn't pay enough attention to others. But this is not only a matter of strengthening the conceptual parts of the paper. Rather, part of the problem was that since Singh focused on two different biographies, he spent relatively little time detailing their trajectory. With so little space to develop each biography, readers could find the alternatives not only conceptually plausible, but also empirically so.

In a sense, then, plausibility reversed the problem of fit. Rather than having an uncomfortable fit between data and theory, the problem of plausibility is that other theoretical explanations fit just as well and, in the eyes of the reviewers, maybe better. Thus, to solve the problem of plausibility, Singh ended up cutting out one of the characters, and focusing on the biography of Nehru. What this allowed him, through added details, was to increase the plausibility of the focus on field transformations. While he still couldn't quite reject other explanations, he could show that focusing on such field dynamics was at the very least one of the important explanatory keys for understanding how Nehru's political strategy and commitments changed over his career.

RELEVANCE: SO WHAT?

The "so what?" question is the trickiest reviewer concern to anticipate because it more than the other evaluation criteria is a judgment call. In terms of fit, reviewers can marshal evidence from the manuscript that the evidence does not meet the author's claims. For plausibility, they can point to the literature to note alternative explanations but whether the analysis makes a strong contribution is often more difficult to assess. The exception is the situation where the reviewer as expert in the field can show that the author is saying something that is already well-established in the literature. In most other cases, the question of relevance turns around the more nebulous concern of whether the analysis and theorization are a compelling contribution to the literature. In essence, the paper needs to allow other people in the discipline to solve other problems: it needs to be able to travel elsewhere (Timmermans and Tavory, 2022). In a sense, like any text or cultural object, it needs to resonate with its audience (McDonnell et al., 2017) by helping them work through the puzzles they face.

Many manuscripts that lack relevance are filtered out by the journal's editor. The editor has to imagine an audience for the work that, if everything works out, renders the manuscript citable by a group of scholars that goes beyond the most immediate subject audience. A lack of relevance is one of the major reasons editors desk-reject manuscripts. *Social Science and Medicine* received 6,497 submissions between July 2020–2021 across its seven disciplinary offices (the medical sociology office received 1,037 of those). About 85 percent get desk rejected and the editors pick from ready-made phrases in their rejection letter. The most used phrase is: "Although your manuscript falls within the aim and scope of this journal, it is being declined due to lack of sufficient novelty," which is a gentle way to point out the lack of relevance. Those that make it to the review process may encounter a reviewer who is enthusiastic about the work but a bit frustrated that the manuscript does not fulfill its scholarship potential to speak to broader themes. That's what happened in the following situation.

Kelly Holloway, Fiona Miller, and Nicole Simms (2021) received the following reviewer comment for an article they submitted to *Social Science and Medicine*:

> When you are clearer about who you are talking about and what you are doing, you can also clarify the contribution of your paper, especially to a scholarly audience. At times you allude to the significance of all of this for tests and approvals and practitioners. What exactly do you want scholars to learn from this? There seem to be many important implications (about regulation, risk, industry practices, professional practices, patient safety, the impact of the private sector on public wellbeing, about experts, and so on). Which of these many implications are most important to you, and what do you want academics to take from your study to move the literature forward? This could be clarified earlier in the paper, and again in the findings and discussion sections.

In other words, the reviewer saw many potential broader themes that the authors hinted at but found those themes insufficiently worked out. This is the kind of comment that suggests that the author is on board with most of the analysis but would like to have a better articulation of how the research addresses the stakes of the research project: how does the article go beyond the materials presented to intervene in larger theoretical and policy debates.

The manuscript initially focused on demonstrating an "invisible college" of industry and private experts who influenced the regulation of a new genetic test Non-Invasive Prenatal Testing, where blood from a pregnant woman is analyzed for the fetus's genetic conditions. This technology has been heavily marketed as an improvement on more invasive technologies as safe, accurate, and reliable and for-profit manufacturers have rapidly disseminated this test across the U.S. healthcare system. The authors focused on the retreat of government regulatory mechanisms as an independent check on this industry and the discovery of an invisible college of informal experts with industry ties that set standards for test validation, developed clinical practice guidelines, and influenced critical reimbursement and insurance coverage decisions.

Rather than sticking with their discovery of the invisible college (a concept present in this literature drawn from Demortain, 2011), the authors took on the reviewer's challenge to elevate the relevance of their article by introducing a new institutional form—a diffuse, polycentric regulatory regimen permeated by commercial interest—that not only build on their own case study but linked the research to similar studies of conflicts of interest in the pharmaceutical industry. They pointed out the lack of accountability in decisions to disseminate and promote the genetic test, the lack of transparency of scientific data produced by test manufacturers, and the construction of covert clinical and regulatory knowledge. The reviewer's prompt lifted the analysis to a new conceptual level and also gave the authors a stronger rationale for their study: expose the influential backroom regulatory work in order to hold it accountable.

CONCLUSION

A Facebook group with more than 75,000 members, Reviewer 2 Must Be Stopped![2] encourages members to vent about the second reviewer's depredations: thwarting the publication of good science with irrelevant, petty, or mean-spirited objections and demonstrating a lack of methodological acumen or even elementary reading skills under the cloak of anonymity. Obviously, anonymous double-blind peer review is an imperfect gatekeeping mechanism for publication. Abuses and frustrations abound, even if we have surprisingly few studies of the actual review process and most of the complaints remain anecdotal (but, see Hirschauer, 2010).

As journal editors, we also see another side to the review process. When it works well, the review process strengthens a manuscript, sometimes transforming it from a mediocre work into a powerful contribution. It does so precisely by doubling down on the considerations we outlined above: by pushing authors to show how the empirical material supports the theoretical claims, whether other theoretical explanations could not do a better job of explaining the observations, or pushing the author to clarify the broader implications of their study. Engaging such comments often adds another round of analysis to the manuscript with the result that the analysis pre and post review is profoundly different. What the author thought was closed, has been reopened and altered.

The review process often seems to insert a level of conservativeness in a body of scholarship, especially in tradition-rich fields. This should not be surprising. The more people are engaged in a particular disciplinary conversation, the harder it is to convince them that a new explanation is better than existing alternatives. This is not necessarily problematic: the bar for new theoretical work should be high. Of course, such a system can also sometimes be narrow minded, rewarding incremental change (or even repetition) rather than bold new arguments. As Thomas Kuhn (1959) noted more than half a century ago, adhering to a research tradition increases the probability for publication but forgoes opportunities for originality. It's a reliable career path. Taking a higher-risk strategy may lead to higher rejection rates, because such explanations feel "too far" to be considered plausible, and too exotic to help other researchers puzzle out the problems that they face (McDonnell et al., 2017). However, if you do manage to convince your readers that a novel explanation is both better than the plausible alternatives and relevant for other cases, it can have a strong staying power. In a study of 6.5 million abstracts in biomedicine, Foster, Rzhetsky, and Evans (2015) found that while innovation in science is rare, truly innovative articles accumulate in higher rewards—at least in terms of the citations to the work.

Lastly, conservative or not, the review process often leads to an additional analytical loop. As authors have to tackle skeptical readings of fit, plausibility, and relevance, they often have to deepen their analysis, sometimes even collect new data. As early observer of science Ludwik Fleck (1979) noted, scientific experience is collective. At their best, reviewer 2 is this invisible manifestation of the collective, erased after the fact, but leaving their mark on the shape of the argument and the relationship between theory and observations.

NOTES

1. This article elaborates on some ideas from our book (Timmermans and Tavory, 2022). We draw especially from chapter 8.
2. https://www.facebook.com/groups/71041660468.

REFERENCES

Atkinson, Paul. *The Ethnographic Imagination: Textual Constructions of Reality*. New York: Routledge, 1990.

Bourdieu, Pierre. *Sketch for a Self-Analysis*, translated by R. Nice. Chicago: University of Chicago Press, 2008.

Burawoy, Michael. *The Extended Case Method: Four Countries, Four Decades, Four Great Transformations, and One Theoretical Tradition*. Berkeley: University of California Press, 2009.

Charmaz, Kathy. *Constructing Grounded Theory*, 2nd ed. Thousand Oaks, CA: Sage, 2014.

Clarke, Adele E. *Situational Analysis: Grounded Theory After the Postmodern Turn*. Thousand Oaks, CA: Sage, 2005.

Corbin, Juliet, and Anselm L. Strauss. *Basics of Qualitative Research*, 3rd ed. Thousand Oaks, CA: Sage, 2008.

Demortain, David. *Scientists and the Regulation of Risk: Standardising Control*. Cheltenham, UK: Elgar, 2011.

Fleck, Ludwig. *Entstehung und Entwicklung einer wissenschaftlichen Tatsache*. Basel, Switzerland: Schwabe, 1935.

Foster, Jacob G., Andrey Rzhetsky, and James A. Evans. "Tradition and Innovation in Scientists' Research Strategies." *American Sociological Review* 80, no. 5 (2015): 875–908. https://doi.org/10.1177/0003122415601618.

Glaser, Barney G. *Basic of Grounded Theory Analysis*. Mill Valley, CA: Sociology Press, 1992.

Glaser, Barney G., and Anselm L. Strauss. *The Discovery of Grounded Theory*. New York: Aldine, 1967.

Healy, Kieran. "Fuck Nuance." *Sociological Theory* 35, no. 2 (2017): 118–127. https://doi.org/10.1177/0735275117709046.

Hirschauer, Stefan. "Editorial Judgments: A Praxeology of 'Voting' in Peer Review." *Social Studies of Science* 40, no. 1 (2010): 71–103. https://doi.org/10.1177/0306312709335405.

Holloway, Kelly, Fiona A. Miller, and Nicole Simms. "Industry, Experts and the Role of the Invisible College in the Dissemination of Non-invasive Prenatal Testing in the US." *Social Science & Medicine* 270 (2021): 113635. https://doi.org/10.1016/j.socscimed.2020.113635.

Katz, Jack. "From How to Why: On Luminous Description and Causal Inference in Ethnography (Part 1)." *Ethnography* 2, no. 4 (2001): 443–473. https://doi.org/10.1177/146613801002004001.

Knorr-Cetina, Karin. *Epistemic Cultures: How the Sciences Make Knowledge*. Cambridge, MA: Harvard University Press, 1999.

Kuhn, Thomas. "The Essential Tension: Tradition and Innovation in Scientific Research." In *The Third University of Utah Research Conference on the Identification of Scientific Talent*, edited by C. W. Taylor. Salt Lake City: University of Utah Press, 1959.

Lamont, Michèle. *How Professors Think: Inside the Curious World of Academic Judgment*. Cambridge, MA: Harvard University Press, 2009.

McDonnell, Terence E., Christopher A. Bail, and Iddo Tavory. "A Theory of Resonance." *Sociological Theory* 35, no. 1 (2017): 1–14. https://doi.org/10.1177/0735275117692837.

Perrotta, Manuela, and Alina Geampana. "The Trouble with IVF and Randomised Control Trials: Professional Legitimation Narratives on Time-Lapse Imaging and Evidence-Informed Care." *Social Science & Medicine* 258 (2020): 113115. https://doi.org/10.1016/j.socscimed.2020.113115.

Singh, Sourabh. "Can Habitus Explain Individual Particularities? Critically Appreciating the Operationalization of Relational Logic in Field Theory." *Sociological Theory* 40, no. 1 (2022): 28–50. https://doi.org/10.1177/07352751221075645.

Small, Mario L. "'How Many Cases Do I Need?' On Science and the Logic of Case Selection in Field-Based Research." *Ethnography* 10, no. 1 (2009): 5–38. https://doi.org/10.1177/1466138108099586.

Tavory, Iddo, and Stefan Timmermans. *Abductive Analysis: Theorizing Qualitative Research*. Chicago: University of Chicago Press, 2014.

Tavory, Iddo, and Stefan Timmermans. "A Pragmatist Approach to Causality in Ethnography." *American Journal of Sociology* 119, no. 3 (2013): 682–714. https://doi.org/10.1086/675891.

Teplitskiy, Misha. "Frame Search and Re-Search: How Quantitative Sociological Articles Change During Peer Review." *American Sociologist* 47, no. 2 (2015): 264–288. https://doi.org/10.2139/ssrn.2634766.

Timmermans, Stefan, and Iddo Tavory. *Data Analysis in Qualitative Research: Theorizing with Abductive Analysis*. Chicago: University of Chicago Press, 2022.

30

FIVE FEET AT A TIME

DUNCAN J. WATTS

Many years ago, when I was a grad student at Cornell, I attended a lecture on the topic of creativity by the renowned scientist Roald Hoffmann, who was both a Nobel Laureate in Chemistry and an accomplished poet. I don't remember much about the content of the lecture but there was one slide that stuck in mind and to which I have returned to many times over the years for inspiration.

On the slide, Hoffman showed two images side by side. The first was a copy of an early draft of William Blake's poem, *The Tyger*, which Hoffman introduced as one of the most famous poems in the English language (see figure 30.1a). The second was an early draft of Dimitri Mendeleev's periodic table of the elements (see figure 30.1b). What was immediately evident from both images—and Hoffmann's point in showing them to us—was how messy they were. In contrast with the pristine versions that one encounters in textbooks and anthologies, these early drafts revealed authors struggling with their ideas: crossing out words, entries, and even entire lines; writing in new suggestions or moving things around; at times crossing out their modifications and trying yet another idea or reverting to an earlier one.

It was a simple point, maybe even an obvious one. But as a student who often made mistakes and who frequently found myself chasing the same thoughts around in circles for weeks or months on end,

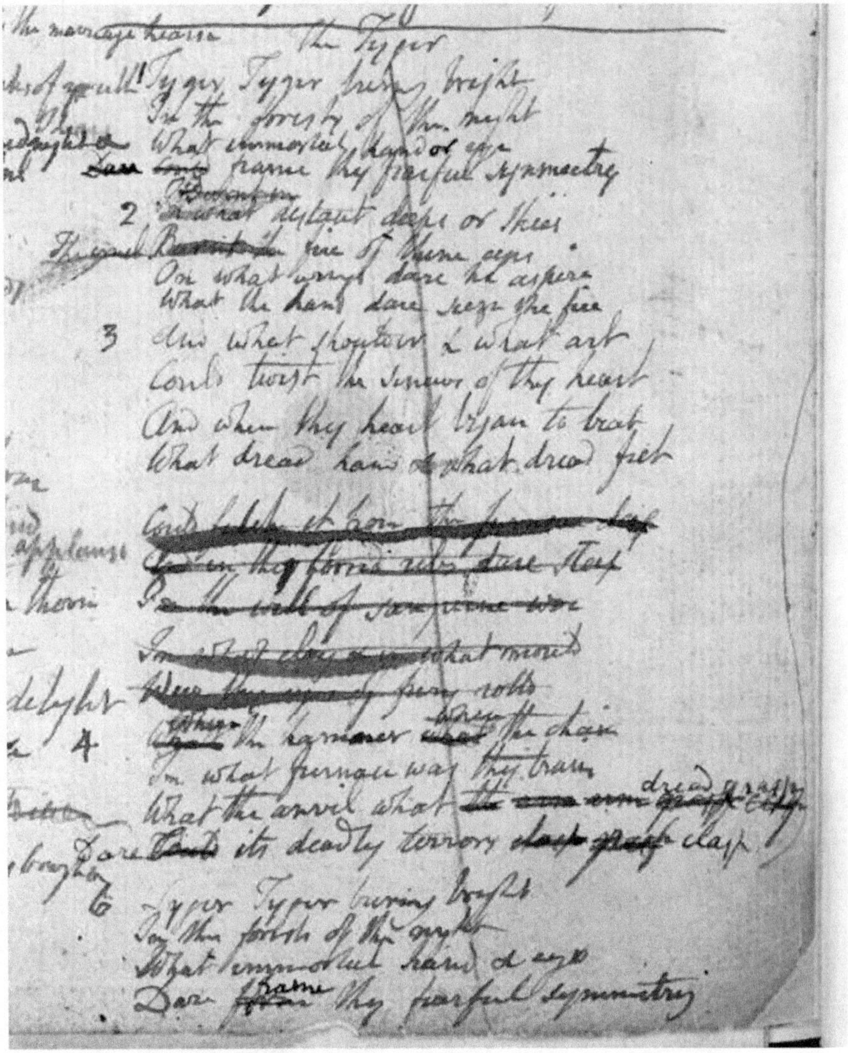

FIGURE 30.1 Example of messy creativity. (*a*) The first draft of William Blake's poem *The Tyger* (https://en.wikisource.org/wiki/The_Tyger_(1st_draft)).

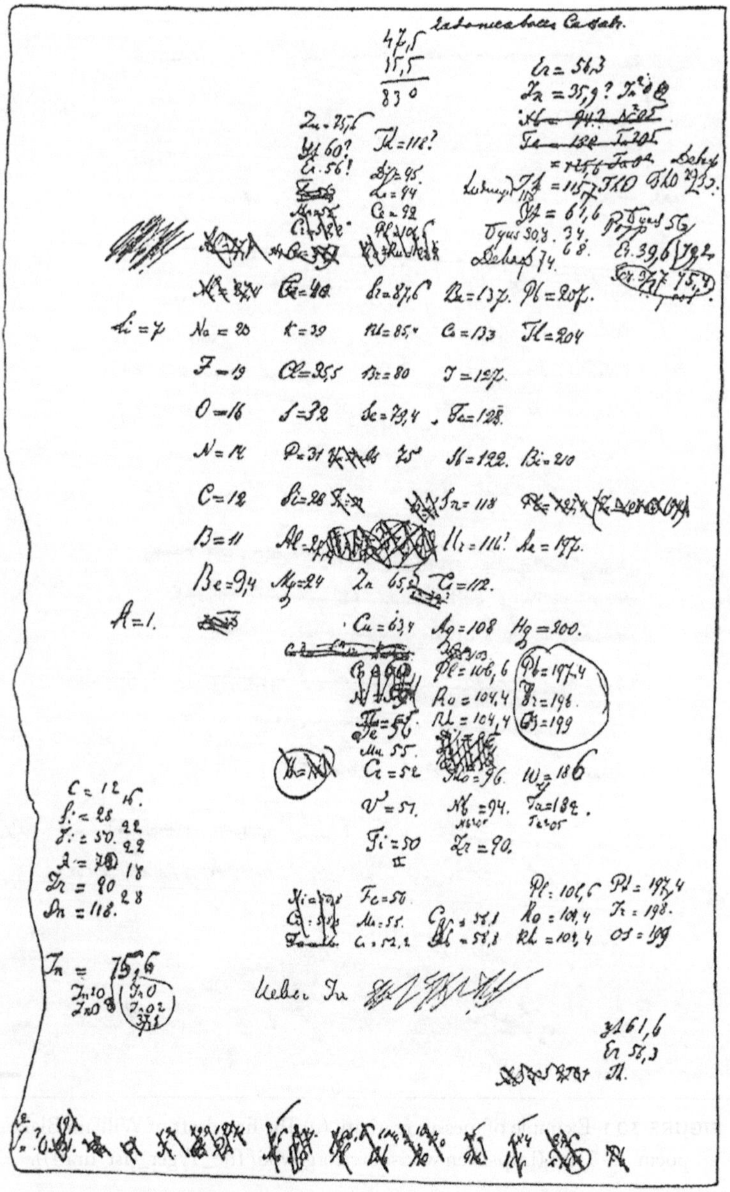

FIGURE 30.1 Example of messy creativity. (*b*) An early draft of Dimitri Mendeleev's periodic table of the elements (https://commons .wikimedia.org/wiki/File:First_Tabla_Periodica.jpg).

I found it nothing short of inspiring. If even the greatest thinkers had had to work through a mess of conflicting ideas and uncertainty about what it was that they were trying to say, then perhaps my own struggles weren't the sign of inadequacy that I had thought they were. Perhaps this process of writing something down, then hating it or realizing it was wrong, and then revising it over and over again until it started to seem OK was actually a perfectly acceptable way to articulate creative ideas. Perhaps it was the only way.

At the time I was also a mad keen rock climber, and I spent a lot of my spare time on climbing trips or hanging out at Cornell's climbing wall. On one such occasion, one of the more experienced climbers was teaching us to climb vertical cracks using a technique called "jamming," which—as the name suggests—involves placing your hands and feet into the crack and then twisting them such that they jam against the sides, allowing you to pull and push yourself up. It's a strenuous technique and I was complaining about how painful it was. "It's OK," he reassured me: "If it doesn't hurt, you're not doing it right." Perhaps, I thought, doing creative science, and writing about it, was the same.

Since those early days I've done a lot of science and a lot of writing about it, but the messiness and the discomfort and the feelings of inadequacy—the lingering suspicion that this time it really is terrible—have never gone away. The difference is that I've internalized all these feelings as a necessary and inevitable part of the process—just as my rock-climbing instructor, and possibly also Hoffmann, intended. Which is not to say that I don't still struggle with them. It's just that I can reassure myself that on the many previous occasions when I've faced the same struggle, everything has worked out fine, and it probably will this time also.

Beyond internalizing the expectation that a certain amount—and possibly a lot—of revising will be needed in any writing exercise, what else can one do on a practical level to get through it? I'm sure all writers have their strategies, but here are five that I've found helpful.

JUST WRITE

My first rule is simple: if you want to write something, you have to start writing. It doesn't matter if you feel ready, or if you know where it's going, or even if you have any plan at all. Just write. It might be terrible and all over the place. You might end up deleting all of it (more on that next). The point is that it is easier to work with words that are written than with nothing at all. It's also my experience that the exercise of committing your ideas to the page helps clarify your thinking. So just start getting them down and keep going until they start to catch and flow. You can worry later about whether any of it makes sense.

Of course, "just write" is easier said than done. Sitting down to write something, especially something long, can be a daunting prospect. And on any given day there are a dozen other things—replying to emails, attending meetings, teaching a class, doing that mandatory training, running errands, attending to your kids, scrolling social media, replying to more emails—that seem more urgent, or at least easier to do, than starting at a blank screen or diving back into a big messy document. And because each day is much like another, the combination of prioritization, procrastination, and distraction can drag on for weeks or months. The problem gets even harder when your deadline is far off, or there is no deadline at all, while for everything else, there is someone who will be disappointed or annoyed today if you don't do it.

For these situations, the best advice I can offer is to plan. Block out time on your calendar—a few hours at least—and decide ahead of time that you will use the time to do nothing but write. Turn off your phone, quit out of email, close your web browser, and find a physical space where nobody you know can interrupt you. It could be your home, your office, a library, a coffee shop, even a plane or a train— it doesn't matter as long as it's somewhere that allows you to make the mental transition from whatever you were doing before into your "writing mode." Personally, I prefer to plan my writing time before lunch, so that at least I can enjoy the rest of my day knowing that I got some productive work done. But if you feel more awake and focused in the late afternoon or in the evening, that's fine too. The point is create uninterrupted chunks of time that are long enough for you to get into the zone, and stay there for a while, before you're inevitably dragged back to your other obligations. Then repeat as necessary until you make progress.

CUT RUTHLESSLY (BUT KEEP IT SOMEWHERE)

Accompanying the first rule is a critical addendum: you must be willing to cut material that, on reflection, doesn't help your work. This rule is harder to live by than it sounds as written words are very much subject to the endowment effect from behavioral economics: owning something causes you to value it more than an identical thing that isn't yours. Just as it can be hard to go through your old junk and throw out possessions that you're no longer using, the time and effort expended in the "just write" phase can lead you to be more invested in your words than you would be if all you cared about were the final product. As a result, you can end up with lots of junk cluttering up your prose just as your old junk can clutter up your house (or storage container—there's a whole industry that profits handily from the endowment effect!).

Fortunately, there's another trick to help you overcome this psychological bias: create a separate "outtakes" file where you can park all the questionable snippets while you decide whether to permanently remove them or not. In my experience, these outtakes sometimes make it back into the main file, but more frequently

I find that once they are removed, the endowment effect is greatly diminished and they end up in purgatory indefinitely. Continuing with the decluttering metaphor, moreover, I find that the hardest part of cutting is starting. Once I have broken the mental barrier of the first cut, the next is much easier. After all, if those first precious words could go and I still feel OK, surely the next ones can also.

INK BLOTS

One misperception that I had about writing early on was that it proceeded in a linear fashion, beginning at the start, and ending at the end. That makes sense of course, because that is typically how we read documents, and sometimes the writing is like that too. But in my experience, writing is more often like a collection of ink blots: I start in many places in no particular order and develop them in parallel. Perhaps I have an idea for one part of the argument that I want to get down before I forget. Perhaps I think of a nice example that I want to work in somewhere. Or perhaps some pithy turn of phrase occurs to me, and I think I can develop it into something interesting. It doesn't really matter. Going back to my first rule, the main objective is just to get down all the "blots" that come to mind and then start fleshing them out.

Initially the process can be haphazard. Maybe I work mostly on a single blot which eventually turns into the bulk of the manuscript, but sometimes I have several of roughly equal size going at once and I hop around among them, working on whichever one seems to be going well at the time. Mostly I go forward from each starting point, but I also work backward from what I imagine to be a nice ending. Sometimes I think I'm going forward but later realize I was going backward. Sometimes the blots switch order, sometimes switching back and forth several times before settling down.

Regardless, over time, the blots grow and begin to join up. Eventually they form one continuous body that now resembles the overall format of final text, but with a bunch of lumpy joins—awkward segues, clumsy phrasing, sudden shifts in tone or terminology—where the previously separate blots have merged. I then go to work smoothing over the lumps until I no longer notice the transitions. Sometimes this process goes quickly, but sometimes it reveals a deeper problem—for example that two parts of the argument aren't logically consistent or don't help each other as I had thought they would. Then surgery is required, and everything gets pulled apart before being stitched back together again.

It's a messy process, but if it all goes well, the result is indistinguishable from the clean linear flow from beginning to end that I had once imagined. My favorite example of this process is a paper that I worked on, in fits and starts, for several years. Over that time, I wrote ten major draft versions, each of which I revised many times before even submitting it to a journal. It then went through two major revisions at the journal, incorporating dozens of pages of referee and editorial comments and completely overhauling the argument and even the title in the process. In the end, I had pulled it apart and put it back together again so many times that it was almost unrecognizable from the original. So, I was thrilled when a respected colleague mentioned sometime later that when he read it, he assumed I'd just sat down one day and blurted it all out.

EVEN UNCONSTRUCTIVE FEEDBACK IS STILL FEEDBACK

As with the other contributors to this volume, when I talk about writing I'm mostly talking about academic writing, which in turn mostly means writing articles to be published in peer-reviewed journals. As you probably know, the typical process for these journals is that one submits a draft manuscript and an editor either rejects the work outright or sends it out to review. In the latter case, one then waits for a few months and then receives some number of (usually anonymous) referee reports from experts in the field—usually two or three but sometimes just one and sometimes more (I think my record is eight). Based on these reports and the editor's own evaluation, the editor either rejects the paper or invites a revision, which could be "minor" or "major" (in theory it could be accepted off the bat, but that has never happened to me or to anyone else that I know of).

Either way, you now have some feedback. And as you may have heard, or experienced yourself, that feedback can be harsh. Sometimes it is very constructive and helpful and you're grateful to the referee for effectively helping you to improve your paper. But sometimes it is misguided, condescending, disingenuous, or outright malicious. Every academic has horror stories about how badly they were mistreated by such and such journal and "Reviewer 2" jokes are literally a meme on Twitter. Reading referee reports is one of my least favorite activities and responding to them can be as painful as it is painstaking. Nonetheless, my experience is that no matter how off base and unfair the criticism seems, the paper almost always ends up better off for it. I'm honestly not sure why this is. Perhaps it's that first drafts are always in need of improvement and so any revision, even an unwelcome one, is likely to help. Perhaps I'm just rationalizing the countless hours I've spent writing out detailed responses to the thirteen sub-sub-bullets of R2's objection 7, part b. Regardless, what I've convinced myself of is that if one reader has a particular reaction to my writing, other readers are likely to also. So even if I think what I said was perfectly fine the way I wrote it, and the reviewer's reaction is unwarranted, it's incumbent on me to try to head off that same reaction in others. It might be a little thing, but if fixing it helps you to avoid an unnecessary negative reaction in even some of your potential readers without compromising your overall message, it's probably worth it.

FIVE FEET AT A TIME

In closing I want to return to my main point about learning to live with your misgivings—especially when those misgivings amount to prolonged feelings of hopelessness. More importantly, I want to use it an excuse to invoke another rock-climbing metaphor.

During my time at Cornell, I got pretty involved in the university's outdoor education program, where I taught climbing and cross-country skiing among other things. One year, the program decided to host a conference and the organizers invited the legendary climber Royal Robbins to give the keynote. Robbins had earned his fame as one of the early pioneers of "big wall" climbing in Yosemite Valley, home to the giant cliffs of Half Dome and El Capitan. Among his many notable achievements were his 1960 ascent of *The Nose*, a 3,000-foot El Cap classic that was and still is the most famous climb in the world, and a particular brutal ten-day solo ascent in 1968 of the Muir Wall, also on El Cap.[1] As a young climber hoping one day to get up something as big as *The Nose*, I was delighted that Robbins was visiting Cornell and thrilled when one of the organizers asked me if I would pick him up from the airport. I was nervous to meet the great man, but he was very friendly and disarmingly unpretentious. He asked if I could recommend a restaurant for dinner and invited me to join him. I couldn't believe my luck! Over dinner, Robbins regaled me with climbing stories just as I'd hoped, eventually getting to his solo ascent of the Muir Wall. And here, some background is in order.

Rock climbing is usually conducted in pairs, where one climber (the "lead") ascends first, placing protection as they climb, while the other one (the "belayer") plays out rope through a braking device from a safe anchor below. If the lead climber falls, the rope will catch on their most recently placed piece of protection and the brake will stop them falling more than a short distance. When the lead climber runs out of rope, they create a new anchor in the rock (usually three or more pieces of protection), and they then become the belayer while the "second" climbs up, removing the protection as they climb. The whole process, called a "pitch," then repeats as many times as necessary to reach the top. Short climbs are often just a single pitch, but long climbs can have many. Standing at 2,900 feet, the Muir Wall on El Capitan has 33 pitches.

All of this sounds daunting enough, but when you're climbing solo, you have to do the whole thing yourself: place an anchor; set a "self-belay" (a brake that moves on the rope with you); climb up as the lead; set another anchor at the top; rappel back down; break down the bottom anchor and then ascend your rope, removing all the protection. In other words, you must climb every pitch twice plus the rappel. Adding to the burden, on a multiday climb you also must bring all your food, sleeping gear, and—critically, because it is so heavy—water. All this stuff goes into a large sack called a haul bag, which, as the name suggests, must be hauled up after you pitch by pitch, typically by running the rope through a pulley and using your body as a counterweight to overcome the friction (for a ten-day expedition a haul bag could easily weigh 80 pounds at the start). So, in addition to doing all the climbing yourself, twice, a solo climber must also do all the hauling. Finally, there is the extra psychological strain. Climbing is dangerous as well as physically and mentally challenging—far more so on a big wall like El Cap, where you're so exposed you feel you're going to get sucked off into space by the sheer emptiness around you. Even when you have a partner you trust, it's scary as hell. On your own—well, I couldn't even imagine it. What I wanted to know was: How on earth did he do it?

His answer surprised me. He said that for most of the climb he didn't think he *could* do it. He was moving much slower than he'd expected and kept encountering difficulties he hadn't anticipated. A couple of days in the whole thing seemed hopeless and he figured he'd have to go down. But then he thought: "Even if I can't make it up, I *can* climb another five feet. Five feet is no big deal, and I can go down just as easily from five feet up as I can from here." So, he'd climb another five feet. Not because he was trying to complete the climb—again, he didn't believe that he could—but just to get a bit further. But then of course he was in the same situation as before and the same logic applied. So, he'd repeat the mantra and climb another five feet, and then another, and another, and so on. And that's how he did it, as he told me: "five feet at a time."

It's a simple insight, but I've found it useful many times—especially when writing. In the middle of any large or ambitious project, there is always a moment—sometimes many moments—when it feels hopeless. In one case, I had spent almost two years working on a book and was a month or two away from my deadline. When I sat down and read the whole thing through, I was appalled at what a disaster it was, from basic sentence structure all the way up to the overall narrative. I remember sitting in my office in a state of disbelief, marveling at how something I had worked on so hard for so long could be so bad. The project felt like a giant hole in the ground into which I had shoveled years of my life, and I couldn't even see the bottom. For all I knew I could spend another two years on it and not be any closer, and I only had a couple of months. Failure was inevitable.

What should I do, I wondered? Call my editor? Tell him I couldn't do it? Cut my losses and move onto other projects? Return my advance? I seriously considered all these options, but then I remembered Robbins. I couldn't finish my book, but I could start at the beginning and make a small change. It wouldn't make much difference—not nearly enough to matter—but it would make it a tiny bit better and, more importantly, it was something that I could do: "five more feet." And then once I made that change, I found the next small thing to fix and fixed that also. And over, and over, and over again. At no point did I feel that I was changing anything important. There was never any big moment where it all clicked or came together, no rush of creativity or frenzy of writing like they show in the movies. Just hundreds of little changes accruing over weeks of painstaking revisions. And yet, when I read the manuscript less than two months later, I realized that the giant hole had been filled. In climbing terms, I had "topped out."

This is the lesson, more than anything, that I'd like to leave you with. When you're flailing in a project and you're miles from the top and nothing you can imagine doing will solve the problem, stop imagining. Just go up five feet at a time and keep going. You might be surprised where you end up.

NOTE

1. For Robbins's own account of this epic climb, see http://publications
.americanalpineclub.org/articles/12196931900/Alone-on-the-John-Muir
-Wall-El-Capitan.

31

ABOLISH THE R&R

CHRISTINE L. WILLIAMS

Publishing an article in a sociology journal requires extensive revising. It is not uncommon for articles to go through multiple rounds of peer review and revision before they see the light of day. Does all of this revising actually improve a paper? It is debatable. But the unintended consequences of this publishing system are not. This norm of multiple "revise-and-resubmits" is time consuming, demoralizing, and stifling of creativity.

Here is a primer on journal publishing in sociology (skip this paragraph if you know how the system works). An initial submission to a journal must first pass the editor's determination of its suitability for review. As many as half of all papers are "desk rejected"—deemed inappropriate or insufficient for scholarly review. The rest are sent to three reviewers (the "peers" in peer review). Sociology journals are "double blind," meaning that neither the author nor the reviewers are known to each other. The reviewers read the article and offer written comments. Sometimes these comments are perfunctory; sometimes they are multiple pages long. Based on the reviewers' assessments, the editor decides if the article should be accepted (rare), revised-and-resubmitted (more common), or rejected (most common). If invited to R&R, the author rewrites the paper to address the reviewers' concerns, writes a "letter to the reviewers" explaining the changes made, and resubmits a new version of the paper to the journal. Then the process begins anew. On the advice of the second-round reviewers (who may or may not be among the original reviewers), the editor may decide to reject, to issue another R&R (in which case the process begins anew for the third time), or to conditionally accept the paper. In the latter case, the author makes the requested revisions and if the editor is satisfied, the paper is accepted for publication. The goal of this labyrinthine and lengthy process is to publish scientifically sound sociology, but it has significant downsides. Many scholars can tell horror stories about revising a paper for years, only to have it rejected after multiple rounds of reviews. What can be done to improve the publication process?

The first step is to eliminate the R&R. After peer review, editors should have two options: reject or conditionally accept. A conditional acceptance means that the editor or their deputy commits to working with the author until the paper is published.[1] There could never be a second round of anonymous reviews, which only encourage reviewers to dig in their hills, pick at nits, become combative, etc. There may be occasions when the editor needs to consult with a specific reviewer a second time to verify that the author has correctly answered the questions raised by the review. However, in this case, the editor has already become a negotiator and advocate for the author, not a disinterested arbiter.

This approach will bring sociology journal publishing more in line with book and magazine publishing. Some academic journals currently follow this model (*Sociological Science* is one example).

This approach assumes a good faith effort by both the editor and the author to work together to produce a publishable paper. I realize that is not always an appropriate assumption and there will be times when one or the other party feels aggrieved and unsatisfied. But unlike our current system, in which the author revises without the promise of future publication, in my model, both editor and author share responsibility for bringing an article to fruition. I believe that these changes could make the publication process more humane and encourage more creativity.

Eliminating the R&R is more humane than our existing system because it builds relationships between the editor and the author, who are known to each other. The anonymity of our current review process can breed abuse. Scholars are scarred by insensitive and sometimes brutal comments from anonymous reviewers sent to them by disinterested editors who pass them on with dispiriting form letters. I know people who have dropped out of graduate school because of this demoralizing experience.

As a post-doc, sociologist Allison Wynn wrote about the insensitivity of academic reviewers, drawing an analogy to Twitter trolls. After suffering at the hands of both, she invented a game, "Twitter Troll or Academic Reviewer?" See if you can pick which statement came from which source (this excerpt is reprinted here with her permission):

1. "I find the discussion undisciplined, with many unsubstantiated claims. . . . Where's the evidence?"

2. "I encourage you to realize asserting reality doesn't affect reality. I especially encourage you to realize changing the words you use to describe that reality definitely have no effect on that reality."

3. "They have no data to support their conclusion."

4. "Are you a mind reader? How do you know the male presenters used technical info to 'intimidate' women into leaving?"

5. "It is unclear what your piece adds to our knowledge."

6. "This is the researcher making up information and pretending it's objective truth."

7. "Even a sympathetic reader has reason to question the objectivity of the findings."

The odd numbers are reviewer comments; the even numbers are anonymous tweets she received about the paper after it was published.

If academic publishing has become a humiliating gauntlet, it is time to change the process. In our current system, authors are in thrall to multiple waves of these anonymous reviews. Eliminating the

R&R limits them to a single wave. This change will not civilize cruel reviewers, but it could lessen their power. After the reviews are in, the editor issuing a conditional accept becomes the only person that the author must satisfy. Revising would become more focused and less dependent on the assessments of unnamed future reviewers.

Eliminating the R&R could also make journal articles more creative. Currently, authors are asked to satisfy reviewers who may disagree among themselves about the value of the contribution. This is especially a problem when editors deliberately choose reviewers who lack expertise about the topic of the manuscript. Trying to appease a wide range of scholars representing conflicting perspectives can water down the contribution, resulting in publication of banal results and stifling controversy. The system of R&R shackles authors to a formulaic approach to writing so as not to raise the ire of reviewers. In my proposed system, editors could empower authors to experiment with new forms, something few scholars dare attempt in the face of anonymous review.

Abolishing the R&R will have drawbacks. It will increase the power of the editor, which will not eliminate (and may exacerbate) the arbitrariness of the current system. It will also result in more work for editors, not all of whom are currently equipped to devote themselves to this expanded role. In my opinion, if editors assume a more active role in shaping the content of their journals, they should be compensated accordingly. Today, many journals pay a nominal "stipend" to editors, which is adequate if all they do is act as conduits for peer review, but it will not be enough if they are editing papers for publication. Abolishing the R&R is not a popular opinion. When I have made this case publicly I have been accused of dangerously degrading the scientific process. But I am not arguing against revision; only resubmission. I do not believe that multiple R&R's improve sociology.

NOTE

1. An editorial collective might replace a single editor structure.

ACKNOWLEDGMENTS

Elena Esposito offered guidance for this project from the beginning. I'm most grateful for her advice and encouragement at each step of the process. Thanks also to Filippo Barbera, Ivana Pais, Flaminio Squazzoni, and others on the Editorial Board of *Sociologica* who supported the initial idea of broadening the journal to include reflections on the sociological craft. We at *Sociologica* are all pleased that Columbia University Press is now publishing it in book form. It has been wonderful to be part of a community so passionate about ideas and how to express them. For helpful comments on my introductory chapter, my thanks to Chris Anderson, Jonathan Bach, Emma Cavazzoni, Victoria Johnson, and Pieter Vanden Broeck. As always, the members of the CODES seminar at Columbia's Center on Organizational Innovation rose to the occasion with insights about the overall project and suggestions about my introductory chapter. James McNally provided valuable editorial and logistical assistance throughout the project. Eric Schwartz championed this book. It meant a lot to me, knowing that his advice on all editorial matters, large and small, was grounded in a shared understanding of why this book could be valuable for the discipline of sociology.

ABOUT THE AUTHORS

EDITOR

David Stark is Arthur Lehman Professor of Sociology at Columbia University, where he directs the Center on Organizational Innovation. Using a broad range of methods—ethnographic, network analytic, and experimental—he studies how people answer the question: What's valuable? Stark has studied factory workers in socialist Hungary, new media employees in a Silicon Alley start-up, electronic music artists in Berlin, derivatives traders in a Wall Street investment bank, Nebraska farmers, securities analysts, video game producers, and megachurches that look like shopping malls. Among other books, Stark is the author of *The Sense of Dissonance: Accounts of Worth in Economic Life* (Princeton University Press, 2009), and *The Performance Complex: Competition and Competitions in Social Life* (Oxford University Press, 2020). He serves as a coeditor-in-chief of *Sociologica*.

CONTRIBUTORS

Andrew Abbott teaches at the University of Chicago. Known for studies of professions, Abbott also pioneered the algorithmic analysis of social sequence data. He has written on the foundations of methodology and on the evolution of the social sciences, the academic system, and research libraries. His current projects include books on the future of knowledge and on processual social theory.

Delia Baldassarri is a professor in the Department of Sociology at New York University. Her research interests are in the fields of economic sociology, political sociology, social networks, and analytical sociology. Her current research includes a study of the emergence of cooperation in complex societies and a book project that investigates the demographic and social network bases of partisanship in American public opinion.

Peter Bearman is Cole Professor of Social Science at Columbia University. He leads the Obama Presidency Oral History Project, as well as a project on the value of the liberal arts. In addition, his new work focuses on poverty in the United States and the network foundations of trust. With Adam Reich, he is the author of *Working for Respect: Community and Conflict at Walmart* (Columbia University Press, 2018).

Jens Beckert is a professor of sociology and director of the Max Planck Institute for the Study of Societies in Cologne. He works in the field of economic sociology. In 2018, he received the Leibniz Prize of the German Research Foundation (DFG). His most recent books are *Imagined Futures: Fictional Expectations and Capitalist Dynamics* (Harvard University Press, 2016) and *Uncertain Futures: Imaginaries, Narratives and Calculation in the Economy*, edited with Richard Bronk (Oxford University Press, 2018).

Michela Betta is a member of the faculty of business and law at Swinburne Business School in Melbourne, Australia. Her current research is concerned with questions pertaining to the epistemic import of ethical reasoning to people's choices, particularly in relation to whether such import increases people's sense of self. She is also researching the effects of organization on today's social life.

Massimiano Bucchi is a professor of science and technology in society and the director of the Master's program in Communication of Science and Innovation (SCICOMM) at the University of Trento, and has been a visiting professor in Asia, Europe, North America, and Oceania. He is the author of several books (published in more than twenty countries) and papers in journals such as *Nature*, *Science*, and *PLOS*. Among his books in English are *Science and the Media* (Routledge, 1998), *Science in Society* (Routledge, 2004), *Beyond Technocracy* (Springer, 2009), *Newton's Chicken* (World Scientific, 2020), and *Handbook of Public Communication of Science and Technology* (3rd ed., edited with B. Trench, Routledge, 2021). From 2016 to 2019, he was editor-in-chief of the international journal *Public Understanding of Science*.

Bruce G. Carruthers is John D. MacArthur Professor of Sociology at Northwestern University and a long-term fellow at the Swedish Collegium for Advanced Study. He works in the areas of economic sociology and comparative-historical sociology, with research funding from the National Science Foundation, the American Bar Foundation, the Russell Sage Foundation, the Institute for New Economic Thinking, and the Tobin Project. His latest book is *The Economy of Promises: Trust, Power, and Credit in America* (Princeton University Press, 2022).

Barbara Czarniawska is professor emerita at GRI, School of Business, Economics and Law, at the University of Gothenburg, Sweden. She takes a feminist and constructionist perspective on organizing, recently exploring such phenomena as the future of the welfare state, the robotization of work, and personnel management of spies. She is particularly interested in methodology, especially in techniques of fieldwork and in the application of narratology to organization studies.

Paul J. DiMaggio is a professor of sociology at New York University, where he is also affiliated with the Center for Data Science and the Stern School of Business; and the A. Barton Hepburn Professor Emeritus of Sociology and Public Affairs at Princeton University. His research and teaching cover the fields of economic and organizational sociology, sociology of culture, social networks, and social inequality.

Wendy Espeland is a professor of sociology at Northwestern University. She has published in the areas of organizations, culture, law, and science and technology studies, with an emphasis on understanding quantification as a formative social process. Her 2016 book with Michael Sauder, *Engines of Anxiety: Academic Rankings, Reputations, and Accountability* (Russell Sage Foundation), examines how efforts to evaluate institutions reshape them.

Neil D. Fligstein is Class of 1939 Professor in the Department of Sociology at the University of California. He is the author of numerous papers and books, including *The Transformation of Corporate Control* (Harvard University Press, 1993), *The Architecture of Markets: An Economic Sociology of 21st-Century Capitalist Societies* (Princeton University Press, 2001), *Euroclash: The European Union, European Identity, and the Future of Europe* (Oxford University Press, 2008), *A Theory of Fields* (with Doug McAdam, Oxford University Press, 2012), and most recently, *The Banks Did It* (Harvard University Press, 2021).

Marion Fourcade is a professor of sociology at the University of California, Berkeley. She is the author of *Economists and Societies: Discipline and Profession in the United States, Britain, and France, 1890s to 1990s* (Princeton University Press, 2009) and numerous articles. Her current work focuses on the new forms of stratification, morality, and profit in the digital economy. A book from this project, *The Ordinal Society* (with Kieran Healy), is under contract with Harvard University Press.

James M. Jasper has written about culture and politics for almost forty years. His main topic has been social movements, especially their emotional dynamics, which he has explored in books such as *The Art of Moral Protest: Culture, Biography, and Creativity in Social Movements* (Chicago University Press, 1997) and *The Emotions of Protest* (Chicago University Press, 2018). His most recent book is the coauthored *Gains and Losses: How Protestors Win and Lose* (Oxford University Press, 2022), about the complicated packages of impacts that movements can have. He recently retired from the CUNY Graduate Center.

Shamus Rahman Khan is Willard Thorp Professor of American Studies and Sociology at Princeton University.

Eric Klinenberg is Helen Gould Shepard Professor in the Social Sciences and director for the Institute for Public Knowledge at New York University. His books include *2020: A Social Autopsy* (Alfred A. Knopf, forthcoming), *Heat Wave* (University of Chicago Press, 2015), *Going Solo* (Penguin, 2013), *Modern Romance* (with A. Ansari, Penguin, 2015), and *Palaces for the People* (Penguin, 2019).

Kristian Kreiner is professor emeritus at the Copenhagen Business School (CBS), Department of Organization. He received his MSc at CBS and his PhD at the Technical University of Denmark. His research has focused on such topics as decision-making, project management, and the role of knowledge when the implications of knowing are problematic. Lately, architecture competitions have been his chosen empirical field of study.

Michèle Lamont is a professor of sociology and African and African American studies, as well as the Robert I. Goldman Professor of European Studies at Harvard University. She is the author or coauthor of more than a dozen books on group boundaries, worth, dignity, culture, and inequality. Her most recent book, *Seeing Others: How Recognition Works and How It Can Help Heal a Divided World*, was published by Simon and Schuster (U.S.) and Penguin (UK) in September 2023. Recent honors include a Carnegie Fellowship (2019–2021), the 2017 Erasmus Prize, and honorary doctorates from six countries. She served as the 108th president of the American Sociological Association in 2016–2017.

Jennifer Lee is Julian Clarence Levi Professor of Social Sciences at Columbia University, and the author of four award-winning books, including *The Asian American Achievement Paradox* (with M. Zhou, Russell Sage Foundation, 2015), *The Diversity Paradox, Civility in the City* (with F. D. Bean, Russell Sage Foundation, 2010), and *Asian American Youth* (edited with M. Zhou, Routledge, 2004). Her most recent project focuses on the surge in anti-Asian hate incidents since the wake of COVID-19, in which she shows how this moment of anti-Asian racism reflects a legacy of exclusion that is embedded in laws, institutions, and the history of science and medicine.

Celia Lury is a professor at the Centre for Interdisciplinary Methodologies, Warwick University. She has just completed a study of personalization called *People Like You: Contemporary Figures of Personalisation*, funded by a Collaborative Award in the Medical Humanities and Social Sciences from the Wellcome Trust, 2018–2022. The latest publication from this research is Sophie Day, Celia Lury, and Helen Ward (2023), "Personalization: A New Political Arithmetic? in *Distinktion: Journal of Social Theory*. Her most recent book is *Problem Spaces: How and Why Methodology Matters* (Polity, 2020).

John Levi Martin is Florence Borchert Bartling Professor of Sociology at the University of Chicago. He is the author of *Social Structures* (Princeton University Press, 2011), *The Explanation of Social Action* (Oxford University Press, 2011), *Thinking Through Theory* (Norton, 2014), *Thinking Through Methods* (University of Chicago Press, 2017), *Thinking Through Statistics* (University of Chicago Press, 2018), and, forthcoming from Columbia University Press, *The True, the Good and the Beautiful: On the Rise, and Fall, and Rise, of an Architectonic for Action*.

Mignon R. Moore is Ann Whitney Olin Professor of Sociology and Special Advisor to the President at Barnard College in New York City. She has written the book *Invisible Families: Gay Identities, Relationships, and Motherhood among Black Women* (University of California Press, 2011) and articles examining race, gender, and sexuality; family formation for sexual minority populations; intraracial relationships and conflict; and interracial variation in the health of racial minority elders. Her current work examines the development of sexual communities for African American sexual minority women. A book from this project, *In the Shadow of Sexuality: Social Histories of African American Lesbian and Gay Elders, 1950–1979*, is under contract with University of California Press.

Christine Musselin is a researcher at the Centre for the Sociology of Organizations, a Sciences Po and Centre National de la Recherche Scientifique (CNRS) research unit. She leads comparative studies on university governance, higher education policies, and academic labor markets. She was a Deutscher Akademischer Austauschdienst (DAAD) fellow in 1984–1985 and a Fulbright and Harvard fellow in 1998–1999. Her last book, *La Grande Course des Universités*, was published by the Presses de Sciences Po in 2017.

Amalya L. Oliver is George S. Wise Chair in Sociology at the Hebrew University of Jerusalem. Her research interests are in the fields of social networks, organizational sociology, and the sociology of innovation and entrepreneurship. Her current research includes a study of gender and ethnicity in the Israeli high-tech industry, innovation in the periphery, and organizational platforms for enhancing innovation over big societal problems.

Johannes F. K. Schmidt is the scientific coordinator of the long-term research project *Niklas Luhmann—A Passion for Theory* (2015–2030) at Bielefeld University. The goal of the project is to preserve Luhmann's literary legacy and make it accessible for research. In addition to the digital edition of the *Zettelkasten* (card index file), he has coedited several of Luhmann's publications from the literary estate in recent years, including *Systemtheorie der Gesellschaft* (Suhrkamp, 2017); *Differenz–Kopplung–Reflexion: Beiträge zur Gesellschaftstheorie* (de Gruyter, 2021); and *Die Grenzen der Verwaltung* (Suhrkamp, 2021).

Eric I. Schwartz is editorial director at Columbia University Press. He is the acquiring editor for sociology and handles special projects including the *Black Lives in the Diaspora* series, a partnership between Columbia University and Howard University. He has a PhD in political science from the New School for Social Research in New York City.

Mario L. Small is Quetelet Professor of Social Science at Columbia University and is an elected member of the National Academy of Sciences, the American Academy of Arts and Sciences, the

American Academy of Political and Social Sciences, and the Sociological Research Association. He has written award-winning publications on networks and decision-making, urban inequality, and the relation between qualitative and quantitative methods. His recent books include *Someone to Talk to: How Networks Matter in Practice* (Oxford University Press, 2017), winner of the James Coleman Best Book Award; and, with Jessica Calarco, *Qualitative Literacy: A Guide to Evaluating Qualitative and Interview Research* (University of California Press, 2022).

Lucy Suchman is professor emerita of anthropology of science and technology in the Department of Sociology at Lancaster University. Before taking up her present post, she was a principal scientist at Xerox's Palo Alto Research Center, where she spent twenty years as a researcher. Her research at the intersections of anthropology and the field of feminist science and technology studies is focused on cultural imaginaries and material practices of technology design. Her current research extends her long-standing critical engagement with the fields of artificial intelligence and human-computer interaction to the domain of contemporary militarism.

Richard Swedberg is professor emeritus of sociology at Cornell University. His two specialties are economic sociology and social theory. He is currently working on various aspects of theorizing: how to do it and how to teach it to students.

Iddo Tavory is a professor of sociology at New York University and the editor of *Sociological Theory*. He has published *Abductive Analysis: Theorizing Qualitative Research* (Chicago University Press, 2014) and *Data Analysis in Qualitative Research: Theorizing with Abductive Analysis* (Chicago University Press, 2022) (both with Stefan Timmermans); *Summoned: Identification and Religious Life in a Jewish Neighborhood* (Chicago University Press, 2016); and *Tangled Goods: The Practical Life of Pro Bono Advertising* (Chicago University Press, 2022).

Marta Tienda is Maurice P. During Professor in Demographic Studies and a professor of sociology and public affairs, emerita, at Princeton University. Her research focuses on the demography of inequality, educational stratification, and international migration. Her current research is based on a diary study of adolescent romantic relationships.

Stefan Timmermans is a professor at the Department of Sociology, University of California, Los Angeles, as well as a professor at Information Services Group (ISG). His research draws from medical sociology and science studies and uses ethnographic and historical methods to address key issues in the for-profit U.S. health-care system. He has conducted research on medical technologies, health professions, death and dying, and population health, and is the medical sociology editor of the journal *Social Science & Medicine*.

Duncan J. Watts is Stevens University Professor and the 23rd Penn Integrates Knowledge Professor at the University of Pennsylvania, with faculty appointments in computer and information science, the Annenberg School of Communication, and the Operations, Information and Decisions Department of the Wharton School of Business. In the summer of 1996, he and two friends climbed The Nose of El Capitan over five very long days.

Christine L. Williams is a professor of sociology at the University of Texas at Austin and a former president of the American Sociological Association. Her latest book is *Gaslighted: How the Oil and Gas Industry Shortchanges Women Scientists* (University of California Press, 2021).

INDEX

Abbott, Andrew, 28, 201
academia: English in, 125; in Germany,
    126–127; hiring in, 181–182
academic books, audience for, 216
acceptance, conditional, 268
actor orientation, in historical work, 47–49
administrative responsibilities, 180–181
Adorno, Theodor, 38, 39
agency, 72; local action and, 36;
    technology relation to, 120
AJS. *See American Journal of Sociology*
ambiguity: identities and, 35–36; in
    social relationships, 33–34; social
    roles and, 34–35, 39
American Journal of Sociology (AJS), 140,
    164, 165, 233
American Sociological Association,
    238–239
American Sociological Review (ASR),
    139, 143, 164, 239
anonymity, of reviewers, 269
anxiety, deadlines and, 163
argument: in editorials, 172; as forms,
    152; innovation in, 204; peer review
    and, 191; qualitative shifts to, 163;

reviewers relation to, 139, 251;
    revision of, 189; simplicity of, 139; in
    The Triple Package, 168–169
articles: data-analysis in, 237; essays as,
    177; monographs compared to, 163;
    PhD and, 182
ASR. *See American Sociological Review*
attention: focus and, 8–9; surprises
    and, 12
audience: for academic books, 216;
    authors relation to, 214; framing for,
    145; of journals, 22, 143; knowledge
    of, 140; market potential and, 217;
    of papers, 141; publication strategy
    and, 13–14, 16–17; relevance to,
    247–248; reviewers compared to,
    21, 144; writing for, 14–15, 167–168,
    199–200
authors: audience relation to, 214;
    consultation with, 210–211; criticism
    for, 234; data-analysis by, 241–242;
    editors relation to, 213–215, 216,
    217, 218, 268–269; expectations of,
    217–218; reviewers relation to, 236,
    240, 248–249; twin, 134–135

Printed and bound by CPI Group (UK) Ltd, Croydon, CR0 4YY

22/05/2024

14505717-0001